BELLE STARR

BELLE STARR
"The Bandit Queen"

The TRUE STORY of the ROMANTIC and EXCITING
CAREER

Of the DARING and GLAMOROUS Lady

Famed in Legend and Story throughout the West
As the BEAUTIFUL GIRL Who Would never have WENT WRONG
if THINGS HADN'T GONE WRONG

The TRUE FACTS about the DASTARDLY DEEDS and
THE COME-UPPENCE

Of Such Dick Turpins, Robin Hoods and Rini Rinaldos

——— AS ———

The Youngers, the Jameses, the Daltons, the Starrs, the Doolins and the Jenningses

The REal StORY

With court RECORDS and cONtemPoraRY
NEWSPAPER ACCOUNTS
And Testimony of Old Nesters, here and there, in the Southwest

A VERITABLE Exposee of
BADMEN and MARSHALS
and Why Crime Does Not Pay!

By BURTON RASCOE

(Deputy Sheriff of Pottawatomie County, Shawnee, Oklahoma)

Introduction by Glenda Riley

UNIVERSITY OF NEBRASKA PRESS
LINCOLN AND LONDON

First Nebraska paperback printing: 2004

Library of Congress Cataloging-in-Publication Data
Rascoe, Burton, 1892–1957.
Belle Starr "the Bandit Queen": the true story of the romantic and exciting career of the daring and glamourous lady famed in legend and story throughout the West as the beautiful girl who would never have went wrong if things hadn't gone wrong / Burton Rascoe; introduction by Glenda Riley.
p.   cm.
Includes bibliographical references and index.
ISBN 0-8032-9003-9 (pbk.: alk. paper)
1. Starr, Belle, 1848–1889.   2. Women outlaws—West (U.S.)—Biography.   3. Outlaws—West (U.S.)—Biography.
4. West (U.S.)—Biography.   5. Frontier and pioneer life—West (U.S.)   I. Title.
F594.S8R375   2004
978'.02'092—dc22   2004015824

WHO WAS BELLE STARR?

Glenda Riley

Was the female outlaw Belle Starr largely a fabrication, or was she an authentic, gun-toting horse thief,
a desperado of the worst kind? As one might expect,
the answer varies according to the "expert" con-
sulted. Early writers maintained that Belle Starr
kept company with the likes of bad men ranging from
Cole Younger to the lesser-known Jim Reed and Sam
Starr; that she cussed and handled weapons like a
man; and that she stole horses, an arch crime in the
Old West. More recent analysts argue that Belle
Starr was more hyperbole than fact, like such over-
done male figures as Doc Holiday and Billy the Kid.
Who is right?

In a sense, both views are correct. Belle Starr did
in fact know and like Cole Younger; likewise, she
married Jim Reed and later Sam Starr. She had an
acerbic personality that frequently resulted in a blis-
tering verbal tirade or a quick grab for her pistol.
And, on occasion, she took a horse when she believed
its owner owed her something. Clearly, however,
Belle Starr's exploits were inflated, her image limned
and expanded to feed a reading audience hungry for
tales of derring-do and moral precepts from the Wild
West as well as of western women who broke gender
bonds to do whatever they darn well pleased.

Introduction

In his 1941 book *Belle Starr "The Bandit Queen,"* the writer, journalist, literary critic, and playwright Burton Rascoe (1892–1957) attempted to reveal the authentic woman. Because Rascoe was also a deputy sheriff of Pottawatomie County, near Shawnee, Oklahoma, he appeared to have additional authority regarding the subject of an Oklahoma outlaw. His title page promised to include court records, the "testimony of Old Nesters," and original accounts from such newspapers as the *Dallas News* and editor Richard K. Fox's widely read and influential *National Police Gazette*. Not only would Rascoe give what he called the "true story" of a "daring and glamorous lady" who went wrong, but he would also expose a number of bad men and marshals, telling why crime did not pay. Certainly, Rascoe's promotional vows were enough to intrigue female and male readers alike.

Rascoe's book soon played an important part of a long-standing Belle Starr tradition. As Rascoe notes in his excellent analytical introduction, the first tome about Belle Starr appeared in 1889, a few months after Starr's death. The anonymously authored *Bella Starr, the Bandit Queen; or, The Female Jesse James*, published by editor Fox, overflowed with tall tales and factual errors yet offered excitement and sexual innuendo. Predictably, it attracted people who professed to be good Victorians but had grown bored with romantic notions of hearts, flowers, and family. In reality, the late Victorian era was turbulent— brimming over with business scandals, labor unrest, dramatic reform movements, the Panic of 1893, the Spanish-American War of 1898, and a rising divorce rate (about one in thirteen marriages ending in divorce)—and many readers sought didactic tales that would guide their own behavior in the troubled world of the 1890s.

At the same time, changing literary traditions made acceptable the gossipy approach found in *Bella Starr*. The rise of realism, as practiced, for example, by William Dean Howells and Frank Norris during the 1880s and 1890s, dictated the inclusion of lurid details. Dime novels—small pamphlets that first appeared in the United States in 1860 and sold for ten cents—increasingly took as their topics western people and events. By the 1870s and 1880s such authors as Prentiss Ingraham and Ned Buntline cranked out novel after novel. At the same time, the newspaper magnate William Randolph Hearst added "yellow," or sensationalistic, reporting to the mix, while such "muckrakers" as Upton Sinclair and Ida Tarbell laid bare the dark underside of American society. Little wonder that editor Fox and the unnamed author of *Bella Starr* felt free not only to enhance Starr's story but to give it moral twists whenever possible.

Subsequent writers followed the lead, contributing rumor and speculation to Starr's story, which passed from popular literature into the realm of folklore. Over the years the imagined Belle Starr grew as fierce and strong as a man, as determined and bold as a soldier, as hardened as a convict, and as promiscuous as a prostitute. When Burton Rascoe came to the subject of Belle Starr, he admitted that the legendary woman was far more fascinating than the real one. Consequently, Rascoe included the more risqué legends and several conjectures along with his "factual" account of Belle Starr. Rascoe aimed his interpretation of Starr at a different audience than had Fox, yet social ills, including changing roles for women and a rising divorce rate (about one in five or six marriages ending in divorce), bedeviled the era. As a result, Americans of the early 1940s were steeped in searing social criticism, especially as practiced by Edmund Wilson and Lionel Trilling during the 1930s. Furthermore, the beginning of World War II beleaguered Americans in 1941, the same year that Rascoe's book appeared. As a result, they, like their forebears, hoped for an intriguing read that would take them back to the mythical and exciting Wild West and at the same time offer moral direction during another bewildering era.

Thus did Rascoe, a reasonable researcher but not a trained historian, put together a book that still lives today as much for what it tells about Belle Starr as it does about the World War II generation of Americans, who faced such issues as war, crime, and morality in the modern United States. Accordingly, Rascoe presented Belle Starr as being born into a pre–Civil War society overwhelmed by the issues of slavery, taxation, states rights, and people's allegiance to regions—the North, the South, and the West. He showed her life encompassing the Civil War era and the Progressive Era, filled with conflict, crime, and attempts at reform. Rascoe was at his best when supplying the historical context for Starr's life. He filled in the details of daily living and gave long quotations from newspapers, describing the political and economic climate of the time. His descriptions of William Clarke Quantrill and his "Raiders" shine as do later accounts of the James brothers, the Youngers, and the Daltons, all larger-than-life outlaws from Missouri, Belle's home state. Rascoe also took care to debunk what he judged inaccurate accounts, ranging from *Bella Starr* to those of a newspaper reporter known as Flossie, who claimed to be Belle Starr's granddaughter.

Even though Rascoe proceeded along a generally chronological line, his storytelling technique sometimes led him to depart from Belle Starr's life for so many pages that it is difficult to piece together a biography. In addition, he was not privy to what is known today about Belle Starr. The bare-bones data is that Belle Starr was born Myra Maybelle Shirley near Modoc, Missouri, on February 5, 1848. Her stubborn and single-minded father, John Shirley, had divorced his first wife in 1818, after a ten-year marriage that had produced two children; in 1829 he remarried but soon divorced again; and sometime during the 1830s John married a teenage woman, Myra's mother, Elizabeth Hatfield. On the Shirley homestead lived John, Elizabeth, Preston, and Charlotte Amanda from John's first marriage, and three children from John's third marriage: John Addison (b. 1841), Myra Maybelle (b. 1848), and Edward Benton (b. 1849).

During the 1850s John kept a hotel and saloon in the nearby town of Carthage, comprising about five hundred people, mostly pro-slave in sentiment. Indeed, the Shirleys themselves were slave owners. Visitors to the hotel provided a ready audience for the mischievous Myra. Located on a new route of the Santa Fe Railroad, it attracted slave owners, planters, merchants, lawyers, and those trying to escape the law. Although John and Elizabeth added two more sons to the family, Mansfield and Cravens, during the decade, they gave some attention to Myra's education. Like any proper Southern woman of the era, Myra learned female graces and such "female accomplishments" as piano playing at the Carthage Female Seminary, organized in 1855, as well as at a private school held in Carthage's Masonic Hall.

Even during these early years Myra exhibited dominant personality traits. A schoolmate said that the ten-year-old Myra "would fight anyone, boy or girl" with whom she had a disagreement. Myra did not practice female reticence at home either. She much preferred to ride horseback across the open fields in the company of her brother John Addison, known as Bud. He taught Myra to ride, use firearms, and never to walk away from a challenge. After the Civil War erupted in 1861, Missouri disintegrated into internal warfare between supporters of the Confederacy and of the Union. The eldest Shirley, Preston, moved to secessionist Texas, but Bud remained in Missouri. He became a bushwacker and was aided by his clever and daring sister, Myra, who carried intelligence across the lines. When Bud fell from a miltiaman's bullet in June 1864, Myra strapped on a gun belt holding two large revolvers and swore to avenge Bud's death.

Within days, however, John Shirley packed his family and belongings in covered wagons and fled a burned and sacked Carthage. John settled his brood in Scyene, south of Dallas and near his son Preston, where he established a mixed-crop farm and raised horses. The Shirleys did not seem to fit in, however. At school Myra's fellow students judged her cranky and badly behaved. In their neighborhood the Shirleys were thought selfish and clannish; John had grown petulant and even fractious, often ranting against the carpetbagger rule that followed the war's end in 1864, claiming it persecuted Southerners who had fought for their cause. When the fugitives Jesse and Frank James appeared at the Shirleys' door seeking a haven, John willingly gave refuge to the two men and four of their gang who could be arrested as former Quantrill's Raiders. Among them was Cole Younger, who later denied the rumor that he had had any involvement with Myra, especially fathering her first child.

It was Jim Reed, another former guerrilla, who snagged Myra's attention and eventually her affection. The handsome and dashing Jim resembled her late brother, Bud, in that he rode well, shot often, and took frequent risks. On November 1, 1866, the eighteen-year-old Myra married twenty-year-old Jim; in 1868 she bore their first child, Rosie Lee, soon known as Pearl. Although Myra was a devoted wife, farm woman, mother, and churchgoer, Jim absented himself a good deal. In Forth Smith, Arkansas, he gambled and raced horses. In Indian Territory, west of Forth Smith, Jim joined the Cherokee Tom Starr, known throughout the area as a horse and cattle thief, in his illegal activities.

Life failed to improve for Myra after the couple bolted to California because Jim had assisted in the assassination of his brother's killer. In 1871 Myra bore a son, James Edwin, soon known as Eddie; the

same year federal officials charged Jim with passing counterfeit money and running from a murder
charge in Arkansas. After Jim fled, Myra moved her
small family back to Texas. Jim rejoined her in Sy-
cene, where the couple farmed a small patch of land
that the Shirleys gave them. Although Myra was determined to be a "good" woman and a faithful wife,
Jim defeated her efforts. In Indian Territory in 1873
he participated in the infamous Grayson robbery. Because Myra decided that she wanted no more of Jim's
criminal activities, she moved with her children into
her parents' home. In the meantime, Jim took a mistress and used aliases in a number of robberies. On
August 9, 1874, a distraught Myra identified the
body of a man that a deputy sheriff had shot and
killed; it was her husband. The following day the
Dallas Commercial described Myra Reed as a "highly
educated and accomplished lady" who lived with her
children in her parents' home. Myra and her children remained quietly with the elder Shirleys until
1876.

During these years Myra Maybelle Shirley Reed
was free of a wild man leading her astray, but other
troubles beset her. Her father died; her youngest
brother, known as Shug or Doc, fled from illegal activities; and her mother decided to move into Dallas, where Myra's daughter, Pearl, attended school.
Myra was left with the Shirleys' land and her son
Eddie, who she said "very much" resembled his father. In a series of letters that Myra wrote to her late
husband's family, she showed herself a nervous and
ill woman. When Eddie departed from home at age
twelve, Myra sold the Shirley farm and proceeded

to pay relatives extended visits. She was next heard of in a mining camp in Galena, Kansas, seemingly doomed to repeat her fascination with men who walked outside the law. In Galena Myra cohabited with Bruce Younger, a half-brother of Cole Younger's father. The couple lived in the Evans Hotel, where the owner remembered her as "a mighty good-lookin' woman . . . not tough like the newspapers made out." Other residents remarked that she was always nicely dressed and well behaved.

The year 1880 was cataclysmic for Myra. Somehow she reestablished contact with members of the Starr clan, with which her husband, Jim, had once run. She especially admired Tom Starr's son, Sam, who, like Bud Shirley and Jim Reed, could ride and shoot with great flair. Myra not only married Sam but lopped five years off her age and began calling herself Belle. Belle and Tom Starr moved to an allotment provided by the Cherokee Nation, of which Tom was a member. They built a cabin and established a small farm near Eufaula, along the Canadian River. Here Belle tried to live undisturbed, but, as she put it, "it soon became noised around that I was a woman of some notoriety from Texas, and from that time on my home and actions have been severely criticized." Belle, often her own enemy, contributed to her already bad reputation by housing Jesse James for three weeks. Sam was also in a tenuous position; as a Starr and a Cherokee he was automatically suspect in almost any situation.

Still, Belle and Sam managed to live peacefully until 1883, when the U.S. Commissioner's Court in Fort Smith put out a warrant for the couple's arrest.

Introduction

Allegedly, they had stolen a white man's horse, worth about eighty dollars. When Belle and Sam fled to the north, sheriff's deputies pursued them. In arresting and disarming the couple, the officers found a six-gun in Belle's skirt pocket and two derringers secreted in her blouse. Because journalists speculated that Belle led a "band" of horse thieves who followed her as their "queen," the courtroom was packed with curious spectators. In court a tale of misunderstanding, based largely on Belle's temper, unfolded. During a four-day trial before Judge Isaac Charles Parker, notorious as a "hanging judge," Belle sent frequent notes to her attorneys, glared at Judge Parker, and generally let her disdain show. The upshot was that Judge Parker, taking into account that it was Belle's and Sam's first offense, sentenced her to two six-month terms and Sam to one year in the House of Corrections in Detroit, Michigan.

Because of good behavior for nine months, the couple gained release in late 1883. Although Belle had gained weight, her face was thin and wizened. The first thing she did was pick up Pearl and an orphan friend from the Missourians with whom they had been staying. The group headed for the Starr cabin on the Canadian River, where Belle hoped for seclusion. But rumors followed her everywhere. As the size of Belle's reported gang grew and Belle's supposed adventures reached unbelievable magnitude, she seemed to give in at last. She took to wearing a man's sombrero, gold earrings, and a Colt .45 pistol, which she called her "baby." Atop a tooled sidesaddle, she rode a black mare named Venus. On special occasions, she sported a black velvet riding habit.

Introduction

In other words, Belle Starr apparently accepted her largely fictitious identity.

In 1885 Belle made another bad decision concerning a man. When the alleged murderer John Middleton asked Belle to shelter him from the law, she agreed. Belle had known the twenty-nine-year-old Middleton previously and admired him as venturesome and brave. Sam also came to like Middleton and helped Belle secrete him for four months. When the law eventually closed in on the Starr cabin, Middleton tried to escape by swimming a half-blind mare across the flooded Poteau River south of Forth Smith. Middleton died in the attempt, thus closing his case but further tarnishing Belle's image.

The year 1886 proved even worse. Implicated in a series of robberies, Sam spent most of his time hiding, especially from the Indian police officer Frank West, in the wild landscape around the Starr cabin. Meanwhile, the U.S. Marshall's office in Fort Smith issued an order for Belle's arrest. Reportedly, she had stolen the horse on which Middleton had made his abortive escape, though she pled not guilty. Now labeled the leader of the Starr gang, Belle was soon arrested again, this time for robbery. After she posted bond, she agreed to pose for photographs for the *St. Louis Globe Democrat*. One of the shots featured Belle with the Cherokee Blue Duck, who had recently been convicted of murder. This became one of the most widespread of Belle Starr photographs and seemed to make clear her status as a female outlaw. She also gave an interview to the *Dallas Morning News*, but when the story appeared, an infuriated Belle was said to have fallen on the reporter, lashing at him with her riding whip, in the courtroom on the first morning of her hearing.

Oddly enough, the court exonerated Belle. Although Fort Smith citizens were sure of her guilt, a jury declared her not guilty of stealing the horse involved in the Middleton escape. The second charge, that of theft, remained pending. When Belle returned to the Starr cabin, she learned that Frank West had shot and killed her horse Venus and wounded Sam, who was at his brother's house. Sam surrendered to the U.S. Marshall in Fort Smith and posted bond. He and Belle then attended the town's Seventh Annual Fair, where a hastily arranged Wild West show featured Belle shooting at clay pigeons and glass balls. Shortly after, Judge Parker's court convicted Sam's father, Tom, of liquor violations and stealing stock, sending him to the Southern Illinois Penitentiary.

Shrugging off their troubles, the couple along with Belle's children, Pearl and Eddie, attended a Christmas party, where Belle accompanied the fiddler on a pedal organ. When deputy Frank West appeared, chaos erupted. According to the *Muskogee Indian Journal*, Sam Starr and Frank West argued, then Starr shot West, who, staggering, returned the fire. Both men fell dead on the floor, bringing an abrupt end to the party, to the Starr marriage, and to Belle's position as an intermarried citizen of the Cherokee Nation. Before officials could force her off the Starr allotment, however, Belle invited one of Tom Starr's Cherokee men, Bill July, to live with her. Because the Bureau of Indian Affairs accepted such marriages, Belle retained her land. For an inexplicable reason, she renamed her new mate July Starr and proceeded with her life.

Things did not go well for Belle and July. Eddie especially resented July, who was only seven years his senior and fifteen years Belle's junior. Eddie, who looked like his father, Jim Reed, began to act like him too, courting trouble wherever he went. Belle administered several demeaning whippings to Eddie, which made the humiliated lad more troublesome than ever. In the meantime, things went sour with Belle and her daughter as well. After Belle encouraged the young man Pearl loved to marry another, Pearl got pregnant by the now married man and Belle ordered her to leave home. When July was arrested in mid-1887 for stealing horses, Belle reached her limit. She refused to help, and the court put him in jail with a bail of five hundred dollars. Eddie was then shot resisting arrest, so Belle called Pearl home, but without her child.

Belle appeared out of control. She beat Eddie with a bullwhip on several occasions and badgered Pearl to give up her daughter, Flossie, for adoption. And when Belle heard that a tenant on her land was wanted in Florida, she cursed and threatened the man, making yet another enemy. Belle's difficulties peaked early in February 1889 when she went to Fort Smith to answer a long-standing charge of theft. As she rode back toward the Starr cabin on February 3, shots toppled her to the ground. Belle Starr lay dead in the road, just two days shy of turning forty-one years old.

Even though Burton Rascoe's biography lacks some of these details, he saw clearly that Belle Starr was a pathetic and tormented woman who exercised poor judgment time after time. He points out that she was not a murderer and barely a horse thief. She was convicted only once, for which she spent nine months in prison. Rascoe also demonstrates that, in a sense, Belle Starr created much of her own misery. Belle was a bright, attractive woman who rejected the female world and its interests. Instead she was drawn to men, all of them resembling her bold and audacious brother Bud. Her choices did not serve her well; they carried her outside the law and "proper" late-nineteenth-century society. Even when she retreated into the Cherokee Nation with her second husband, Sam, and later with July, she found herself in the midst of illicit liquor trading, horse stealing, and petty robbery, and this at the very time that Indians and whites alike were trying to eliminate from the area such criminals as those of the Starr clan.

In his revisionist approach to Belle Starr, Rascoe further explains that at the time of her death Starr was "no more than a local character." Yellow journalists and dime novelists, always in need of new material, pounced on her story and turned her into a national figure. Of course Belle Starr died at a fortuitous time for legend making. In 1890 the U.S. Bureau of the Census declared the West "closed," meaning that because the region had an average of two people per square mile it could no longer be considered a frontier. Americans of the 1890s were left devoid of the mythic frontier that had so long provided them with romance, adventure, and a primal sort of morality. Americans who were anxious to see and smell the Old West flocked to Buffalo Bill Cody's Wild

West Exposition and its scores of imitators. They also voraciously consumed dime novels about the West. Into this milieu dropped Belle Starr's story, replete with her violent death in 1889. It is little wonder that she became fodder for those churning out western popular culture.

Fifty years passed after Starr's death before Burton Rascoe attempted to untangle her legend—fifty years of exaggeration, extrapolation, and outright falsehood. Although the Ozark folklorist Vance Randolph had tried to analyze Belle in a 1931 essay, Rascoe's study was the first book-length treatment. It pioneered in the revision of long-accepted western American myths. It demonstrated a desire to cut through the mists shrouding anything western. And it showed compassion and understanding for the anguished woman known as Belle Starr. Long before the women's history movement erupted during the 1960s and scholars subsequently rethought customary views of women in American and western history, Rascoe judged Starr with unusual insight. It was not, he wrote, her reputation as a petty horse thief and "harborer of criminals" that led to her downfall. It was Belle's "eccentricity of conduct" as a woman for which she paid.

Rascoe's book sold well, yet only a few listened to his underlying message. Writers, artists, and even songwriters continued to immortalize Belle Starr as an intrepid bandit queen. Not until 1982 did an unusually reliable book on Belle Starr appear that supplanted Rascoe in facts, but not style. In *Belle Starr and Her Times: The Literature, the Facts, and the Legends*, the now deceased author Glenn Shirley, pre-

Introduction

sumably a descendant of Belle Starr, put side-by-side actual court records and bombastic newspaper accounts. From public records he established the basic facts of Belle Starr's life. Also, because Shirley researched and wrote about criminals and law officers in Oklahoma Territory, he was able to weave a useful historical context for Belle Starr. Unfortunately, his organization was difficult to follow, and he gave no interpretative framework for her actions.

If Rascoe was still alive he might agree that it is too late to transform Belle Starr into a factual historical figure. As Rascoe remarked, she remains immortalized "in the folk legend of the Southwest . . . part of the romantic heritage of the region, where no rules of fact govern the telling of a person's story." The creation of the legends concerning the Mississippi River boatman Mike Fink and the Minnesota lumberman Paul Bunyan are two good examples. As a result, Belle Starr ranks with Calamity Jane, the Rose of Cimarron, and Pearl Hart, other women who chose to live at the edges of the law and more in a world of men than of women.

SUGGESTIONS FOR FURTHER READING

The Belle Starr obituary that provided much grist for the mill is reprinted as "The Weekly Elevator, Fort Smith, Arkansas, February 15, 1889," in Jerry J. Gaddy, comp., *Obituaries of the Gunfighters: Dust to Dust* (San Rafael CA: Presidio Press, 1977), 67–73.

The books that originally shaped Belle Starr mythology were the anonymously written (sometimes the author is listed as Alton B. Meyers) *Bella Starr: The Bandit Queen; or, The Female*

Introduction

Jesse James (New York: Richard K. Fox, 1889) and S. W. Harman, *Hell on the Border* (Fort Smith AR: n.p., 1898).

Other authors besides Burton Rascoe who delved into the Belle Starr legend were the Ozark folklorist Vance Randolph, who published under a pseudonym, Anton S. Booker. See his *Wildcats in Petticoats* (Girard KS: Little Blue Books, 1931), 52–63, and William Yancey Shackleford, *Belle Starr, The Bandit Queen* (Girard KS: Haldeman-Julius Publications, 1943). A writer who treated Belle Starr with sympathy and proclaimed that his details were accurate (but who is generally unreliable) was James D. Horan. See *Desperate Women* (New York: G. P. Putnam's Sons, 1952).

During the 1970s Carl W. Breihan with Charles A. Rosamond put Starr stories in a highly readable format for a general audience in *The Bandit Belle* (Seattle: Hangman Press, 1970). Charles W. Mooney's *Doctor in Belle Starr Country* (Oklahoma City: Century Press, 1975) claims to relate the author's physician father's experiences with Belle Starr but contains many local fables. The work of Robert G. Winn, *Two Starrs: Belle, the Bandit Queen, Pearl, River Front Madame* (Fayetteville AR: Washington County Historical Society, 1979), which was later reprinted as *Who Killed Belle Starr?* (Fayetteville AR: Washington County Historical Society, 1994), contains information regarding Pearl Starr, and speculates on Belle Starr's assassins, but is full of errors.

Published more recently, William Watkins's *Was There a Real Belle Starr?* (n.p.: n.p., 1986) is full of fifteen pages of tall tales from "Belle Starr country," where Watkins claims to have grown up. Glenn Shirley's *Belle Starr and Her Times: The Literature, the Facts, and the Legends* (Norman: University of Oklahoma Press, 1982) is reliable but difficult to read. Glenda Riley's essay "Belle Starr: Queen of the Bandits," 139–58, in Richard W. Etulain and Glenda Riley, eds., *With Badges and Bullets: Lawmen and Outlaws in the Old Wild West* (Golden CO: Fulcrum Publishing, 1999) offers a feminist interpretation. Carl R. Green's and William R. Sanford's *Belle Starr* (Hillside NJ: Enslow, 1992) is a version of Belle Starr's life for young adult readers. Phillip W. Steele's *Starr Tracks: Belle and Pearl Starr* (Gretna LA: Pelican

Introduction

Publishing Co., 1992) combines Belle's and Pearl's stories and includes some family letters as well.

For other articles on Belle Starr see, James A. Browning, ed., *The Western Reader's Guide: A Selected Bibliography of Nonfiction Magazines, 1953–91* (Stillwater OK: Barbed Wire Press, 1997), 293–94.

There are a number of books by and about Burton Rascoe worth mentioning as well. *Titans of Literature, from Homer to the Present* (New York: G. P. Putnam, 1933) is the author's best-known book, a widely acclaimed assessment of thirty important writers; *Before I Forget* (New York: Literary Guild of America, Inc., 1937) is an account of the author's literary life; *The Dalton Brothers and Their Astounding Career of Crime, by an Eye Witness* (New York: Frederick Fell, 1954) was edited by Rascoe and chronicles the career of the notorious criminals the Dalton Brothers; Donald M. Hensley, *Burton Rascoe* (New York: Twayne, 1970), examines Rascoe's life and work; and James Branch Cabell, et al., *Burton Rascoe* (New York: Wildside Printing, 2001), also analyzes the author's life and work.

For Ruth Rascoe

ACKNOWLEDGMENTS

———————

My indebtedness to many people for help in preparing this book is great; but I wish especially to acknowledge my thanks to these:

To Mr. Nat Fleischer, editor and publisher of *Ring*, New York City, for his courtesy in permitting me to make use of his incomparably complete files of the *National Police Gazette;* to Mr. Jerry Rand, of the New York *Sun;* to Mr. Wayne Gard of the Dallas *News;* to Miss Elaine Boylan, librarian of the Dallas *News;* to Miss Stella N. Drumm, librarian of the Missouri Historical Society, St. Louis; to Sheriff C. C. Hawk of Pottawatomie County, Shawnee, Okla.; to Mr. Victor Harlow, president of the Harlow Publishing Co., Oklahoma City., Okla., to Mr. Walter M. Harrison, managing editor of the *Daily Oklahoman*, Oklahoma City, Okla.; to the staff of the Oklahoma Historical Society, Oklahoma City, Okla.; to Mr. Savoie Lottinville of the University of Oklahoma Press, Norman, Okla.; to Professor Kenneth C. Kaufman of the University of Oklahoma and literary editor of the *Daily Oklahoman;* to Mr. M. Harzof of the G. A. Baker & Co., booksellers, New York City; to Mrs. George Rogers Fluke of Ponca City, Okla.; to Dr. Angelo C. Scott of Oklahoma City, Okla.; to Mr. Charles Bragin, whom I have dubbed "The King of Dime Novel Collectors," who

Acknowledgments

offered me unrestricted use of his incomparable collection of 30,000 items; to the Messrs. Bennett A. Cerf, Donald S. Klopfer and Saxe Commins of Random House, New York City, for their generous co-operation; and very especially to my secretary, Miss Diana Grant, who was constantly, though sympathetically, critical of my text, and who therefore saved me from more blunders than I might otherwise have committed. I make no special acknowledgment to my wife, Hazel Rascoe, because no formal acknowledgment of the aid given by the wife of an author to her husband could possibly indicate the special burden that is put upon a wife when a writer is composing a book. Suffice it to say that Mrs. Rascoe bore the trial with equanimity and read the manuscript with approval. My indebtedness to writers who have been in the field before me, I have acknowledged, amply, I hope, in the *Bibliographical Review*.

CONTENTS

ILLUSTRATIONS

———•———

PART ONE

FOLKLORE AND HISTORY

FOLKLORE AND HISTORY

—————•—————

Vernon Parrington's monumental three-volume history, *Main Currents in American Thought*—especially the volume devoted to *The Romantic Revolution in America*—is guilty of a glaring omission. It contains no reference to Richard K. Fox and his *National Police Gazette*.

That sprightly, well-edited, highly moral and romantically imaginative illustrated news-weekly had a much more profound influence upon the national culture of its period than had the work of all the romantic writers discussed by Parrington put together.

The *National Police Gazette* was read presumably by the male half of the population only, and was to be found in bordellos, saloons, gambling houses, poolhalls, livery stables and barber-shops. Nonetheless, it crystallized and sustained a national code of morals and honor. It provided a way of thinking, a pattern of conduct, a point of view and a rationale of sentiment that were adopted by at least ninety per cent of the male population of the United States—and, by a sort of spiritual contagion, ninety per cent of the female contingent, also.

From the *National Police Gazette* (with the hearty support of brewers, distillers and saloonkeepers) American men learned that it was immoral, degrading and ungentlemanly to drink alone, whether at a bar or in the privacy of one's home; that it is cowardly to shoot your enemy in the back or to shoot at him, face to face, until he has made a move to draw his gun or a knife; that you must knock a man down (or try to) if he says anything more profane than "shuckin's" in the presence of a lady, i.e., anything in skirts, including, especially, the inmates of a bawdy house; that a man who cheats at cards deserves to be shot down like a dog (an injunction that, if it were consistently carried out, would have reduced the professional gambling population to zero within a month's time); that when a gentleman is walking down the street with a lady, he should walk on the side nearest the curb (so he won't have to fire a shot of tobacco juice across her bow in order to hit the gutter, thus endangering the lady's apparel; and so that he can make a quick get-away if an emergency arises); that if some vile reptile seduces your sister, even at her invitation, you have to take the law into your own hands and see to it that the viper becomes your brother-in-law right away; that you must never hit a man with his glasses on—you must make him take them off first so he can't see to hit you at all; that you must never smoke in the presence of ladies, even if they themselves dip snuff; that you should never let your children see you intoxicated or under the influence of strong drink—better to sleep it off on the floor of a saloon; that if your mustache hangs down over your lower lip you should always genteelly part it before drinking coffee out of a saucer; and that the most sacred word in the language is the word "mother"—anybody's mother.

Week in and week out the *National Police Gazette* impressed this code of conduct upon the minds of its gentlemen readers, both directly by precept and indirectly by narrative—but even more effectively by pen-and-ink illustrations.

The *National Police Gazette,* especially during the editor-ownership of Richard K. Fox, was the source of a vast deal of our native folklore, particularly as it involved crime and retribution, the vices of the rich, the sins of the cities and the exploits of gunmen and outlaws. Much that was invented for the columns of that pink-paper illustrated weekly has passed into legends that have come down the years by word-of-mouth and have been embellished by lonely oldsters residing among bleak hills, remote bayous, scanty prairie settlements, jerkwater railroad stops, lumber camps and desert way-stations.

Belle Starr

In the swamps of Arkansas, old nesters still tell weird stories they heard from the lips of their grandfathers, "true" stories of the infamous Murrell gang which these grandfathers, or more likely, someone else, had read in the pages of the *National Police Gazette* as early as 1850, long before Richard K. Fox got hold of it.

In shanty towns along the Brazos and in the Texas Panhandle, men whose memories have been dimmed by the years tell of their "personal experiences" with such fabulous and notorious characters as John Wesley Hardin, Sam Bass and the Thompson brothers. They insist that what they tell you is something which actually occurred to them in their youth. Quite naturally, they have long since forgotten, through so many retellings, that their experience was vicarious, thanks to the vivid pages of the *National Police Gazette*.

In New Mexico, it would probably be hard to find an old-timer who, on being questioned as to whether or not he remembers any stories or legends about "Billy the Kid," will not perk up and tell you that he knew "The Kid" intimately. Pressed for details of this intimacy, nine times in ten he will swear that "The Kid" stayed overnight many times at the narrator's cabin and, indeed, considered it a second home. And invariably the descriptions of "The Kid," and even the episodes in his career that these narrators "remember," are virtually the same.

Folklore and History

The reason is not far to seek: the sources of these descriptions and narrations were the *National Police Gazette*. "The Kid," in these oldster's descriptions, was slim, neat and handsome, with beautifully small hands and feet, light brown, wavy hair, and clear, gray, steady eyes, a smilingly expressive mouth; he was quiet, unassuming, modest, gentle, good-natured except when aroused, courteous and gallant in his bearing toward all women and therefore the Galahad of women young and old; his mind and muscle were so marvelously co-ordinated that his act of drawing and shooting a pistol was a quicker-than-the-eye action, like that of an expert sleight-of-hand performer; he was generous, loyal to his friends, well poised and aristocratic in his bearing.

"Billy the Kid's legend in New Mexico," wrote the late Walter Noble Burns, in *The Saga of Billy the Kid,* "seems destined to a mellow and genial immortality like that which gilds the misdeeds and exaggerates the virtues of such ancient rogues as Robin Hood, Claude Duval, Dick Turpin and Fra Diavolo. From the tales you hear of him everywhere, you might be tempted to fancy him the best-loved hero in the state's history. His crimes are forgotten or condoned, while his loyalty, his gay courage, his superhuman adventures are treasured in affectionate memory. Men speak of him with admiration; women extol his gallantry and lament his fate. A rude balladry in

Spanish and English has grown up about him, and in every placeta in New Mexico, Mexican girls sing to their guitars songs of Billy the Kid. A halo has been clapped upon his scapegrace brow. The boy who never grew old has become a symbol of frontier knight-errantry, a figure of eternal youth riding forever through a purple glamour of romance.''

Walter Noble Burns was a serious-minded and conscientious newspaperman, never given to faking or distorting his facts. He spent months traveling through the territory known to be the scene of the operations of Billy the Kid; he interviewed old-timers who claimed to have been on intimate terms with the bandit; he read old paper-bound books alleging to set forth the true story of the young outlaw's life; he patiently went through old newspaper files; he searched through dusty, badly scrawled public records in remote county court houses; he accumulated masses of legend and folklore but only a few grains of authentic fact. Burns had a problem on his hands.

The facts he was able to obtain about Billy the Kid could be stated in a paragraph: he appeared out of nowhere in Lincoln County, New Mexico, in the fall of 1887, when he was eighteen years old, giving his name as William H. Bonney, but preferring the sobriquet, ''Billy the Kid''; he was supposed to have been born in New York and to have been taken west at the age of three by his widowed mother; on his arrival in Lincoln County, he apparently had practiced pistol shooting until he was an expert shot; and he himself had spread the rumor that he had killed his first man when he was twelve years old and had made the total of his homicides twelve by the time he was eighteen; that he hired out as a killer in the Chisum faction in the Chisum-Murphy cattle feud that became known as the Lincoln County War; that his killings became so notorious that he was summoned into the presence of General Lew Wallace (later the creator of *Ben Hur*), newly appointed Governor of the Territory of New Mexico, who promised to grant Billy the Kid a pardon for any crimes of which he might be convicted if he would surrender and stand trial— an offer The Kid refused; that he was arrested by Sheriff Pat Garrett and held in Lincoln County jail, awaiting trial for the murder of Bob Beckwith, and that he escaped from there after killing the jailer, J. W. Bell, and Deputy Sheriff Bob Ollinger; that he was shot to death by Marshal Pat Garrett at Pete Maxwell's house near Fort Sumner, Texas, and that his body was buried in a little cemetery in that now deserted spot; that although The Kid boasted of having killed twenty-one men in his twenty-one years, only three of his killings can be authenticated; that, although legends have it that The Kid was neat, handsome and dashing, the one known authentic photograph of him shows him to be a nondescript, ade-

noidal, weasel-eyed, narrow-chested, stoop-shoul-
dered, repulsive-looking creature with all the out-
ward appearance of a cretin.

But, ah, the legends! They were glorious! Forty-
five years after Billy the Kid's death, which was
when Burns began to write his book, the legends had
made of this probably undistinguished cowhand (who
hired out as a killer in a cattleman's feud) a hero, a
Rob Roy, a loyal avenger with unerring aim, a friend
and protector of the poor, an agent of justice, although an outlaw.

Burns' book is a genuine contribution to Americana and American folklore, partly because copies of
the *National Police Gazette* containing contemporary accounts of The Kid's career, are so rare that
he undoubtedly never had an opportunity to study
the Fox writers' treatment of the subject. If he had,
Burns' story of Billy the Kid might well have been
entirely different.

Curiously enough, the Fox staff, although they invented episodes and anecdotes to build up and point
the character of the heroes and heroines of their
crime biographies, ordinarily were careful to get
essential dates, names and pertinent facts correct.
Unfortunately, it was not the truth that was remembered—only the legends the *Police Gazette* writers
created.

In its handling of the story of Billy the Kid, the

staff of the *National Police Gazette* had more reliable sources of information than those later available to Walter Noble Burns. While The Kid was still alive, the *National Police Gazette* was running almost weekly accounts of the whereabouts and activities of the bandit, telegraphed by its far-flung correspondents. The *National Police Gazette's* account of The Kid's escape from the Lincoln jail was vivid and succinct. When Pat Garrett's Colt .45, Navy pattern, six-gun put an end to the career of Billy the Kid, Richard K. Fox's staff writer of criminal "biographies" had ready at hand the essential known facts in The Kid's career. There remained only the imaginative work of filling in those episodes that were later to become absorbed into folklore. These episodes, illustrative of The Kid's bravery, quick thinking, loyalty, expertness with a gun and essential good character, followed a fixed formula.

It was a rigid formula that fitted in with the conscious needs, aspirations and ideals of the commonality. Any other would not have been acceptable to the audience of the Richard K. Fox publications, and Fox would have failed. Indeed, the Fox publications went bankrupt when the scene, the complexion of the country, changed, the American mind became more civilized and adult, and Fox neglected to modify the expression of the formula in consonance with the change in the times and the public mind.

◄§ 11 §►

The essentials of the formula are fairly constant. They are the same today as they were, not only fifty years, but a thousand years, ago; only the manner of presentation changes. The essentials embrace fundamental psychological facts: (1) civilized man, no matter how circumspect, law-abiding, conventional and tamed he may be, has a subconscious desire for revolt against law, against restraint, against the civilizing forces of life; (2) thus, even when he deplores, he always has a measure of admiration for the outlaw, the man who is definitely at odds with the restraints of civilization and inimical to them; (3) if the outlaw hero is depicted as having been a naturally good and very superior man who was forced into outlawry through an event that outraged his sense of justice, particularly if the outrage was perpetrated by a representative or representatives of the forces of law and order, the civilized man is able to make the outlaw hero his vicar in the righting of injustice by spectacular revenge; for every civilized man is, at times, or feels himself to be, the victim of an injustice which he cannot right, or of forces against which he cannot take revenge; so his outlaw hero performs *for him,* cleansing his emotions of hate by vicariously killing (in a brilliant, courageous and superior manner) the representatives of the persons or forces the civilized man hates; (4) the outlaw hero must die, preferably through treachery or against terrific odds and never in a fair and open fight; for there must be retribution for the outlawry, not only to satisfy the moral conscience of the civilized man, but also because the vicar, or the scapegoat, who bears the weight of one's sins, must die so that civilized man may live.

The murder of Belle Starr caught Richard K. Fox's staff writers unawares. When Belle died she was no more than a local character in Fort Smith, Arkansas, in Dallas, Texas, and in the Cherokee Nation of Indian Territory. She was known in her own bailiwick merely as a horse thief and a harborer and consort of horse and cattle thieves and outlaws, although a forceful, showy, exhibitionistic and clever woman who had kept out of the tangles of the law, except for one prison sentence, and who was well liked by many people.

But Belle's mother and some of her kinfolk were still living in Dallas or near Scyene (two miles west of what is now Mesquite), Texas, and they were interviewed by correspondents of the *National Police Gazette* for information as to Belle's life and career, after the Dallas, Fort Smith and Kansas City newspapers began to make a sensation out of the murder. Obviously Belle's kinfolk tightened their lips and refused to divulge any information, or gave versions of Belle's history least likely to bring discredit upon themselves; and the newsmen had to resort to other and less reliable sources among Belle's acquaintances.

In order to exploit the public curiosity about this female bandit, whose murder had suddenly thrown her into the national limelight, and make it possible for him to sell twenty-five-cent, paper-bound books about her life, Richard K. Fox could not follow his usual procedure of serializing the biography in his weekly. It would have to appear "cold," without previous serialization. And so it did. Among all of Fox's biographical books about bandits, *Bella Starr, the Bandit Queen, or the Female Jesse James* is unique. This narrative does not have a single essential fact correct: her name and date of birth are both wrong in the Fox story, and from there on, the yarn is a masterpiece of a hack writer's invention. Unhampered by restricting facts, and inspired by having a female bandit to write about, the anonymous Fox Publications genius really went to town. His opening paragraph gives you the key:

Of all women of the Cleopatra type, since the days of the Egyptian queen herself, the universe has produced none more remarkable than Bella Starr, the Bandit Queen. Her character was a combination of the very worst as well as some of the very best traits of her sex. She was more amorous than Anthony's mistress; more relentless than Pharaoh's daughter, and braver than Joan of Arc. Of her it may well be said that Mother Nature was indulging in one of her rarest freaks, when she produced such a novel specimen of womankind. Bella was not only well educated, but gifted with uncommon musical and literary talents, which were almost thrown away through the bias of her nomadic and lawless disposition, which early isolated her from civilized life, except at intervals, when in a strange country, and under an assumed name, she brightened the social circle for a week or a month, and then was, perhaps, lost forever.

Thereafter the story lives up to the elaborate promise of the opening paragraph. Having claimed so much for Belle, the author had to prove all his points by realistic narrative, involving dialogue as well as action. He went to work with zest and abandon, filling in gaps with faintly plausible excerpts from what was alleged to be Belle's private diary, in which she is pictured as writing down the horrifying details of her daring robberies and the mirthful details of some of the exploits in which she was the heroine and others were the discomfited victims. Needless to say, the diary was as mythical as almost all the episodes related in the Fox book.

So highly imaginative, so good, in its way, was *Bella Starr, the Bandit Queen, or the Female Jesse James,* that it became the treasure chest of other fabulists in writing or talking about Belle. Years later, people repeated the inventions from this book as facts they knew about Belle from personal experience. Other people, who professed to be historians, credulously and solemnly set down some of these oft-repeated legends as historically true episodes in the career of Belle Starr.

After I had completed my investigation of source material for this book, letters began to come to me from many people who claimed to have authentic and exclusive information about Belle Starr from persons who had known her.

In nearly every instance it turned out that these "true" stories were garbled versions of the apocryphal anecdotes invented by the anonymous hack in Fox's employ a half-century ago. Occasionally, the correspondent would send something he or she had heard direct from the lips of a grandfather or grandmother.

These anecdotes at least proved that the grandfather or grandmother was not lacking in creative imagination. Typical of these generous offers of help in preparing my book about Belle Starr is this ingenuous bit:

I have some true happenings in the life of Belle Starr in which my grandfather, unfortunately, participated. All this information came from him. I heard him tell it no less than forty-nine times.

It is a little difficult to write so I am going to write as if I were writing a book. Note description of Belle Starr's clothes. I thought this was something you might not have.

Chandler, Oklahoma, on July 2, 1894,[1] was like any other day in July—warm and almost sultry. Mr. Blank [Name omitted—B.R.] wiped the perspiration from his forehead as he entered the city bank's one large room. His law office was on one section off a wooden fence. From the other offices in the bank came greetings.

"Good morning, Mr. Blank," one called. "You seem to be in a big hurry this morning."

"Yes," he answered. "I've some letters to write. Have to get them off in the early morning mail."

At nine-thirty o'clock that morning the letters were ready for mailing, and Mr. Blank was walking out of the bank. As he stepped out to the sidewalk, he was confronted by one of the most handsome men he had ever seen. Blank recognized the face of Bill Doolin who was leveling a gun at his heart.

"Keep going, but don't bat an eyelash, or I'll send you straight to hell."

Mr. Blank was so frightened he could scarcely move. He saw four other men with revolvers. Since none of them were masked, and since he had seen many pictures of Cherokee Bill and Lucas, he immediately recognized them.

Carefully putting one foot in front of the other, Mr. Blank thought each step might be his last as he considered his past life. He later reported that it seemed a year before the walk to the end of the block was at an end.

In the middle of the road sat Belle Starr on her brown and white horse. Dressed in a black riding habit and a crisp white blouse, she rode side saddle, her high top laced shoes

---

[1] The robbery Mr. Blank told about took place, according to his account, on July 2, 1894. Belle Starr was murdered February 3, 1889.

showing beneath her skirt. Her black eyes blazed at Mr. Blank.

Her guns were concealed in the folds of her dress, and Mr. Blank saw them move as he passed by. He felt sure she intended to kill him then, but at that instant Mitchell, a barber, saw the bank robbers and rushed out yelling,

"Bank robbers! Bank robbers!"

Belle Starr stormed, "Get back in there or I'll blow your head off."

He disappeared, then returned, screaming, "Bank . . . !"

That was his last word, for he fell at the feet of Mr. Blank who was forced to step over his body and continue down the street.

As the robbers were leaving the bank and mounting their horses, Lucas was injured and his horse killed. He fell to the ground. The robbers picked him up and started to take him on with them, but he was so badly wounded, he begged them to leave him. They did that, so Lucas was captured.

My correspondent's grandfather's yarn, although repeated forty-nine times, is entirely fictitious on the face of it. The robbery the narrator tells about is alleged to have taken place in 1894. Belle Starr was murdered on February 3, 1889. Belle Starr *never* participated in the robbery of a bank. There was *never* a warrant out for her charging her with murder.

If the narrator witnessed what he says he witnessed, he would have sworn out a warrant for Belle Starr and her two companions; and the three miscreants would have hanged for the robbery, for the narrator was a lawyer; therefore he was a substantial eye-witness, and his testimony would have convicted the trio. The only Lucas tried for a capital offense in Judge Parker's Federal Court at Fort Smith (where the robber would have been taken for trial) was Eli Lucas, who was convicted on June 11, 1895, and sentenced to die October 1, 1895, the conviction afterward being reversed by the Supreme Court and Lucas returned to the Choctaw Nation. . . . One detail in my correspondent's grandfather's yarn *may* have been true: "July 2, 1894, was like any other day in July—warm and almost sultry."

The Richard K. Fox employee who wrote the anonymous *Bella Starr, the Bandit Queen, or the Female Jesse James,* very early in his narrative introduced a masterpiece of erotic invention which was so implausible, yet so titillating, that it was lifted intact or embroidered upon or paraphrased boldly by nearly every person who chose to write even a newspaper article about Belle over a period of fifty years.

The Fox writer's story was, in brief, that once, in a crowded hotel in Dallas, accommodations were so scarce that Belle, christened Myra Belle Shirley, and at the time married to Jim Reed (or Bella, as the Fox writer had it), who had disguised herself as a young man, was forced to share a room with a prominent judge, who, of course, was not aware of his roommate's identity.

Throughout the evening, so the Fox writer's story went, there was much talk about the notorious "Bella" Starr and her ability to disguise herself as a man so that no one could recognize her. To which pronouncement the judge allowed that no woman living could fool him. "Bella," according to the story, listened to all this talk with great apprehension because she had to devise some means whereby she could get her night's rest in the same bed with, and alongside of, the judge without his discovering that she was a woman—let alone "Bella" Starr.

Suffice it now to say that a good night's sleep was enjoyed by "Bella" and the judge in the same bed; that "Bella" was awake early in the morning and fully dressed while the judge was still snoring, and that, before making her get-away, she could not resist the temptation to awake the judge, inform him of her identity and enjoy his discomfiture:

After partaking of a hurried meal, Bella saddled her horse and hitched him to the gate in front of the house, after which she ascended the stairway to the Judge's room and awoke him.

"Judge," said she, "Mrs. Reed, of whom you were speaking last night, is downstairs waiting to see you. Get up at once. She hasn't a moment to spare."

"Dear me," said he, "I wonder what in the mischief she

wants at this hour of the morning.'' Saying which he crawled from beneath the blankets and proceeded to dress.

''My friend,'' said he, as Bella was leaving the room, ''you must be mistaken. I can't believe such a thing until I see for myself.''

Our heroine was on the porch awaiting Thurman, who descended with a cautious step, till he reached the door. Looking out and seeing nothing of ''his own dear Myra,'' as he had called her last night, he broke out with the following remarks:

''Young man, it ill becomes you to play practical jokes on your elders. I was particularly anxious for sleep this morning, and you . . .''

''Wait a minute, Judge,'' said she. ''Just step as far as the gate and you'll see the Bandit Queen.''

Bella opened the gate, and laying one hand on the withers of her horse, vaulted into the saddle.

''Where? Where is she?'' asked the judge.

''Look right into my face—look well. I am Bella Reed, and you—well you are a consummate old fool. Your own self-conceit will damn you without the devil's help. Dallas has reason to be proud of its judiciary. Go right home and tell your friends that you have had the honor and glory of sleeping with the Bandit Queen.'' With these words Bella put spurs to her horse and struck westward like a blue streak.

Anyone familiar with the smutty stories which are part of our cultural heritage will recognize the folklore pattern of this narrative and will also recognize that it falls into the category of those stories which have a homosexual cast. In the higher realms of literature, one finds variations on the theme in Théophile Gautier's *Mademoiselle de Maupin,* wherein the hero's moral anguish is relieved when he discovers that the beauteous person he loves is not a boy but a girl in disguise.

In the word-of-mouth repertory of off-color stories there are infinite variations of this theme of the crowded hotel, wherein the complication arises because two strangers have to sleep in the same bed. In the story about Belle and the judge, the Fox writer has "cleaned the story up" for family-fireside consumption.

It is amusing to read the variations in the subsequent versions of this story by those who purport to give us "authentic" accounts of Belle Starr's life. One of these writers is a woman who began to write about Belle Starr in 1933 under the name of "Flossie," alleging that she had only recently discovered that she was the long-lost granddaughter of Belle Starr, the granddaughter who, one legend has it, was given away to gypsies and who, another legend has it, was placed in an orphan asylum. "Flossie" claims that she was brought up in an orphanage and adopted therefrom by some good people who never disclosed to her the fact that she was not her adopters' child; but that the true facts were revealed to her in a mysterious way.

It is quite possible that what "Flossie" says about her being Belle's granddaughter is true. But it is unusual, to say the least, for one to claim that her grandmother was an outlaw and that her mother was a whore and keeper of a bawdy house. Inferentially, this is what "Flossie" asserts when she alleges that she was the daughter of Pearl Younger, who was the daughter of Belle Starr. "Flossie" circumvents any mention of her mother's profession.

In her accounts of the life of her grandmother, "Flossie" did not trouble to do any original research. She merely paraphrased what others had written. She relied mainly upon Ward L. Schrantz's *Jasper County, Missouri, in the Civil War,* and S. W. Harman's *Hell on the Border.*

When "Flossie" first began to publish newspaper stories of Belle Starr's career, she was obviously unaware of Harman's sources, the principal one of which, of course, was the Fox Publications' "biography," mentioned above, and extremely rare even in 1933. It is interesting to observe how "Flossie" used only a slightly paraphrased version of the Fox story of Belle and the judge and how she "cleaned up" Belle's parting shot to the judge. In "Flossie's" story, the dénouement is given thus:

Up in the room, Myra lay awake facing the risk of discovery. Before daylight she was out in the stable caring for her horse. She sent a boy into the hotel to ask Judge Blank to come out, that Myra Reed wanted to see him. Imagine his astonishment when the "young man" that had been his bedfellow came toward him, saying, ''Tell the folks that you have had the honor of meeting Myra Reed.'' And striking him with her riding whip, she mounted her horse and rode off like a streak.

Other versions of this yarn from which ''Flossie'' lifts hers, and which itself was derived from the Fox Publications' fiction, differ from ''Flossie's'' in that the judge is depicted as being a married man and Belle's parting shot is given as, ''Go home and tell *your wife* that you had the honor of sleeping with the notorious Belle Starr!''

One of the most persistent legends created about Belle by the Richard K. Fox staff writer and later reworked by numerous ''historians,'' because it was perhaps the most dramatic of his inventions, had to do with the identification of Jim Reed's body. We have no record of the marriage, and the stories vary as to the date, but it would appear that Belle might have been married, somewhat unconventionally to be sure, some time between 1866 and 1871, to Jim Reed, who was a notorious outlaw. Some stories date the marriage as 1866, some in 1867, some in 1868, some in 1870 and some in 1871.

At any rate, Jim Reed was killed by John T. Morris on August 6, 1874, about fifteen miles north of Paris, Texas. Morris, a newly appointed deputy sheriff, who was related to Reed, had a warrant for his arrest for participation in the robbery of the Austin-San Antonio stage on April 6, 1874. We know the date of Jim Reed's death and the circumstances surrounding it from the contemporary newspaper accounts.

There was a $7,000 reward offered for the apprehension of the robbers connected with the hold-up of the Austin-San Antonio stage. But where rewards were offered for notorious bandits, dead or alive, identification of the body was necessary, when a bandit was killed, before an officer could collect the reward. Here was a golden opportunity for the imagination of the Richard K. Fox writer. He could make it appear that Belle was the only one who could identify the body. In order to cheat Morris out of the reward, he made her lie valiantly, dramatically.

This is Harman's version of this breath-taking event in *Hell on the Border* as he rewrote it from *Bella Starr, the Bandit Queen, or the Female Jesse James:*

An event in connection with this cold-blooded murder [the killing of Jim Reed by Deputy Sheriff John Morris] exhibits the steady nerve and the powerful command which Belle had over herself. It was necessary for the assassin, in order to secure the reward offered for Reed "dead or alive," to furnish proof of his death, and as the murdered man was a stranger in that portion of the country where he was killed there was none to identify the body. The weather was sultry, making an early burial imperative, and word was sent to

Belle Starr

Belle informing her of her husband's death, the supposition being that she would weep, as would ordinary wives, over the remains, thus establishing their unquestioned identity. But Belle was far from "ordinary." When she received word to come and take charge of her husband's dead body her eyes took on a hard look and she said, "They've killed him for the reward but they will never git it," and rode to the house where the body lay. As she entered the room where a number of men, Morris among them, were gathered about the corpse, one of their number removed the covering, exposing the features, while the others silently fell back expecting to witness a heartrending scene of weeping. They also expected to make oath to what they saw, and thus assist the murderer to obtain the reward. Belle walked to the body, gave a glance at the face of her loved one and without the least sign of emotion, but with a scornful curve of the lips, quietly remarked:

"I am very sorry, gentlemen, that you have made such a mistake and killed the wrong man; very sorry, indeed. John Morris, you will have to kill Jim Reed if you desire to secure the reward offered for Jim Reed's body."

Since Morris had but a few days previous visited the man who now lay before them dead, at his own home, and Belle's, this was a turn in affairs on which he had not counted. Belle rode calmly away, suffering the anguish she would not indicate, and her husband's body was buried in the potter's field.

This is a good example of "slanting" a story in order to make a heroine out of a notorious woman by transforming everyone connected with her into a hero —a hero-martyr, in this case. Contemporary accounts give the facts about the shooting of Reed: he was under arrest and was, in fact, being treated too leniently by the arresting officer, who finally had the choice between killing him and getting killed himself.

Duncan Aikman in *Calamity Jane and the Lady Wildcats,* falls for the *Police Gazette* fiction. His version is this:

Belle came and looked at what was left of Jim dry-eyed and casually, but at Morris scornfully and for an uncomfortably long while.

"Mr. Morris," she said in her best Dallas evening-party irony, "I am very sorry, but you have killed the wrong man. If you want the reward for Jim Reed's body, you will have to kill Jim Reed."

"Flossie" gives this version in the Dallas *News* for April 30, 1933:

In order for him [John Morris] to collect the award, it was necessary for the body to be identified and so Myra was sent for. Morris expected her to break down when she saw James Reed lying there dead. Throwing her head back, with flashing eyes, she said, "If you want the reward for Jim Reed, you will have to get Jim Reed. But this is not him."

An account by Walter Biscup in *The Tulsa World* for March 17, 1929, gives this version:

A group spread apart as Belle walked to the body of her husband. She glanced longingly at Reed; appealingly, beseechingly, but her damask face reflected nothing. She only smiled at grief.

"I am very sorry, gentlemen, that you have made a mistake and killed the wrong man, very, very sorry indeed. Mr. Morris, you will have to kill Jim Reed if you desire to collect the reward offered for his death," said Belle calmly, suffering the anguish she refused to reveal.

Mr. Biscup gallantly and rhetorically contributes a "damask face" to our heroine, but otherwise his account is orthodox.

The trouble with the pretty legend is that Jim Reed's body was identified by a full quorum of competent witnesses.

Belle, who was either in Dallas or in the Indian Territory at the time and undoubtedly was notified by the authorities of her husband's demise, thought so little of the event that she did not even go to Paris, Texas, to take charge of the remains or attend the obsequies when the body was taken to McKinney.

It was probably just as well that Belle did not show up, for we have this gruesome bit of information from a telegraphic dispatch to the Galveston *News* from McKinney, Texas, two days after the killing of Reed:

McKinney, Texas, Aug. 8—Last night the remains of Jim Reed, the mail robber, arrived here from Paris, near which place he had been apprehended and shot; and were buried today after having been fully identified by those who knew him. . . . Reed's body had been very much decomposed, particularly about the head, having been shot between the nose and right eye. The drayman, in carrying him to the potter's field mistook the place, and in returning, with the breeze to the windward of the corpse, he took sick, and was compelled to abandon it on the roadside. It was, however, taken charge of by the sheriff, and finally interred. It is hoped that the others [Reed's outlaw companions] may be taken and dealt with in like manner.

The foregoing variations of a contrived legend should persuade the most credulous reader that fact and folklore have little relationship.

If the conscientious historian's task is a needle-in-the-haystack venture when he is dealing with a personage of folklore, there is some reward in finding something a famous pundit of science has written about a character like Belle Starr and enjoying the spectacle of a renowned writer convicting himself of charlatanism.

The heartiest laugh I have enjoyed in my research work incident to the composition of this book was on reading the following from *The Female Offender,* by Professor Caesar Lombroso and William Ferrero, translated from the Italian:

The born criminal is rarely inclined to write much. We know but of three instances among them of memoirs: those of Madame Lafarge, of X., and of Bell-Star, while male criminals are greatly addicted to these egotistic outpourings. Madame Lafarge, the Woman X., and Bell-Star, particularly the last, were certainly endowed with superior intelligence. . . .

Belle Starr

But when by an unfortunate chance muscular strength and intellectual force meet in the same individual, we have a female delinquent of a terrible type indeed. A typical example of these extraordinary women is presented by Bell-Star, the female brigand, who a few years ago terrorized all Texas. Her education had been of the sort to develop her natural qualities; for, being the daughter of a guerilla chief who had fought on the side of the South in the war of 1861-65, she had grown up in the midst of fighting, and when only ten years old, already used the lasso, the revolver, the carbine, and the bowie-knife in a way to excite the enthusiasm of her ferocious companions. She was as strong and bold as a man, and loved to ride untamed horses which the boldest of the brigands dared not mount. One day at Oakland she twice won a race, dressed once as a man and once as a woman, changing her dress so rapidly that her ruse remained unsuspected. She was extremely dissolute, and had more than one lover at a time, her admirer *en titre* being always the most intrepid and daring of the band. At the first sign of cowardice he was degraded from his rank. But, however bold he might be, Bell-Star dominated him entirely, while all the time having—as Varigny writes—as many lovers as there were desperadoes in four States. At the age of eighteen she became head of the band, and ruled her associates partly through her superior intelligence, partly through her courage, and to a certain degree through her personal charm as a woman. She organized attacks of the most daring description on populous cities, and fought against government troops, not hesitating the very day after one of these raids to enter some neighbouring town unaccompanied, and dressed—as almost always—in male attire. Once she slept in the same hotel as the judge of the district, without his once suspecting her identity or even her sex. And as during the *table d'hote* dinner he had boasted that he would undoubtedly recognize Bell-Star if he ever met her, and would arrest her on the spot, the following morning, when mounted, she sent for him, told him who she was, called him a fool, and after lashing him twice across the face with her whip, galloped away. She wrote her memoirs, recording in them her desire to die in her boots. This wish was granted, for she fell in a battle against the government troops, directing the fire to her last breath.

Lombroso, you may remember, was the professor at the University of Turin who founded the "science" of criminology as an independent subject of research dealing with the nature and causes of crime. When he published his *L'Umo delinquente* (Criminal Man) in 1876, he set the enlightened world by the ears. He had measured a great number of skulls of the living and the dead, and announced the astounding "discovery" that a man's career as a criminal was predetermined by the shape of his head! There were some secondary characteristics possessed by the criminal type, he wrote, such as short ear-lobes and eyes set close together. He went into the psychological and psychophysical determinants and identification marks also, giving elaborate case histories. These were probably as imbecile as the above "case history" of Belle Starr.

Lombroso was so careless that he accepted the shoddiest lira-a-line yellow journalism for his "scientific data." The Varigny he quotes was an Italian journalist in New York who acted as a correspondent for the Rome and Milan newspapers in the nineties. He was paid at space rates. The Italian newspapers, like all newspapers on the Continent, were interested in little else from America besides crime news. Varigny stole his stuff from the *National Police Gazette,* the *Police News,* James Gordon Bennett's *Herald* and Joseph Pulitzer's *World;* but in lifting, he always managed to rewrite what he took with the most sensational twists his mind could devise. Lombroso accepted it literally as a perfect demonstration of his theory about the criminal type!

Varigny improved upon the domestic legend creators; he mixed up the story of Belle Starr with the story of Mrs. Rose O'Neal Greenhow, the beautiful Confederate spy, who, by the way, though arrested by Allan Pinkerton, the Federal detective, on August 26, 1861, and imprisoned after trial, was not shot, but, on the contrary, escorted beyond the Union lines on June 2, 1862, and set at liberty.

The Caesar Lombroso analysis is my prize exhibit in obfuscation; but I cannot forbear to give you my runner-up for the honors in complete nonsensicality. It is *Frank James: The Only True History of the Life of Frank James, Written by Himself.* It was published in Pine Bluff, Arkansas, in 1926.

Folklore and History

Of course, Frank James had been dead eleven years when this book was published, so I at first tossed it aside as one of those horrible examples of meretricious trash, fabricated by some hack to capitalize on the notoriety of the James brothers, by putting out a book alleged to have been written by Frank James himself. In such cases the victim of the imposture has no redress because he is an outlaw and perhaps a dead one. In the nineties, and even earlier, there were many such books. Richard K. Fox published an anonymous "true" story of the career of the James brothers in 1881, while the brothers were still at large and active. The Arthur Westbrook Company, publishers, of Cleveland, Ohio, issued in the nineties *Jesse James, My Father,* by Jesse James, Jr., which was advertised as being "the inside history of the life of Jesse James," written for the Westbrook Company and distributed by them as "the authorized and exclusive publishers for Jesse James' only son." The Westbrook Company also published a series of thirty-six books, each one dealing solely with *one* "daring exploit" of the James Brothers, and all written by one William Ward. Besides that, the same company advertised in their Adventure Series: "You can get the absolutely true and authentic history of the lives and exploits of the Younger Brothers, Harry Tracy, the Dalton Gang, Rube Burrow, and the Other Notorious Outlaws of the Far West."

Such books showed, in the first few pages, incontrovertible evidence that they were pure fabrications. Even the story of John Wesley Hardin, allegedly published from a manuscript left by himself, seemed (and still seems) to me so obviously a forgery that I cannot understand how serious historians have dared to use it. Nor can I believe that the text Stuart N. Lake introduced into his *Wyatt Earp: Frontier Marshal* derives from a manuscript Wyatt Earp left behind him when he died. My credulity doesn't extend that far. Although Wyatt Earp may have left some sort of manuscript, Lake himself or somebody else must have doctored it up, for it seems extremely improbable to me that Wyatt Earp, an almost illiterate gunfighter, whose entire adult life was spent in strenuous action, could have written a book about his career in a style worthy of Ernest Hemingway.

Upon rereading *Frank James: The Only True History of the Life of Frank James, Written by Himself,* something told me that this piece of shoddy, for a wonder, was just what it was alleged to be. It is maudlin, illiterate, vague, confused, pathetic. It is just the sort of thing that Frank James, in his distressful, diabetic, last days might write, when sufficiently urged to do so by the down payment of a few dollars and the promise of some more. You must remember that after Frank James got his release from prison (after having served twenty-one years) he had a tough time making a living. He was 60 years old and he had never worked a day in his life except while he was in the penitentiary, and about all he had done there was to sort gunny-sacks. It is disconcerting, to say the least, for a man 60 years old to apply for a job and then have to say, when asked: "What can you do?", "I am a gunny-sack sorter." It doesn't help much to add, "I am an expert at it; I've been doing it for twenty-one years," for there are not many places outside of a penitentiary where they have gunny-sacks to sort.

Frank's first job, after he got out (which is to say, the first salaried job he ever had), was that of shoe salesman with an enterprising shoe-store proprietor in Nevada, Missouri, who must have felt that he was being very noble in giving the notorious bandit his first job as a reformed man; and, besides, even if Frank couldn't read the size-codes and hadn't any true salesmanship talent, the mere fact of his presence ought to have brought in a lot of people, who would come in to get a look, and buy shoes out of sheer embarrassment.

Somehow, though, Frank didn't last long at that job. Pretty soon everybody had seen him. He drifted on to Dallas, Texas, where he got another job, as a shoe salesman, curiously enough. Then "Colonel" Ed Butler, Democratic ward boss in St. Louis, who owned a burlesque theater called The Standard, gave Frank a job as doorman at the stage-entrance leading into the alley behind the theater. The job paid $70 a month, and Frank had to support a wife and child on that. He couldn't think of pulling a stick-up, because, in effect, he was on parole; he had to be satisfied that nobody else pulled a stick-up and pinned the job on him. "Colonel" Jack Chinn, official race starter at the St. Louis tracks, gave Frank a job as assistant starter, and from then on until he crept back to the Old Samuel's Homestead in Clay County, Missouri, to die, he pursued the profession of assistant race-track starter and race-track starter in various cities.

It is quite probable that, when he was on his uppers, he wrote this story of his life as it was published eleven years after his death. Only one portion of this document, Chapter XV, pages 117-120, need concern us here. It is about our heroine. There is something so pathetic about its general style and information, that I have a deep suspicion that Frank James may actually have written it and that no "ghost" or collaborator helped him out in the least.

Who was Bell Star? is asked by the newspapermen. Bell Star was a native of Kansas. Her maiden name was Shirley. She was known as the broncho rider.

At the age of sixteen years, her brother Captain Shirley, sent her to the camp of Federals, a distance of twenty-five miles [From where? B. R.], to learn their movements. She soon learned, after arriving at camp that her brother's camp would be attacked. Late that afternoon when the soldiers found out that Bell was Capt. Shirley's sister they had her arrested and put under guard, with orders that she not be turned loose until after the raiders who had been sent out to visit her brother's camp had been gone one half hour.

When the half hour had expired Bell was turned loose. When she gained her liberty she mounted her pony and was off like the wind, through fields and pastures, jumping fences, on and on, until she was hid from view among the low hills of the Kansas prairies. When the detachment of soldiers arrived at Shirley's camp he was gone. Bell had got there first. This famous ride gave Bell the name of bronco rider.

When the civil war was over Bell married Jim Reed, a noted highwaymen, who had served under Quantral. Jim Reed and my father were brothers. I was a base begotten child. It was never known to the world. My parents came from Tennessee to Missouri. I was born a short time after they arrived in Clay County, Missouri, and the people there never knew or thought anything about the child that was called Frank James. My mother was promised to be married secretly to a man named Edd Reed. He was killed before I was born, and to save the disgrace my mother married Robert James and then moved to Missouri. So the people of this old world did not know that Frank and Jesse James were only half brothers.

After Bell married Jim Reed old man Shirley told her that he would never forgive her for marrying Reed, and that he would give her all the trouble that he could. They were run out of Illinois and Iowa and they went to Texas, where Reed was killed a short time after they moved there. They had one child and named him Edd Reed. Edd, after he was grown to be a man, served for years in Oklahoma, as United

Belle Starr

States Marshal, and a bandit at the same time. He was a killer when imposed on.

A short time after Jim Reed died Bell married Henry Starr. Henry Starr was killed in a pistol duel with a United States Marshal. After Henry Starr was killed Bell married John Starr. He also went the pistol route. She afterwards married Sam Starr, a son of Tom Starr. Bell had a girl by Cole Younger, named Pearl Starr. Her name should have been Pearl Younger, after her father, Cole Younger, according to nurse papers handed out to the world. Pearl was killed several years ago in an automobile smashup at Fort Smith, according to the newspapers, but I don't count on what the newspapers say, I have read so much about myself in newspapers. Bell Starr was waylaid and killed by a man named Watson. Bell knew about him killing a man in Kentucky. They got into a dispute about some land. Watson was living on Bell's place. Bell told him if he did not do what was right she would tell what she knew about the killing in Kentucky.

Bell ate dinner at Watson's the day she was killed, near her home on the Canadian river in Oklahoma. Bell was a bandit, and knew how to handle a gun, but in other respects she was as true as steel.

Cole Younger was captured in Minnesota while he and his band were trying to rob the Northfield bank. He was given a life sentence in the penitentiary. He served twenty years and was pardoned. He repented and joined the church, lived a useful life and died surrounded by loving friends.

Cole had three brothers, John, Jim and Bob. John was killed in a duel with a detective just after the civil war. Jim died of wounds received at the Northfield bank. Bob Younger received a life sentence in the pen, and was pardoned the same day, with Cole. Bob died the next day after receiving his pardon. He died from hemorrhage of the bowels.

George Shepherd was killed in Texas for turning traitor to the James and Youngers. The whereabouts of Cell Miller is unknown.

Listen, readers, I have read about Cell Miller's death but I know it to be false. He is unknown today.

Sam Starr, Bell's last husband, was a robber, and died at the end of a six-shooter at a dance, in Whitefield, Choctaw Nation. The man that killed him didn't know at first that he had killed the most dreaded man in Oklahoma.

Bell had only two children. One by Reed, her first man. She named him Edd Reed, as I have stated before, he served as U.S. Marshal and highwayman at the same time, for years, without being detected. He was a killer when imposed upon. He killed John and Jake Chritention, two U.S. Marshals, one morning, after giving them a chance to shoot first, but he finally met his fate and died with his boots on.

What is genuinely startling about the above is not the misinformation about Belle Starr, or the fact that Henry Starr did not gain prominence until after Belle was dead, but the disclosure—if it is a disclosure and not a fabrication:

"Jim Reed and my father were brothers. I was a base begotten child. . . . My mother was promised to be married secretly to a man named Edd Reed. He was killed before I was born, and to save the disgrace my mother married Robert James."

Jim Reed did have a brother named Ed Reed, but the Ed Reed who was Jim's brother couldn't very well have been Frank James' father. Frank James was born in 1843 and Belle Starr was born (probably) in 1848. If Jim Reed and Frank's father, Ed Reed, were brothers, and near in age, that would make Belle marrying Jim Reed when he was old enough to be her father. But, after all, maybe he was. I don't know. All I know was that Jim Reed was described as being only 29 years old when he was shot and killed on August 6, 1874. Perhaps the father of Frank James was an Ed Reed who had sons named Ed Jr., Jim and Scott. . . . Perhaps we have a genuine disclosure there. It is not to be found in any other book or article I have seen; and it doesn't sound like one of those things the hack writers were in the habit of inventing. When they invented a juicy morsel, it was always to make a point, and this alleged story of Frank James about his being the bastard of Edd (sic) Reed is so entirely pointless that it sounds like the truth.

If Frank James was the bastard son of an Ed Reed, whose son later married Myra Shirley, more familiarly known as Belle Starr, we have a strange link in this consanguineous chain of Missouri families that produced notorious outlaws. The mother of the Dalton brothers was Adelaide Younger, a half-sister of the father of the Younger brothers, who were first cousins of the James brothers. There you have the most sensational bandits of the stage-and-train robbery period in our history—Cole, Jim, Bob and John Younger; Frank and Jesse James; Bob, Grat and Emmett Dalton; Jim Reed and Belle Starr and their outlaw son, half-brother to the presumptive bastard daughter of Cole Younger and Belle, Pearl Younger, who became a harlot. Quite a family!

The task of the conscientious historian, who ventures to deal with popular heroes and heroines or popular villains and villainesses whose careers have been left almost entirely to the creators and expanders of folk legend, is beset with difficulties. Not much more is known about Billy the Kid or about Wild Bill Hickok from documents that can be verified than is known about Robin Hood, Dick Turpin, Fra Diavolo or Rini Rinaldo, even though a vast literature sprang up about Wild Bill Hickok and Billy the Kid during the time they were still alive, flourished luxuriantly after their deaths and, in time, largely died out as literature of great popular interest, but nonetheless passed into folklore.

In trying to disentangle the real Belle Starr from the legendary one, I am frank to admit that the legendary Belle Starr is a more enticing person than the one who emerges from a recital of the cold facts. So I have given the legends, as legends, along with the ascertainable facts. I have even contributed a conjecture (about Myra Belle Shirley's first sweetheart) which I admit is pure conjecture, but which may, in time, become part of the folk legends about "The Bandit Queen."

PART TWO

"QUEEN OF THE BANDITS"

CHAPTER ONE

BIRTH AND BACKGROUND

If the traditionally accepted date—February 5, 1848—is correct, Myra Belle Shirley was born at a time when frontier banditry was rapidly becoming a major anxiety to the pioneers. While Mrs. John Shirley, in a log cabin in the Missouri wilderness, was feeling the first birth pangs before Myra Belle was brought into the world, doings were afoot that were to have an important bearing on the career the baby was to follow in later life.

Down in the Ozarks, about a hundred miles due south of the Shirley farm, the now fabulous John A. Murrell and his band of cutthroats and thieves were setting the pattern for later outlawry and establishing a record in villainy which the Quantrills, the Youngers, the Jameses, the Daltons, the Doolins and all subsequent gangs of organized murderers and bandits tried to emulate.

Murrell had the doubtful distinction of being ahead of his time. Not only was he cruel and vindictive, but he showed considerable inventiveness in his rapacity.

Belle Starr

It was he who devised a racket too subtle for his immediate imitators, but one which was adopted nearly a hundred years later and brought to perfection in Chicago by Al Capone—the "protection" racket. Victims were made to pay for "protection" against the very gang to whom their money was given.

Murrell and his gang levied weekly or monthly tribute from farmers in the immediate vicinity of their hangouts in the Ozarks for "protection" against robbers, incendiarists and murderers. Those who did not pay the tribute were robbed and murdered, and their homes and barns were set afire.

Mark Twain, writing in *Life on the Mississippi* (1883) paid his respects to Murrell (or Murel) and his imitators in these words:

There is a tradition that Island 37 (in the Mississippi River) was one of the principal abiding places of the once-celebrated "Murel's Gang." This was a colossal combination of robbers, horse-thieves, Negro-stealers, and counterfeiters, engaged in business along the river some fifty or sixty years ago. While our journey across the country towards St. Louis was in progress we had had no end of Jesse James and his stirring history; for he had just been assassinated by an agent of the Governor of Missouri, and was in consequence occupying a good deal of space in the newspapers. Cheap histories of him were for sale by train boys. According to these, he was the most marvellous creature of his kind that had ever existed. It was a mistake. Murel was his equal in boldness, in pluck, in rapacity, in cruelty, brutality, heart-

Birth and Background

lessness, treachery, and in general and comprehensive vileness and shamelessness; and very much his superior in some larger aspects. James was a retail rascal; Murel, wholesale. James's modest genius dreamed of no loftier flight than the planning of raids upon cars, coaches, and country banks; Murel projected Negro insurrections and the capture of New Orleans; and furthermore, on occasion, this Murel could go into a pulpit and edify the congregation. What are James and his half-dozen vulgar rascals compared with this stately old-time criminal, with his sermons, his meditated insurrections and city-captures, and his majestic following of ten hundred men, sworn to do his evil will!

The depredations of the Murrells, according to the more reliable traditions, began about 1835 and continued to about 1860. Even more than the history of later notorious outlaw bands, the truth about the Murrells has become so confused and identified with folklore that a reliable historian would have to content himself largely with little more information than Mark Twain gives and discount that by ten, for few records are available. Murrell operated before the use of the telegraph became widespread and in sections of the country which were not to be penetrated by railroads for many years after the Murrells were disbanded.

Where Murrell came from no one seems to have known or even to have heard (a rare omission in folklore). The tales tell that he had a great house, large enough to accommodate his band of one hundred men, deep in the woods, near what is now Forrest City, Payne County, Arkansas. That would be forty-one miles southwest of Memphis on what is now U.S. Highway No. 70, which was built over an old trail which may (or may not) have been the Murrell trail, said to have been dotted by lone pines, in a country where pines are rare. The tales tell also that the farmers who paid tribute to Murrell planted pine saplings before their houses, so they would be identified as "friendly" by the divisions, or lone members, of the gang. A single pine tree in the front yard of an Eastern Arkansas farmer's house is said to have indicated to Murrell's men that, within, they might find food and lodging and, what was more important, unwagging tongues.

The tight-mouthed "loyalty" of the farmers of Jackson and Clay counties in Missouri to the James "boys," which proved so baffling to peace officers and detectives in their efforts to apprehend those murderous outlaws, may not have been "loyalty" at all, but fear. Thus the post-mortem sentiment that grew both in fact and in legend most likely had its origin in intimidation. Even a man who had paid craven tribute to a scoundrel might, after the scoundrel was dead and had been made into a dime-novel hero, have the kind of vanity that makes him want to shine in another's reflected glory.

The tales tell that beneath Murrell's huge but

somber house, there was a dungeon, with a trapdoor, into which he cast traitorous members of his gang to die of starvation, and that when they died, he buried the bodies in quicklime.

This story of the Murrell dungeon is, to be sure, part of the stock descriptions in folklore concerning nearly all bandit gangs and even concerning simple, wholesale murders. Legend also has it that Murrell stole more than a thousand slaves and often sold them back to their original owners, who were too frightened or too prudent to protest; that Murrell and his gang murdered and robbed hundreds; and that in these deeds they had a special Murrellian technique in murder—that is, he or some member of his gang first slit the lone traveler's throat, took his money and valuables, removed his clothing and all other possible means of identification, then eviscerated the body, burned the clothing and entrails, filled the body with rocks and sewed it up, and finally dropped the corpse into a deep lake. Thus if a friend or neighbor in the region wherein Murrell operated disappeared, one need have no doubts as to the exact details of what had happened to him.

Varying stories are told, too, about Murrell's end. Some say he was cast by his followers into his own dungeon and left there to starve to death and rot without benefit of quicklime. Some say he was hanged by a citizens' posse in Arkansas, when he was mistaken for another outlaw. Most likely they never would have hung him, if they had known it was the dreaded Murrell they had captured, so greatly was the name Murrell feared by everybody. On hearing such simple folk tales, one wonders why every tyro hold-up man who was captured by a posse didn't say in a deep and awesome voice, "I'm *Murrell*," and thus throw the possemen into a panic and escape hanging.

Before the Civil War began, there was no more of Murrell, if there ever was any at all. It is quite possible that he was invented entire, except for the name —which may have been that of a minor outlaw—by one of the anonymous rewrite men on the original *National Police Gazette,* before Richard K. Fox acquired it. Certainly the activities of the Murrell gang were luridly described in those early issues, and there one finds what is probably the source of many of the Murrell legends that have passed into folklore and have been accepted as authentic by historians as credulous as Mark Twain.

At all events, a girl was born to John and Elizabeth Shirley in Missouri, but not in Carthage or even in Jasper County, as the tales tell. The date generally accepted is February 5, 1848.

That was the date chiseled upon Belle's tombslab after she was murdered while riding home on a lonely road along the old Briartown-Eufaula Trail in the Indian Territory on February 3, 1889.

Presumably in Belle's home at Younger's Bend there was no family Bible which would have given the stonecutter the correct information. And presumably Belle's children, Pearl Younger and Ed Reed, whose education amounted to criminal neglect, were vague and uncertain as to when and where their mother was born. But the stonecutter may have had recourse to the Cherokee Tribal records, and possibly he got his information therefrom; for, when Belle married the Cherokee citizen Sam Starr, it was necessary for her not only to swear allegiance to the Cherokee Nation in the application for a license, but also to give the date and place of her birth. It is not to be imagined that Belle seized this occasion as the one moment in her life in which to be scrupulous. The day and the month she doubtless gave correctly. And it would be easier and more impressive to write down "Carthage, Missouri" than to write that she was born on a farm in Washington County. But if she exercised her woman's privilege of giving an incorrect date for her birth year, we may assume that she subtracted from rather than added to her age.

So, Myra Belle Shirley was probably not born in Carthage, and probably not even in Jasper County, for it appears that her parents had not moved to Jasper County until June, 1848. The books of the

Recorder of Deeds of Jasper County somehow miraculously survived the burning of the Jasper County
courthouse by the Federals in the summer of 1863,
and they also survived the almost complete destruction of the city by "Bloody Bill" Anderson's Confederate guerrillas on September 22, of the same year.

These records show that on June 30, 1848, entry
was made of the United States Government's patent
to John Shirley's land grant of 800 acres of land,
located about ten miles northwest of Carthage and
about four miles southeast of Medoc. The advertisement was one inserted by George W. Broome, to
whom John Shirley sold the 800 acres in 1856.

The farm was described by Broome, when he offered
it for sale in the Carthage *Southwest Times* of March
29, 1861, as "600 acres of Spring River bottom land,
situate in Jasper County about three miles northwest
of Sherwood, and on one of the most beautiful streams
in the west. There is 100 acres in cultivation, has on
it a small apple orchard, dwelling house, kitchen,
stable & c., has a good well. The larger portion of it
is heavily timbered; stone coal is abundant in the
vicinity, and a more desirable stock farm could not
be found in the Southwest." Broome's advertisement
stated that Negroes would be taken in payment for
the land "at the highest cash price."

There is no Sherwood now, but the Shirley farm
was located as described above. The "kitchen" indi-

cates a house probably apart from the main dwelling in which food was prepared not only for the master and family, but for the slaves—if there were any slaves. A "kitchen" was usually large enough to accommodate an open fireplace, a variety of utensils for cooking, and a larder. It also was large enough to serve as the dining room.

It is probable that Shirley at no time owned more than three or four slaves. From the advertisement, it would appear that both Broome and Shirley were at first engaged mainly in stock-raising and not in farming; and a man who bred and reared horses and cattle had not the same need for slave labor as a tobacco or cotton planter: a stable boy, a yard boy, a hostler and perhaps a cook (if his wife did not do the cooking, which, it is likely, she did) would have been all he needed, including help for plowing, planting, cultivating and reaping small crops and tending a garden. And in that part of the country, it was cheaper to hire help than to buy, house, feed and care for human property. The stables on the Shirley farm were probably more elaborate than the "dwelling."

The tales tell that the Shirleys were wealthy and aristocratic slaveholders; that they had come from Virginia, of course (for Virginia was associated in the popular mind with breeding and glamor), and that John Shirley was a judge and that Myra's brother,

Edward, was a captain, no less, in the Confederate forces.

It is likely that John Shirley's people came from Kentucky or Tennessee, for most of Southern Missouri was settled by emigrants from those states. The Shirleys were even prominent enough or numerous enough later to have given the name Shirley to a town in Washington County. And it was in Washington County, perhaps even in the present town of Shirley, that I elect to believe John Shirley and his family lived before filing patent on a land grant in Southwestern Missouri, and that it was probably in Washington County not only that Preston and Ed Shirley were born, but Myra Belle also.

In 1848, when John Shirley had become a stock-raising landowner in Jasper County, Missouri, that part of the country had only recently been vacated by the Osage Indians under treaty with the United States. Only ten years before, the land was a wilderness occupied by the Osages, who so resented the encroachments of the whites that they would descend upon the tiny settlements on the frontier, kill and scalp the pioneer adults, take their children captive and burn their homes.

Even in 1848, the farms in Jasper and adjacent counties were mostly small clearings in the wilderness and many miles apart. The typical home in the region was made of two clapboard houses of one room each, joined by a roof which left a third room open on two sides and serving as a dining room and as an extra bedroom when the weather permitted. Sheds and barns and houses were joined together to form a sort of stockade. The cleared land was usually enclosed by a rail fence, laid in Virginia, or zigzag, fashion.

The furniture of the farmhouses was nondescript —some of it having been brought overland in ox teams, such as bureaus, bedsteads, spinning wheels and looms, home-made chairs and tables and Osage-made blankets and coverlets. The bases of the bed, when a farmer was prosperous enough to own one, were webbings of hemp rope, which usually sagged in the middle like a hammock, and over which were placed feather beds made by the women of the family.

The wilderness thereabouts was plentiful in wild turkey, deer, rabbit, squirrel, quail, bear, 'possum, raccoon and grouse. The streams on which most of the farms were located, were filled with trout, perch, pickerel, crappies and catfish.

Those farmers who had emigrated from the south, usually had their own smokehouses for curing hams and bacon, and unchinked log cribs for storing corn. Money was scarce and was derived mainly from the sale, not of farm produce, but of hides and furs. Travelers through the country of the period noticed a curious absence of cows and a consequent absence of milk and butter from the common diet.

It is possible that the John Shirleys, before moving to Jasper County, had resided in, or near, what is now the town of Shirley, Washington County, seventy-two miles southwest of St. Louis and eight miles southwest of Potosi, on what is now Missouri State Highway No. 8. Two, and perhaps more, families of Shirleys settled in that neighborhood, having emigrated from Ohio, Kentucky or Tennessee, and gave the name to the town of Shirley, even if they did not found it.

That would follow the regular pattern of western emigration of the period. Not until the California gold rush did people take the long jump from the Eastern seaboard to the Pacific Coast or even from the Mississippi Valley to Oregon or Utah. The earlier migrations were gradual. The Lincolns, for instance, moved from Hardin County, Kentucky, to Indiana, thence to two locations in Illinois. People would follow the frontier, moving to the eastern part of a state or territory first, then in the second generation moving a hundred or two hundred miles farther west, and in a third generation moving still farther west, especially after they had exhausted the soil with a succession of single crops in their clearings. They were always on the move for virgin soil or a "fresh start."

Birth and Background

Some, of course, were just naturally restless and wanting to be on the move after a few monotonous years in one locality. Of these one must count, especially, migrants of Scots and Scots-Irish descent—an independent and clannish folk, irked by the presence around them of "furriners," i.e., people not of their blood kin.

John Shirley was certainly of the type that was always moving about, always seeking to better his position in life, even shifting his occupation from farming to stock-raising to tavern-keeping, thence back to farming and then stock-raising again. It is probable that John Shirley first sold the land he had acquired near the present town of Shirley and invested his money in one of those fraudulent land grants comprising a large tract of land in Jasper County, which were finally declared legally valid and patentable; and there is a good chance, of course, that John Shirley had lived on the land as a homesteader and improver of the property long enough to establish his right to patent the title. And thus it may have been that Myra Belle Shirley was born on the Shirley farm in Jasper County; or it may even have been that she was born in the town of Carthage while John Shirley was waiting for his patent to be granted, for the records show that John Shirley acquired title only four months before Myra Belle was born.

John Shirley either was a land speculator and had acquired land only to resell it later at a profit, or else he found stock-raising unprofitable, or perhaps his wife, with three children to take care of, grew weary and discontented with the drudgery and isolation of farm life on the frontier where there were no churches, no schools, no neighbors within miles.

At all events, on March 16, 1850, we find John Shirley and his wife, Elizabeth Shirley, selling off 160 acres of their farmland fourteen miles northwest of Carthage for $700 to one David Martin. Then, on June 18, 1851, we see them making the first move toward becoming townfolk, when they are recorded as having bought from John and Melinda Richardson two quarter-acre lots in the township of Carthage, a town just in the process of development.

In the following year, on May 16, 1852, a school tax of $400 had been levied against the Shirleys, although there were no schools in the district their children could attend. Lacking cash for this tax, John Shirley had to mortgage 160 acres of their land for a loan of $400, for a period of one year. This loan was paid within the time specified.

On September 1, 1855, we find John Shirley mortgaging 160 acres of his land for $500. John renewed this note every six months and finally paid it off on February 2, 1858, after he had moved into Carthage and established himself as a tavern-keeper. That gave him $500 cash for his new venture, and on the same day that he borrowed this $500, he purchased from Archibald McCoy a Negro boy and a Negro girl, putting up his farm property as collateral and giving a note in the sum of $611.

In 1856, John Shirley was no longer a stock-farmer in a dreary, unsettled region that had been only lately abandoned by the Osage Indians. He owned a whole block on the north side of the town square of Carthage (sinister name for a town, and horribly prophetic; for, within a few months of each other, in 1863, both the Federal troops and the Confederate guerrillas were to reduce it to ashes, as was Carthage of old). For a brief time, John Shirley was to prosper so well as an innkeeper that he paid to Archibald McCoy the $611 he owed him for the Negro boy and the Negro girl. These slaves John Shirley would need in Carthage in his capacity as innkeeper; the boy, Jordan Gloss, to act as stable boy, yard boy, errand boy and general utility slave; the girl, Leanner Shaw, to make beds, clean out the rooms, sweep, wash dishes, serve in the dining room, draw water, light the fires and act generally under the direction of Mrs. Shirley.

Carthage, Missouri, in 1856, was a town of about 100 inhabitants. (The population was not to exceed 350 at the beginning of the Civil War.) It was a good location for a caravansary. People were still moving west, not merely to reach the California gold fields, but just to get out west.

In 1852 Captain Randolph B. Marcy, who had been commissioned by the United States Government to make a survey of a new route to Santa Fé, New Mexico, had opened a shorter, almost direct trail from Fort Smith, Arkansas, through the central part of what is now Oklahoma, and straight to Santa Fé.

Gold-seekers, who had come up the Missouri River by boat as far as Independence, flocked south, through Carthage, on the way to Fort Smith, there to equip themselves for overland travel on the shorter, Marcy, route, instead of taking the old Santa Fé or Oregon trails. And people en route from Southeastern Missouri had to pass through Carthage before taking the southern trail, on their way through the Ozarks to Fort Smith. Carthage was a fine location for a wayside inn.

Trail-station or crossroad taverns in those days were barn-like structures, whether brick or frame, usually two stories in height, with one-story wings added for larger accommodations as patronage increased. The main floor served as lobby, living room for guests and family, dining room, bar, game room, and (when crowded) bedroom for those who would rather sleep on a pallet in this room, where there was a large open fireplace, than on a pallet upstairs where, in winter, it was very cold, or in a bed with two or three other people—all fully clothed in winter time except for boots and hats.

Connected with every tavern, and owned or leased by the proprietor, would be a livery stable and blacksmith shop for the accommodation of those who traveled horseback or who came through, not by stage, but in their own wagons. John Shirley, owning the whole block, had a livery stable behind his tavern and a blacksmith shop which he either owned or for which he rented space to a smithy.

John Shirley was the tavern host. He registered the guests, presided at the till, saw to it that the guests' horses were properly fed, watered, stalled for the night, fed, currycombed and made ready for the journey in the morning; he dispensed the liquor, kept the accounts and made out the bills; and Mrs. Shirley presided over the kitchen, cooked, or helped cook, the food, directed the scullions and made herself agreeable to the guests after the work in the kitchen was done.

Food would be game in season and, occasionally, fish; rarely beef, never fresh pork, veal or mutton; almost never milk or butter; fresh vegetables and fruits only in the summer time and dried fruits in the winter. Dried beans, boiled with salt pork, would be a staple, along with fried chicken, bacon and eggs.

When dinner (the main meal of the day, served at

noon) was ready, everything would be put on the table
at once and the dinner bell rung. In the autumn and
early winter there might be many kinds of food on
the table at the same time: wild turkey, quail, 'possum, squirrel, rabbit, venison, bear meat, duck, plover,
ham, salt pork, rutabaga, squash, baked beans,
stewed corn, corn-meal mush, molasses, corn pone
with cracklings, and coffee heavily infiltrated with
chickory. For the oldsters there would be sassafras
tea, on demand. Nearly everything would be fried
in deep grease, often used many times over. The men
would cut this grease with whiskey. Most of the
women would abstain from whiskey except for "the
misery," and get liver-complaint, becoming gaunt,
jaundiced and dry-skinned by the time they were
thirty-five.

Supper would be served at six. It would consist
of the left-overs from dinner, warmed up. At each
meal, the host always sat at the head of the table.
After everybody had sat down, they would fold their
hands in their laps and bow their heads; then the
host would say grace. After that everybody would
pitch in.

In the summer time, the dining room would be
swarming with flies, midges and mosquitoes. The
mosquitoes would be hatched in the rain-barrels
under the eaves of the houses; the flies would be born
in the manure piles of the stables. A girl (and in

the Shirley household it would be the Negro slave girl, Leanner Shaw) would stand by the table, waving a stick back and forth, onto which had been tacked a copy of a weekly newspaper cut into strips—to fan the insects away.

There would be no bath, no toilet, no running water, and, of course, very little privacy of any kind. Twelve or fifteen people, all strangers, perhaps, might be sleeping on the floor in the same room. Winter or summer, one washed one's face in a tin basin on a wooden stand near the pump in the tavern courtyard. If the tavern had private rooms, of course, there would be a pitcher of cold water and a tin basin and a cotton towel, but this would be for very elegant and aristocratic people who could afford to pay for such luxuries.

Inasmuch as Carthage was the county seat of Jasper County, there were more lawyers than other professionals or tradesmen in the town; and when court was in session, the Shirley Hotel probably not only was well patronized by the litigants, but most likely it was a meeting place for transients and townsmen to talk over politics and the affairs of the day.

Bars were not part of the standard equipment of the inns of villages the size of Carthage in that part of the country in those days. Instead, the proprietor usually served whiskey, rum and wine, drawn from kegs, in pewter mugs at table. He also sold whiskey and rum by the half-gallon and gallon jug, but not by the quart or pint bottle; glass bottles were rare and expensive.

Drunkenness at county-seat towns was common, especially during the times when court was in session, and on Saturdays and Saturday nights. Indeed, it was considered the mark of a gentleman to get drunk at least once a week; and fist fights, stabbings, and cutting affrays were the usual diversions in the Saturday-night brawls. Such outbursts of exuberance and energy, however, took place in the streets; and even if a fight were started in a hotel like that of John Shirley, where ladies were present, the antagonists would either be hustled into the street or they would retire to it of their own accord for the actual physical encounter.

Such fights were a combination of pugilism and wrestling; and when the opponents were writhing on the ground, there were no sportsmanship rules to guide their conduct or to inhibit them in any way. They would gouge an eye out, if possible, chew off an ear, kick each other in the groin, and the victor would sometimes stomp his unconscious antagonist in the face.

These fist fights were seldom fatal, even when knives were drawn and the principals succeeded in gashing each other up a great deal; and the fights were not matters of concern on the part of the local constabulary, unless a death ensued, in which case the contestant who emerged alive would be bound on a charge of manslaughter, but usually speedily released on a plea of self-defense.

Guns, however, played no part in these amenities of the 1850's, as they were later to play in the cow-towns of the Southwest. Every man and boy owned a pistol; and a "squirrel," muzzle-loading rifle, was part of the family arsenal before the War between the States; but men did not wear guns conspicuously in the Missouri towns, or carry Winchesters in saddle scabbards until after the outbreak of the border warfare between the Bushwhackers and Jayhawkers.

It is possible that the Shirleys had given up the stock-farm and had moved into Carthage because their daughter, Myra Belle, was eight years old and in need of formal schooling. It was customary at the time for those living on farms in remote regions to employ a tutor, if they could afford it, who would come and live at a farmer's house, help with the crops in planting, cultivating and harvest time, split wood, do chores, mend fences, shuck corn, carry water, feed the hogs and generally make himself useful, and, during certain hours of the day or evening, teach the children their ABC's, penmanship, elementary arithmetic, reading and singing.

The texts for such instruction, by 1853, had become

standard. They were *Ray's Arithmetic, Part First,*
"simple mental lessons and tables for little learners";
*McGuffey's Eclectic Pictorial Primer; McGuffey's
Eclectic Spelling Book,* "for primary and common
schools"; *Pinneo's Primary Grammar* "on the an-
alytic method; a complete work for beginners in the
study"; and *McGuffey's Eclectic Readers,* which ran
from first to fifth, inclusive. The *McGuffey Readers*
were marvelous introductions into the delights of
reading for the children capable of profiting from
such instruction.

It is not probable that Myra Belle had progressed
much beyond elementary spelling, reading and writing, when the Shirleys moved into town. She had at
least two brothers, Preston, aged 20, and Ed or
"Bud," aged 18, when her father opened his hotel
in Carthage. Their formal schooling must have been
on the general level of other boys' in the region at
the time; that is, it was almost nil. Most likely they
could write their names, spell and write simple un-
grammatical letters with painful effort, and it is probable that they could add, subtract and multiply in
their heads, but not on paper.

It is fairly certain, however, that they knew much
about horses, mules and cattle, and at least a little
something about farming. And it may be surmised
that Myra Belle, whom tradition makes something
of a hoyden even as a girl, knew considerable about

horses also. Daughters of stock-farmers and horse traders (particularly an only daughter, as Myra Belle was) were even more thoroughly instructed by their fathers in the handling and riding of horses than sons. Boys had to learn to handle and ride horses by trial and error; but fathers who were horsemen or horse fanciers, gave their daughters the benefit of all they knew about horseflesh. Myra Belle must have known how to handle a horse before she was ready for the higher learning of McGuffey's *Second* or *Third Reader*.

The year before John Shirley opened his hotel in Carthage, the Missouri legislature passed an act incorporating the Carthage Female Academy. This institution was under the management of a number of trustees, all local men of substance, who considered it cheaper to provide for their daughters' education locally than to send them to St. Louis, Springfield or Independence.

The Carthage Female Academy was a solid, two-story brick structure, divided into four classrooms on each floor. The president of such an academy, or the "professor," usually lived with his wife and family in a fairly commodious frame house adjoining the school, and provided room and board at the current rates for the extra instructors, when extra instructors or instructresses were required. The pupils whose parents lived in the country or in other towns found board and lodging in recommended homes in Carthage at from $8 to $10 a month, depending upon the accommodation.

Tuition in such an academy ranged from $18 to $36 a year, with an extra charge of $50 for instruction in piano and/or organ, plus (strangely enough) $6 a year for the privilege of practicing on the piano or organ outside of instruction hours. Oil painting was also taught, but the cost was $40 a year, whereas the extra cost for instruction in Ornamental Needle Work was only $20 a year. The curriculum included instruction in Reading, Spelling, Grammar, Arithmetic, Algebra, Deportment, Greek, Latin and Hebrew. Instruction in the dead languages cost nothing extra, but instruction in French was considered essential for young ladies of quality attending a "finishing school," and its social importance was emphasized by the fact that it cost $20 a year extra to acquire a vague and quickly forgotten smattering of French.

Mark Twain in *Life on the Mississippi* grew rather bitterly sarcastic about these Southern "she-colleges," as he called them, which advertised to turn out, in short order, young women fully instructed in all branches of knowledge including Greek, Latin, French, Hebrew and music, and trained "according to the Southern ideas of delicacy, refinement, womanhood, religion and propriety," the Southern ideas being, according to the advertisement that Mark

N. H. Rose

THE BANDIT QUEEN AND HER FRIEND, THE BLUE DUCK

Birth and Background

Twain quotes, "the highest type of civilization this country has seen." Mark then proceeded to give some examples of this "highest type of civilization" by quoting excerpts from the Southern press detailing slugging matches, gun-fights, drunken brawls, etc., among the gentry of the most prosperous and enlightened cities of the South.

There is no way of proving Myra Belle Shirley attended the Carthage Female Academy, but it is probable she did, for the legends make much of her piano-playing talent, even having her playing all night in a saloon in Fort Smith, Arkansas, on one occasion, in celebration of her acquittal on a charge of horse-stealing, of her playing the piano while a guest at the home of "Hanging Judge" Parker (a most improbable story), and of her having a piano in her log-cabin at Younger's Bend (a fantastic supposition).

Myra Belle, however, did attend a private school in Carthage, conducted by one William Cravens, in a room on the second floor of Masonic Hall, on the northwest corner of the public square. Tuition at Cravens' school was from $1 to $1.50 a month. On September 7, 1922, the Carthage *Press* carried an interview with Mrs. James Brummett of that city, who was brought up in Carthage before the War between the States and who recalled Myra Belle as one of the students at Cravens' school. Mrs. Brummett said: "Among my schoolmates I recall Mattie and

Belle Starr

Lucy Hood, Robinette Langley, Myra Shirley, two Shirley boys, and others. Myra Shirley, as everyone knows, later became the notorious Belle Starr. At this time she was about ten years of age, I think, and small and dark. She was a bright, intelligent girl but was of a fierce nature and would fight anyone, boy or girl, that she quarreled with. Except for this trait, she seemed a nice little girl, however. In fact, the entire Shirley family were nice people, as I remember them.''

The peaceful prosperity of the Shirley Hotel was not to continue long. Missouri was to have an undeclared civil war with its neighbor, Kansas, before the outbreak of hostilities in the War between the States.

There was a fellow named John Brown who was destined to stir up bad blood between Missourians and Kansans. Brown was a lanky, fanatical, ne'er-do-well from Torrington, Connecticut, who was twice married and had a score of children, none of whom he ever undertook to support. In his crazy brain there burned such a desire to better the lot of black folk that he was content to let his own great litter of children starve, or let them embrace a slavery worse than that of the Negroes of the South.

Missouri was mainly populated by Southerners, and was almost overwhelmingly a pro-slavery state. When the Abolitionist movement was in full swing,

Birth and Background

the senatorial representations of the Northern and the Southern States were so nearly evenly balanced that, with the accession of one more state to the pro-slavery group, there would have been a deadlock in the Senate.

Missourians sent propagandists into Kansas in an effort to make Kansas a pro-slavery state.

The Abolitionists countered by financing the transfer of a great number of New Englanders into Kansas.

Anti-slavery immigrants into Kansas founded the town of Lawrence on July 30, 1854, and soon John Brown was in their midst organizing and agitating for abolition.

So great was John Brown's zeal that, on the night of May 24, 1856, he marshaled a few fanatics and descended upon the homes of five innocent Southern sympathizers at Pottawatomie, Kansas, none of whom owned a slave, and murdered them. His own home in Osawatomie, it gives me a humanly malignant pleasure to record, was burned in reprisal three months later. The Kansas war was on.

CHAPTER TWO

QUANTRILL'S PUPILS

The seeds of hatred and distrust sown in that frightful Border War between Missouri and Kansas have not been entirely eradicated to this day—nearly a hundred years after the first sacking of Lawrence, Kansas, by pro-slavery men from Missouri on March 19, 1856.

In the South, one occasionally finds old gentlemen who are still vocally fighting the War between the States; but in Missouri and Kansas, the Civil War itself has ceased to be a cause for dispute, whereas the inter-state feud is kept alive by those of the second and third generation.

Many contemporary Missourians who profess a hatred for Kansans, and many contemporary Kansans who profess a hatred for Missourians, have long forgotten, even if they ever knew, the historical basis of their quarrel. They keep alive a senseless tradition of hate, even if the hate is only rhetorical. Kansans are still opprobriously referred to as ''red-legs'' because during the Civil War the Kansas guerrillas, operating nominally on the Federal side, were derisively named "Jayhawkers" by the Missourians, after the predatory bird, the jayhawk. Jayhawks have red legs.

This interstate prejudice is even observable in the writings of the officials of the two state historical societies. In the eyes of William Elsey Connelley, secretary of the Kansas State Historical Society, William Clarke Quantrill was an ogre. "Of the Civil War in America," says Mr. Connelley, "he was the bloodiest man. Of the border he was the scourge and terror. Idolized for his ferocious blood-madness, he forgot his mother. Embarked in savagery, he foreswore his native land. Professing allegiance to an alien cause, he brought upon a fair land fire and sword, desolation and woe. To manifest a zeal he did not feel, he had recourse to slander, betrayed his companions and aided in their murder. With red hands he gave fair cities to the torch and pillage, and reveled in the groans and cries of the helpless and innocent victims of his ruthless and inhuman crimes."

When Missourians write of Quantrill (or of Quantrell as he is better, though erroneously, known), they picture him as a greatly misjudged hero and point out the fact that in his guerrilla band there were not only the James and Younger brothers, who became outlaws, but some of the finest men the State has produced. Missourians point to the Federal guerrilla chiefs, Lane, Jennison and Montgomery, who, at the head of bands of Jayhawkers laid waste to Missouri towns before the Quantrill bushwhackers fired and looted Lawrence; and they point out, too, that after the war, those who had espoused the Southern cause under Quantrill's banner, were hunted down, hanged or shot by the self-constituted Vigilantes of the period, thus making unwilling outlaws of the more independent and spirited men who had served under Quantrill.

Augustus C. Appler, editor of the Osceola, Missouri, *Democrat,* writing about the Younger brothers in 1875, says:

The Youngers went home after the surrender of the Southern armies, and tried to live at peace with their old neighbors and friends. They were residents of Jackson County in Missouri, and for months it was a question whether this country would be held altogether by the Kansas people, or go back to Missouri. The county was in a state of anarchy. A vigilance committee went one night to the home of the Youngers, surrounded the house, attacked the female members, but found none of the men at home. Again and again this was done. Threats were made of certain death if any of them were caught, and word was sent them that they should not remain in the county. They were waylaid, and hunted down in every conceivable manner. They were compelled to protect themselves, to go heavily armed, and thus were forced to assume the character of outlaws. Other bad men took advantage of this condition of affairs to pillage and murder in their names. Every highway robbery in the West, especially if there was about it a deed of boldness and dash, was placed to their account, almost without knowing why, and suddenly these proscribed men were made both famous and infamous.

Propositions were made to both Governors McClurg and Woodson, only asking protection from mob violence as the sole condition of a surrender. Neither of the Governors gave the required guarantee, and so nothing came of the efforts made, in good faith, to be once more at peace with society and the law. There was abundant reason why these men should not surrender unless the guarantee of protection was given, for men who had served in the same guerrilla band had been taken out at night from their places of imprisonment and hung by masked and unknown men. Tom Little was hung at Warrensburg, Johnson County; McGuire and Devon were hung at Richmond, Ray County; Arch Clemens was shot in Lexington, Lafayette County; Al Shepherd and Payne Jones were shot in Jackson County; in the same county Dick Burns was surprised, while asleep, and murdered. Many of Quantrill's men had to flee the country; many were hung and shot in other places. For months after hostilities had ceased, predatory and bloodthirsty bands, under the guise of vigilance committees, swept over the border counties, making quick work of Confederate guerrillas wherever they could be found.

For all crimes committed during the war the Congress of the United States had absolved the Federal soldiers. By a special law, Kansas granted absolution to all who had killed, robbed, burned or plundered, and held the militia free from any trial or prosecution for deeds done or crimes committed during the war. The present Constitution of Missouri provides that no person shall be prosecuted in any civil action or criminal proceeding for, or on account of any act by him done, performed, or executed after January 1st, 1861, by virtue of military authority. Happening to be on the wrong side, however, these men are cut off from the benefits of all such amnesties or protective acts, and are outlaws simply because they were forced into an attitude of resistance in that transition period in Missouri when the very worst element of the population were gratifying their private feuds and vengeance.

Little, however, can be said in extenuation of the guerrilla gangs whether of the North or of the South during the four-year period when the outcome of the war was undecided. Repeated efforts were made by the officers in command of both the Federal and Rebel forces to get the irregulars to join up either with one side or the other; but these efforts were mostly in vain because the regulars on both sides were subject to army discipline and to recognized rules of warfare, which were too irksome to the predatory bushwhackers and jayhawkers. Regularly enlisted men in both armies were required to pay for food and forage whenever they commandeered it; and they were not permitted even to sleep overnight in a farmer's house without offering to pay for the accommodations. Pillage was a capital offense.

The guerrilla bands, however, preyed upon the defenseless without regard to political belief or sympathies. Quantrill's large troop of desperadoes, for instance, while nominally operating on the Cenfederate side, helped to create anarchic conditions, and, having created them, used the state of affairs to rob the homes and steal the horses and cattle of Union and Confederate sympathizers alike. Their easiest prey, naturally, were the farmhouses from which all the able-bodied men had gone to enlist in the regular armies, leaving only women, children and aged men at the mercy of the marauders.

Quantrill's band was the most notorious, but there were others, notably, Todd's and "Bloody Bill" Anderson's gangs of bushwhackers, nominally fighting in the Confederate cause; the "Pin" Indians under the command of Colonel N. F. Ritchie, U.S.A.; Jennison's jayhawkers nominally fighting on the Union side; and Kinch West's murderous band of outlaws who made little pretense of fighting on either side and who simply terrorized the whole countryside, seizing supplies from both armies, robbing farms of horses, mules and harvesting machinery, looting homes and shooting old men and boys indiscriminately.

We are particularly concerned with Quantrill because under his tutelage and command, the James and Younger brothers got their training in murder and pillage, and the careers of the Jameses and Youngers are definitely linked with Belle Starr.

William Clarke Quantrill was born in Canal Dover,

Ohio, in 1837. If the legends are to be believed, he came of a family of peculiarly criminal tendencies, there being among his forebears forgers and confidence men, professional gamblers, one pirate, an assortment of horse thieves and wife deserters. In spite of this, however, his education was such that he was able to become a school teacher, and it is as a school teacher in Kansas that we first hear of him as a renegade. In the ante-bellum Border Strife, he abandoned pedagogy for horse stealing and minor outlawry. He seems first to have preyed upon Missourians and then later to have got together a group of eight men in Jackson County, Missouri, in January 1862, as a nucleus of a band of Confederate marauders, who later comprised four hundred and fifty men. Thomas Coleman Younger, known in history as Cole, was one of these original eight organized under Quantrill's leadership as a Rebel guerrilla. Quantrill is said to have made himself captain and to have designated William Haller as his first lieutenant, Cole Younger as his second lieutenant and George Todd as his third lieutenant.

From the best authenticated records, it would appear that Quantrill, in organizing his Confederate guerrillas in Clay, Jackson and Jasper Counties, Missouri, found it necessary to invent a pretty story about himself to explain his desertion of the Union for the Rebel cause; for it was known, among some of those whom he wished to recruit, that in the Border war which preceded the outbreak of hostilities between the North and South, Quantrill had led raids into Missouri to free slaves and steal cattle.

He said he was a Southerner by birth—giving Maryland as his native state—and that his sympathies were entirely with the South. He had joined the Kansans, like a spy within the ranks, he said, pretending to fight with them but actually seizing every chance to assassinate as many Jayhawkers as he could, one by one; for they had killed his older brother, and he believed in blood-revenge. He had learned the names and identity of all of the Kansans who had participated in the raid that had resulted in his brother's death, and, having shot each one of them down secretly, he was ready to come out under his true colors and lead Missourians in blood-revenge against the Abolitionists of Kansas.

His whole account of himself was later proved to be pure fabrication, but it was believed implicitly by ingenious Missourians of good character as well as by those naturally lawless, unscrupulous and unprincipled; and at least until 1923 (the date of publication of Ward L. Schrantz's *Jasper County, Missouri, in the Civil War*) there were survivors of Quantrill's band who could not be convinced that Quantrill's story was pure fiction. More than sixty-five years had passed since these survivors had settled down into placid civilian pursuits after an adventurous and reckless youth spent in the saddle as ruthless marauders; and it is probable that they wished to believe no worse of their leader than they believed of themselves.

But the record against Quantrill is considerable, even if we discount many of the stories of the bloodier deeds that are told of him even by his apologists. Nor, on the principle that two wrongs make a right, does it exculpate him to say that Lane, Jennison, Terrill and other Federal guerrilla leaders were just as unprincipled and just as ruthless as he was, which no doubt they were.

It so annoyed Stand Watie (the leader of an irregular band of Confederate Cherokees and who, for his generalship and bravery, was made a brigadier-general of the Confederate army on the advice and consent of President Davis on May 10, 1864) to be compared with Quantrill, that he was obliged to protest: "I am not a murderer," and to cite an instance where Quantrill, having penetrated into the Indian Territory for no sensible military reason but only to kill and steal, had, near the Creek Agency, killed eight defenseless Creeks, including a small boy. Watie said he was bound to protest against the killing of women and children. Moreover, he strongly implied that Quantrill could not be trusted to be loyal to either side, since he killed, and allowed his men to kill, Indian men, women and children without inquiring about their allegiance.

Such was the instructor of the Youngers and the Jameses, and, as their later records were to show, they were apt pupils.

The Youngers, the Jameses and the Daltons of Missouri all appear, from legend, at least, to have been related, either as blood kin or by marriage. And from this, it would also appear that there was something as imponderably wrong with the family as there was with the descendants of Laius, in Greek legend. The Youngers, with whom the James brothers were associated by consanguinity as well as banditry, have certainly done their share to provide an American variant to the Oedipus story.

The tragic death of their parents persists in our folklore. The father of the Younger brothers was Colonel Henry W. Younger, a Union enthusiast and a man of considerable wealth. The story is that he was murdered and robbed by Federal soldiers, or Federal guerrillas, from Kansas, while he was driving back alone on July 20, 1862, from Independence, Missouri, to Harrisonville (where he had a prosperous livery business as well as 35,000 acres of farm land near by); that the Federal soldiers "turned his pockets inside out, stole $400, missed several thousand which Colonel Younger carried in his belt beneath his outer clothing, and left his body by the roadside"; and that shortly after this, Federal soldiers, after looting her home, forced Colonel Younger's widow to set fire to her own house, burning it to the ground; and that the widow Younger "died in 1870 after many years of semi-invalidism due chiefly to the results of harsh treatment at the hands of Kansas Jayhawkers and Red-legs and the Jackson County Federal Militia."

So runs Robertus Love's story in *The Rise and Fall of Jesse James,* taken from previous accounts in two-bit, paper-back books. "Bob" Love was a well-known newspaperman so constantly assigned by his city editor on the St. Louis *Post-Dispatch* to cover news concerning bandits and their exploits that he was known in the newsroom as "The Outlaw Editor." When he came to write his history of the James brothers, he waxed exceedingly indignant at the "irresponsible errors," "fictitious accounts" and "misrepresentations" of those who had written before him. It is obvious that Robertus Love made a sincere, and possibly even an exhaustive, effort to get at the facts; but, nevertheless, his book is burdened with statements just as "irresponsible" as those of his predecessors. Some of these statements I have noted in the Bibliographical Book Review, which forms part of Book III of this volume. The point is: How did Robertus Love learn all of these things for certain?

In the first place, Henry W. Younger is given the

title of "Colonel." Although Love doesn't say so, in some of the more obviously "irresponsible" accounts it is stated that the elder Younger achieved the title of colonel in the Mexican War. But there is no Younger from Missouri on the enrollment lists in the War Department archives for the period of the Mexican War; and no Colonel Henry W. Younger in the United States Army at any period from the War of 1812 through the Civil War.

We can safely say that the male parent of the notorious Younger brothers was not a promoted or breveted colonel in any army, at any time. He probably wasn't even an army man. His title, "Colonel," was doubtless one of those numerous examples of the custom of the country in those days, which conferred upon nearly everybody, of high or low degree, some sort of title.

A title, in the Mississippi Valley, was, and still is, likely to be a nickname. Thus a man whose exterior aspect was anything but judicial might be called "Judge," just as a young man six feet, four inches in height would be called "Shorty."

There was no rule about it. A male person might be known to everybody as "Major" or "Judge" or "Colonel" or even "General." Yet never, except when he was a sort of no-account person around town, would he be degraded to the rank of "Captain" in address or salutation, for "Cap'n" was the way every

Negro addressed every white man, indiscriminately.

Victor Tixier, writing of his travels through Missouri and the Osage country during the years 1839-41, speaks of having spent the night at the home of a General Duglass and then comments: "General Duglass is an excellent, very peace-loving man. He had never been in the army, yet his rank is very high . . . In this country a captain takes the title of general, a sergeant that of captain; everybody boasts of his democratic feelings, but everyone has a distinctive title. Such usages are spread all over the United States."

It would probably strike Tixier as being a tacit disavowal of our democratic principles to discover that the "madame" of nearly every bagnio in New Orleans, St. Louis, Chicago and points East and West, is addressed, "Yah Highness" or "Duchess."

Historians are inclined to forget such folk amenities. There is not an account of the career of Belle Starr which does not state that Belle's father was "Judge John Shirley," or does not make Belle's brother, Edward or "Bud," a captain in the regular Confederate forces.

The Confederate, as well as the Federal, enlistment rolls are complete and available. There was no Captain Ed Shirley of Missouri on either side. Moreover, we have authentic records of Ed Shirley's status and the manner of his death: he was a bushwhacker, without rank even among the guerrillas, and he was killed in Sarcoxie, Missouri, by men of Company C, of the Seventh Provisional Enrolled Militia on or about June 20, 1863.

But, meanwhile, let's get back to the murder and robbery of Henry W. Younger. According to all the extant accounts, his body was found on the roadside about five miles south of Independence; his pockets were turned inside out; but it was later discovered that the robbers had overlooked a certain amount (the accounts vary from $1000 to $5000) in greenbacks sewed up in his clothing.

But how do the writers of the various accounts *know* that the elder Younger was murdered and robbed by *Federal* guerrillas, or, as Robertus Love's account has it, "by Federal soldiers from Kansas commanded by a captain named Walley"? How do they know that $400 was taken from Younger's body?

There were no witnesses to this murder; and nobody ever confessed to the crime even in the years after Federal soldiers and guerrillas were granted amnesty for crimes committed during the war period.

Here we find ourselves, therefore, in the realm of conjecture when we are confronted with the factors entering into the choice of outlawry on the part of the Younger brothers and the James brothers. And, in this realm of conjecture, we discover that all the writers, whether prejudiced in favor of, or against,

the Youngers, ascribe their taking up a predatory
and murderous career to the spirit of revenge aroused
in them by the murder of their father, the burning
of their widowed mother's home and the cruel and inhuman treatment visited upon their mother by the
Federals!

But, by the accounts of these very same writers
who would exculpate or condone the outlawry of the
Younger brothers, Cole, Bob and Jim Younger and
Frank and Jesse James had joined Quantrill's band
of outlaws at least six months *before* the elder
Younger was murdered.

Some (including Robertus Love) place the approxi-
mate date of their joining at more than a year before
the murder of "Colonel" Henry W. Younger, although, to be sure, Love includes Frank but does not
include Jesse James among those who first joined up
with Quantrill. Thus, Love is permitted to follow the
tradition of the "revenge" motive, in accounting for
the outlawry of the James boys, by recording that the
fiercest and most bloodthirsty of the two brothers,
Jesse, was not impelled to join Quantrill until the
iron sank into his soul through the following events:

He [Jesse James] was cultivating corn, trudging between
the handles of an oldtime bull-tongue plow, one day in June,
1863, when the Hell's imps which for years had been raging
all around him swooped down with specific fingers not alto-

gether phantasmal, clutched him, carried him aloft, shook him violently for a time and then let him drop into the midst of the fiery furnace. . . .

That June day a large squad of Federal militia visited the Samuel farm. Dr. Samuel, stepfather of the James boys, met the visitors and inquired their mission.

"You have been entirely too loud in your disloyal expressions," the leader informed him, "and so has your wife. Furthermore, you folks are friendly to that damn cutthroat Quantrill, and you harbor his men. We've come to teach you a lesson."

One of the regulators produced a stout cord. The doctor's hands were bound behind his back. He was escorted to a tall tree with an overhanging limb. A rope was noosed about his neck. One end was tossed over the limb and caught by several home-staying soldiers as it descended. They pulled hard, drawing the victim up until his feet were well off ground. The pulling end of the rope then was tied around the trunk of the tree, and the regulators of private opinion publicly expressed left the doctor to choke slowly to death.

Mrs. Samuel saved his life. She had followed the execution party, keeping considerably to the rear. As soon as the militiamen departed, she ran forward and cut her husband down. She was an excellent nurse, he a skillful physician. Though about half dead from strangulation, Dr. Samuel recovered. His escape from death was due chiefly to the zeal of his tormentors for haste in completing decimation of the male members of the family found at home. They went looking for little Jesse. They found him in a distant cornfield, plowing as straight a row as any lad of fifteen could be expected to plow. He was a rather baby-faced boy, seeming younger even than his years. The lesson-teacher had another rope along, but when they saw what a little fellow Jesse was they hesitated.

"Don't let's hang him—this time," the leader counseled. "He's too young to go and fight like that tall wild devil Frank. But let's teach the cub a lesson, anyhow."

The lesson comprised a whipping along between the rows of corn. One of the teachers used the stout rope as a lash. Jesse released the plow handles and made toward home, the stern schoolmaster administering a fraction of the lesson at every other step. The militiamen made off before the pupil got to the farmhouse; they went to teach similar lessons to other Southern sympathizers.

The "revenge" motive was not omitted by earlier writers to account for the turning of Myra Belle Shirley into Belle Starr, "The Bandit Queen."

You may look into *Bella Starr*—if you can find a copy of that rare book—to get the full story conceived by the anonymous writer for the Richard K. Fox Publications; but suffice it here to observe that in this earliest of the stories of Belle Starr's career, the revenge motive is duly set forth in this wise: "It was during this time (about 1867, after Belle's marriage to Jim Reed and after the Sherley family had moved to Texas, according to the Richard K. Fox account) that Edward Sherley [sic], Myra's brother, a young man of 17 years of age, was killed when resisting officers. To this unfortunate tragedy may be traced the reckless spirit which then and there seized upon the almost broken-hearted young woman."

Quantrill's Pupils

The trouble with this explanation of Belle's adoption of banditry as a career is that the records show that Ed Shirley was killed in Missouri in 1863, as noted above; that Ed was not Myra's *younger* brother, but was her elder by at least four, and, more probably, by six, years; and that Ed Shirley was never in Texas at any time, at least the Ed Shirley who was Myra's brother was not.

Subsequent writers, seizing upon the Richard K. Fox fiction for most of their character-developing episodes, obviously found some flaws in the Fox chronology as well as in the Fox spelling of names, and, moreover, invented a more plausible explanation of the transformation of a beautiful, talented, well-brought-up, highly educated innkeeper's daughter (as they pictured her) into an avenging goddess— her dead-shot hand and her courageous heart set against all the forces of law and order. One also wonders, incidentally, how horse thievery, which was the only offense that Belle was ever actually charged with and convicted of, can be conceived as an act of revenge against the forces of law and order for the killing of a brother, especially inasmuch as her horse stealing was largely from Indians and from squatters illegally résident in Indian Territory and therefore outlaws like herself.

First in the field of the revisionist school of writers, who improvised variations on the Richard K. Fox writer's theme, was J. W. Weaver, for many years the editor of the Fort Smith, Arkansas, *Weekly Independent* and correspondent for the New York *Herald,* later the author of a series of reminiscences published in the Fort Smith *Weekly Elevator,* to whom S. W. Harman (co-author with C. P. Sterns), of the famous and now very rare source book, *Hell on the Border* (1898), was indebted for this exercise in rhetoric:

On her sixteenth birthday, February 3, 1862, as Belle, returning from a scout, was riding through the village of Newtonia, in the eastern part of Newton County, Missouri, thirty-five miles, as the crow flies, from her home town, Carthage, she was intercepted by a Major Enos who, with a troop of cavalry, was stationed in the village and who had his headquarters at the home of Judge M. H. Ritchery.

It is a quaint old place; the house, a long structure of red brick, with broad verandas and an L. located at some little distance back from the highway, the centerpiece of beautiful grounds, dotted here and there with fine old shade trees. The house is still standing, and is the home of Professor and Mrs. S. C. Graves, the latter being a daughter of Judge Ritchery. The place is a romantic one; scattered here and there are seven solid shot that were dropped on the grounds during the cannonading incident to several lively skirmishes about the time the battle of Pea Ridge, in Arkansas, was fought. The cornice of the house, in several places, still shows where portions of the architecture were carried away by shells; it was the desire of Judge Ritchery that the marks of battle be allowed to remain as they were, and that the cannon balls be not disturbed, and those who came after him have respected his wishes. Across the road from the grounds still stands a large, but considerably dilapidated, stone building, first built for a mill and afterwards successively used for a hospital, first by the Confederate and then by the Federal troops.

On the day of Belle Shirley's capture, as noted above, Major Enos had sent a detachment of cavalry to Carthage for the purpose of capturing her brother, Captain Shirley, who was known to be on a visit to his home. Belle, or Myra, as she was then called, had ridden into that section of the country for the purpose of obtaining information that might be of value to her people, and having discovered that men had been sent to capture her brother, was on the point of hastening to warn him, when she was arrested and detained. She had been in the habit of riding recklessly where she pleased, and as scarce any Union soldier would think of molesting a woman, especially when the woman chanced to be a beautiful and buxom girl, her plans had not, hitherto, been disarranged. It happened that Major Enos, who had resided in Carthage, was acquainted with both her and her brother, as children, and this was why he had ordered her arrest; he rightly surmising that she was about to go to her brother's assistance. The girl was taken to the chamber of the Ritchery home and guarded by the major himself, who laughed at her annoyance. This served to anger her and she gave expression to her rage in loud and deep curses. Then she would sit at the piano and rattle off some wild selection in full keeping with her fury; the next instant she would spring to her feet, stamp the floor and berate the major and his acts with all the ability and profanity of an experienced trooper, while the tears of mortification rolled down her cheeks, her terrible passion only increased by the laughter and taunts of her captor. At last, believing his men to have had plenty of time to reach Carthage ahead of her, Major Enos said:

"Well, Myra, you can go now. My men will have your brother under arrest before you can reach him."

With eagerness, trembling in every lineament, she sprang to the door, rushed down the stairway and out to a clump of cherry bushes, where she cut several long sprouts for use as riding whips. The judge's daughter, now Mrs. Graves, accompanied her.

"I'll beat them yet," said the girl, as with tearful eyes she swallowed a great lump in her throat. Her horse stood just where her captors had left it; vaulting into the saddle, she sped away, plying the cherry sprouts with vigor. A short distance from the house she deserted the traveled road and, leaping fences and ditches without ceremony, struck a bee line in the direction of Carthage. She was a beautiful sight as she rode away through the fields; her lithe figure clad in a closely fitting jacket, erect as an arrow, her hair unconfined by her broad-brimmed, feather-decked sombrero, but falling free and flung to the breeze, and her right hand plying the whip at almost every leap of her fiery steed. The Major seized a field glass and ascending to the chamber watched her course across the great stretch of level country.

"Well, I'll be d——," he ejaculated, admiringly. "She's a born guerrilla. If she doesn't reach Carthage ahead of my troopers, I'm a fool."

The Major was right; when his detachment of cavalry galloped leisurely into Carthage that evening they were greeted by a slip of a girl mounted on a freshly groomed horse. She dropped a curtsy and asked:

"Looking for Captain Shirley? He isn't here—left half an

hour ago—had business up Spring River. 'Spect he's in Lawrence county by this time.''

The famous ride by his little sister availed Captain Shirley but little after all, except that it gave him an opportunity to give up his life in battle; he was killed a few days later while at the head of a band of guerrillas during an engagement in the brush with Federal cavalry.

Her brother's death enlivened all the animosity of which her untrammeled nature was capable, and to her dying day there was nothing so hated by her as a ''Yankee.'' She still continued her rides as a scout as occasion encouraged until the close of the war, and during the three years after her brother's death was frequently with Cole Younger and the James boys, whose acts of recklessness and daring in after years astonished the world.

The Weaver-Harmon school of writers about Belle Starr blithely perpetuate inaccuracies about their heroine. In the above account they depart from the generally accepted date of Belle's birth, perhaps in order to conform to their own assumption that Myra Shirley (Belle Starr) and Ed Shirley were twins. Then, too, they credit Major ''Enos'' with the arrest of Belle. This fiction involves one Major Edwin B. Eno of the Eighth Missouri Militia (Federal) cavalry. This Major Eno made voluminous nightly reports in the vernacular to his commanding officer on his operations for the day, his expectations, his view of the disposition of the enemy forces, and everything that happened to him. His records fail to reveal any mention of having arrested or questioned a girl named Myra Shirley, or any other girl for that matter.

Further evidence of the romantic treatment of this episode is contained in the reference to Ed Shirley as a captain. He was not a captain, nor was he at the head of a band of guerrillas. There can be no doubt that Ed Shirley was a bushwhacker, or Confederate guerrilla. We know the circumstances, if not the actual date, of Ed's death. Mrs. Sarah Musgrave of Sarcoxie, Missouri, in a newspaper interview published in Schrantz's *History of Jasper County, Missouri, in the Civil War,* recalled that she had helped to take care of the dead body of Ed Shirley after he had been killed.

Shirley and Milt Norris, according to Mrs. Musgrave, were bushwhackers whose presence at Mrs. Stewart's home in Sarcoxie had become known to a company of Federal militia encamped at Cave Springs, not far north of Sarcoxie. While Shirley and Norris were eating a meal the militia surrounded the house. "Both men broke and ran. Shirley was shot as he leaped the back fence and fell dead on the other side. Norris got a rifle-ball scratch on his side as he went over the fence, but was not much hurt and escaped in the brush."

The rest of Mrs. Musgrave's narrative concerning Ed is open to grave doubt. "Norris came to Carthage posthaste and told the Shirley family of Bud's death. Next day Shirley's mother and Myra Shirley, the sixteen-year-old sister of Shirley, appeared at Sarcoxie, the latter with a belt around her waist, from which swung two big revolvers, one on each side. She was not timid in making it known among those she saw that she meant to get revenge for her brother's death. As is well known in Carthage, Myra Shirley is the girl who afterwards acquired bandit fame as Belle Starr, and became famous in literature under that name.''

I deeply suspect that it is to her memory of literature that Mrs. Musgrave was trusting, in this instance, and not to her memory of actual happenings. For, although it is entirely possible, and even probable, that she helped to take care of the body of Ed Shirley after he had been killed in the manner she describes, she is incorrect in saying, ''I *think* it was near the close of the war that Bud Shirley was killed'' (for he was killed in June, 1863), and it is incorrect for her to say that Belle went to Sarcoxie from Carthage loaded with revolvers and bent on revenge, for the simple reason that there wasn't any Carthage left at the war's close. The town had been razed to the ground in October, 1863. John Shirley, Mrs. Shirley and Myra were already in Texas or on their way there in 1864. After the Confederate guerrillas burned Carthage in 1863, only the courthouse escaped the flames, but even that was destroyed by Jennison's Jayhawkers on their return through what was left of the town in the spring of 1864. Even the county seat of Jasper County had had to be removed to Cave Springs in 1863, and there wasn't enough of a rebuilt town of Carthage to re-establish the county seat there until September, 1866.

After the close of the war, "There was not much" [in all of Jasper and surrounding counties] "to return to," writes Schrantz. All the towns and villages in the central and western part of the county were in ashes, and those in the eastern part were either destroyed or badly damaged. Most of the farmhouses had disappeared and all over the region were skeleton chimneys, surrounded by weed-grown fields. In the main the district had reverted to the wilds. Deer, wild turkey and game of all sorts had increased tremendously during the last years of the war and early comers after the struggle state that wolves were so tame that they could be shot from the wagon seats of those who at wide intervals drove along the seldom used roads.

It makes a highly romantic story for the fiery Myra, the Carthage innkeeper's later-to-be-famous daughter, to be described as buckling on her six-shooters to avenge the death of her beloved brother. But, alas, the internecine strife, especially the guerrilla warfare, had rendered nearly all Southwestern Missouri and Southeastern Kansas uninhabitable, except for roving bands of murderers, arsonists and robbers. The non-combatants had begun to evacuate the southwestern part of Missouri in the early stages of the war.

"Most of the people who had gone had been driven out by the generally lawless conditions which prevailed at frequent intervals," comments Schrantz, "and others suspected of sympathy to the cause of the South had been required to leave during 1864 by the Federal authorities who feared that they would feed bushwhackers or give them information and thus help to maintain them in the guerrilla warfare they carried on every summer."

In the early part of 1863, John Shirley, with his wife and daughter, had loaded their belongings into ox-drawn Conestoga wagons and, with the money he had been able to salvage out of his hotel and livery-stable investments and out of the sale of most of his horses to regular Confederate cavalry units, had started south to Texas. He had a son, Preston, who had moved to McKinney County, north of Dallas, some time before the outbreak of the war, and he had a brother who had a farm near Scyene, about ten miles east of Dallas. Scyene was his goal. We do not know the route he followed; but it most likely was down through the Ozarks to Fort Smith, Arkansas, and thence by a tortuous route to De Queene and westward on a trail to Dallas and southeast to Scyene, a village now two miles west of Mesquite post-office. It is not likely that John Shirley would have chosen a more direct route through the Indian country, torn as it was at the time by a more awful civil strife than that of Missouri. Moreover, it was a wild region in which white intruders not only were not welcome, but were forbidden by law to trespass, even in time of peace, except by permission of the tribal governments of the Indians. The United States had, at least temporarily, lost whatever authority it had reserved over this land of the Cherokees, Choctaws, Chickasaws, Seminoles and Creeks.

To leave Missouri for Texas at that time was almost like jumping from the frying pan into the fire. At any rate, John Shirley would find in East Texas quite a number of ex-Missourians, even if there would be among them some he would rather not see, or some who would rather not see him.

CHAPTER THREE

HELL AND/OR TEXAS

If John Shirley, his ox-team wagons creaking along the rutted and alternately muddy or dusty road toward Texas, dared strike west from Fort Smith, through the Choctaw and Cherokee country, to the old Texas Road, he would have followed the old Marcy trail across the Canadian River, near where Whitefield now stands, to Briartown. He would have gone over the Briartown-Eufaula trail, and thence to Edwards' Trading Post, about five miles southeast of the present town of Holdenville, Oklahoma, and on to the Texas Trail to the Red River crossing at Preston, and thence almost due south to Dallas.

Thus Myra Belle Shirley would have passed right by the place she was later to name Younger's Bend, on the Canadian River, which was to be her home for the most spectacular period of her life. To the right, on the old Briartown-Eufaula trail about six miles from the ferry-crossing south of Briartown, she would have seen the cabin of her future father-in-law, old Tom Starr, and, to the left, near the river, she would have seen a log cabin, perched on top of a bluff overlooking the river, which she was to own and occupy for eight or nine years until her death.

Moreover, en route to Texas, Myra (no matter what trail her father chose) would have passed through the largest, wildest, toughest, most heterogeneous town she had ever seen—the town probably more associated with her career than she could have wished—Fort Smith, Arkansas. It was a town bordering on the Indian country, a garrison town, and a town filled with Indians, whiskey peddlers illicitly running liquor into the Indian Territory, gamblers, sharpers, prostitutes, litigants, outlaws, emigrants heading south and southwest. It was a town with trading stores supplying everything pioneers and frontiersmen could need. Belle might have seen, for the first time in her life, several steamboats, which in those days, when the Arkansas River was more navigable, plied up the river from Fort Smith as far as Fort Gibson and down the river to the Mississippi.

At Edwards' Little River Trading Post, John Shirley would have stopped to replenish supplies, make repairs on equipment, rest up in a comfortable hostelry and make preparations for the arduous two-hundred-mile journey still in front of him, a journey through mountains and heavy wilderness and across streams that were swollen at one season in the year but treacherously filled with innocent-looking quicksand in summer.

The country through which they would pass after leaving Edwards' Trading Post would be the land of the Choctaws, and here and there, at long intervals, the emigrants would doubtless be greatly surprised to see regular mansions of brick or of log and clapboard, far more substantial and elegant than the homes of even the more prosperous class of whites in Southwestern Missouri. These would be the homes of the rich Choctaws, with fine implements, well-cultivated fields, blacksmith shops, stables, cattle, horses and vegetable gardens, tended by Negro slaves. But those would be the homes of only the rich few, who had amassed their fortunes (or had inherited them) in their old lands east of the Mississippi before the Indian Removal.

Squalor, misery, the physical results of hunger and drunkenness would confront the emigrants as they passed the lonely cabins of the less fortunate, great body of Choctaws—those who had been driven from their lands by greedy whites backed by a treaty-breaking, unscrupulous aggressor-government and chased across the Mississippi, across Arkansas and into a wild, uncleared country and turned loose there, without schools, medical care, food supplies and necessities such as they had been used to in the East, where they had absorbed the white man's civilization and had become agriculturists, artisans and civilized men; where they had even, many of them, absorbed white and Negro blood.

James Edwards, proprietor of the trading post, paid a license fee for his concession in the Indian country and could be ejected at any time by command of the chiefs and council of the Choctaw Nation. He cultivated a large tract of fertile land, with the aid of Creek retainers and Negro slaves, and raised corn, squash, pumpkins, watermelons, peas, wheat, sweet-potatoes, string beans, onions, radishes, okra, beets and Irish potatoes, by means of which he could set a fine table for emigrants stopping at his trading post. He sold everything from saddles to kitchen knives, from carbines to snuff, from beef, pork and flour to sunbonnets and calico dresses, from wagon-tongues to blacksmiths' anvils. His was an oasis of civilization in a wilderness.

It was an oasis Belle would have found delightful on this first visit; but, in later years, it would be an oasis to avoid. Going through the Indian country from Texas to Younger's Bend and from Younger's Bend to Kansas, she would have taken the old trail that went through what is now Wilburton, more than a hundred miles east; for Edwards' Trading Post was not a welcome or comfortable place for horse thieves and outlaws. Edwards' success depended upon the good will of his Indian neighbors; he could not afford to shelter outlaws even for the night, much less harbor and have dealings with them.

South of Edwards' Trading Post all the way to the Red River, the Shirleys would have passed through beautiful country. The road would have been excellent, with a well-packed bed, no rock hills and no mires of sand or mud; the woods would give way to a rolling prairie, green and waist-high in fertile grass; there would be clear sparkling streams bordered by walnut, elm, ash, oak and sycamore, as well as cottonwood trees; small herds of wild horses might start up at the sound of the approaching wagon caravan and scamper off through grass and brush; and, if the Shirleys had luck, they might see how a Choctaw brave brought home a wild turkey for dinner.

The Indian would be wearing a breech-clout and astride a horse without saddle or bridle, guiding the animal only by a twist of the mane, and carrying a long pointed stick. When the Indian would sight a wild gobbler on the prairie, he would give chase until the turkey was tired out. Then he would prod the turkey around and drive him at a slow walk back home. A wild turkey never flies more than a short distance at a time and never flies more than twice without becoming exhausted. After that it is easy to catch the bird and drive him back home, to be penned up until one is ready to kill and dress him for cooking.

Most of the current roadmaps of Texas and of

Oklahoma, given away by the oil companies at service
stations, show, very faintly, a town called Preston on
the south side of the Red River, seventeen miles northwest of Denison. The town is so small now it is not
listed in the tables of towns and cities. That is, it is so
small comparatively. I suppose the population now
is as large as, if not larger than, it ever was in any
previous year; but from 1845 on through the
Eighteen-eighties, it was a mighty important little
town.

When there was no Denison, Sherman, Gainesville
or Wichita Falls, in Texas, there was a Preston. Fifty
years before Oklahoma Territory was opened up for
settlement, and twenty years before Jesse Chisholm
and Robert Bean laid out the 175-mile trail that bore
Chisholm's name through West-Central Oklahoma,
Preston was an important little post and settlement;
for it was located at the best, and about the only, ford-
ing place along the Red River and hence was a post
and settlement on the first cattle trail from Texas
through Oklahoma. When the Shirleys drove through
there in 1863 on the way to Dallas, it was the first trading post and white settlement they would have encountered after they left Edwards' Little River Trading Post.

When the Shirleys reached Preston they were in
Texas. They could not only rest, refurnish and relax
in preparation for the last leg of their journey, but

Hell and/or Texas

John Shirley could legally buy himself a drink. The introduction of liquor into the Indian country was a serious Federal offense. In Texas, in those days, very few things were prohibited; and it was considered justifiable homicide to kill a man if he refused to join you in a sociable snort; you didn't even have to bury your own dead.

The Republic of Texas, relinquishing its status as an independent nation, was admitted into the Union by treaty in 1845. Two years later, the United States had to fight a war with Mexico to keep this prize within the Union; and for forty years after that, there were unceasing wars within the state—wars between rival cattlemen, wars between cattlemen and homesteaders, county-seat wars, wars between Texas cowboys and Kansas peace officers, wars between Texas settlers and the Comanche, Apache, Arapahoe, Cheyenne and Kiowa Indians, wars between Federal and Rebel sympathizers, a war with the Union, wars between rival two-gun men, wars of rivalry between Fort Worth and Dallas and between Houston and Galveston, wars between Gringos and Spiks on the Border, and later the Brownsville raid and the incursions of Villa.

It has never taken much to start a fight in Texas.

Long before Texas was admitted as a state, it was the great magnet for sturdy, restless and reckless people. It was the magnificent goal of those who wanted to get as far away from the confinements and comforts of eastern seaboard civilization as possible. There was plenty of space in that vast empire for a man to run around in, yell and kick up his heels.

Naturally, such an attractive place didn't always attract the best element of society. Around 1850 the expression "G.T.T." became as endemic as "O.K." was to become later. It was an abbreviation for "Gone to Texas." It didn't necessarily mean that someone had gone to Texas; it merely meant that he had skipped out. Process servers scribbled "G.T.T." across the backs of summonses for persons they couldn't locate; creditors wrote losses off their books when debtors skipped out owing them money; wife-deserters, forgers, murderers, prostitutes, crooked gamblers, swindlers and deadbeats on the lam—all of them, when their disappearance was noticed, were conversationally described as "G.T.T."

But, although the more recalcitrant element of human society was playfully and sometimes even dangerously present in the general population of early Texas towns and villages, there was a sufficiency of the placid, plodding, vigorous and industrious yeoman type of men and their wives to exercise just enough of a restraining influence to prevent anarchy, and not too much of this restraining influence to make Dallas, for instance, a cowtown imitation of Boston. Texas happily remained healthily crude for quite a long time.

Dallas, as late as 1864, when the Shirleys arrived, was a one-street town, the one street being a mud-hole in rainy weather and a dust bowl during the dry spell. The stores, saloons, restaurants, gambling halls and banks were mainly one-story shanties with false two-story fronts. Plank sidewalks even on Main Street were a rarity to a point of being obtrusive; but the more elegant emporia had wooden "galleries" or porches stretching out over the sidewalk, with post-rails to tie your horse to and with wooden benches out in front which you could whittle as long as there was enough left to a seat to hold you up.

But Dallas was an up-and-coming town in 1864; it had a population of 2000 and was beginning to rival San Antonio, Austin and Fort Worth. All that was needed was to get those cattlemen and caballeros down around Uvalde County to thinking right, so they would come to Dallas to blow their money; and the best way to do that would be to hurry up that project to bring a spur of the Arkansas and Louisiana Railroad up as far as Dallas and stop there.

The Arkansas and Louisiana Railroad project never materialized; but in July, 1872, the Houston Texas Central Railroad brought its first train into town, and a year later the Texas & Pacific completed its construction through Dallas in a system that was ultimately to link Dallas by rail to both the east and west coasts; the town's population rose from 3000 to 6000; the stagecoach was doomed to become extinct within ten years; and Dallas really began to boom.

The Civil War, of course, had retarded progress for many years to come. East Texas was a wonderfully fertile country, suitable for agricultural crops as well as for stock raising. With the outbreak of war, the stream of immigration from Missouri, Arkansas, Kentucky and Tennessee widened. As the war dragged on, the Southern sympathizers who came to East Texas were, almost all of them, impoverished.

From here on the records become more numerous and the memories of aged people who knew the Shirleys in Texas become more reliable. What they have to contribute tends more to conform to the known facts and the scene. The legends, however, the earliest of which were created twenty-six years after the Shirleys moved to Texas, grow more fantastic.

The legends, which always tend to endow Belle with an opulent and aristocratic background, such as didn't exist in Southwestern Missouri or in the whole State of Texas during the period, have the Shirleys living in something of a mansion on an estate which included many well-cultivated acres. There were Negro slaves, blooded stock, equipages—all the familiar claptrap of the sentimental, romantic novels written in the eighties about life in the "Ole South" of ante-bellum days.

The true story as it emerges, incompletely and conjecturally, of course, from the ascertainable facts, has more humanity than the silly legends, and is, therefore, more truly romantic. It is grotesquely absurd to picture, as many of the legends do, "Judge" Shirley as living like a squire of the Deep South on the open prairie between Scyene and Mesquite, while the three "richest" men in Dallas, John Neely Bryan (the first postmaster, whiskey peddler and storekeeper), Judge William Hord (the first realtor) and Alexander Cockrell (the first manufacturer), were living in cabins. Judge Hord's cabin is still standing at the entrance to Marsalis Park in Dallas. For $7,000, Cockrell, who ran a brickyard and a lumber business, bought nearly the whole town of Dallas from Bryan, who had established a trading post on the east bank of the Trinity River in 1841 and had thus founded the settlement which grew up around his post and came to be known as Dallas. This real-estate transaction in which Cockrell bought out Bryan, lock, stock and barrel, took place only nine years before John Shirley's ox-team passed through the main street of Dallas on the way to Scyene.

It would appear that John Shirley moved right in on his son, Preston, who had a farm of a few acres, probably forty, sixty or so, about a mile east of the village of Scyene. The settlers in that region were mostly like Preston Shirley himself, emigrants from Missouri, Arkansas, Tennessee and Kentucky, in search of virgin land, impoverished but industrious and used to toil. For all that Preston's father had been a village tavern-keeper, Preston was not a "townsman"; his training had been on a farm.

Preston's home was doubtless a one- or two-room shack of clapboard. Log houses were rare in that region because timber was scanty and a log house was more expensive than a frame one. It is possible that Preston lived in a dugout. Dugouts were common on the prairies then, and for thirty years or more later, and, in many respects, they were the most suitable dwellings that poor men could build; for they were cool in the summer and easy to keep warm in the winter. In the famous blizzard of 1886, hundreds of dwellers on the prairies from the Dakotas to the Rio Grande were found frozen to death in log, brick and frame houses, whereas those who lived in dugouts were found to have kept snug and fairly warm and to have suffered little more than from hunger, inconvenience and boredom.

A dugout was cheap to build. One simply dug a hole in the ground about fourteen feet square, threw the dirt up into a mound on three sides, built a front of three or four layers of logs with an entrance like that of a cellar door, put a roof over the hole, piled up the excavated dirt upon the sides and over the roof, leaving room for a chimney of some sort, and building—if one cared to take the trouble—a bower-porch in front to serve as an outdoor living and dining room when the weather permitted.

It is likely that John Shirley arrived in Scyene early enough in the summer either to construct a dugout for himself and wife and daughter or to build additions to Preston's frame house, if such was the habitation he had. Meanwhile they could live, as during the weeks of their journey, in their Conestoga wagon.

I regret to report that the Shirleys were not liked by their neighbors. An eighty-eight-year-old resident of Dallas who lived on a farm adjoining the Shirleys' near Scyene and whose memory is remarkably clear and whose imagination is not cluttered up with the Belle Starr legends says the first thing that antagonized the other farmers in the vicinity was the extreme inconsiderateness of the Shirleys. The Shirleys' special action showing a lack of consideration may, on first thought, seem like a small thing; but, once you think about it, it was a very large thing, indeed. The Shirleys had a habit of dragging their water barrels on ground sleds up to the communal well and draining it dry. They wouldn't leave any water for the next fellow, and it took some time for the well to fill up again, or for enough water to seep in for the others to get a bucketful.

This was a just and important grievance. On the open prairie, you can't take a post-hole digger and go down ten or twelve feet into the ground just anywhere and expect to find water. Prairie wells are deep and costly, and you may dig twenty of them and still find no water. You have to hit an underground spring or the seepage from a stream. There was a South Mesquite Creek about halfway between Scyene and Mesquite, and a North Mesquite Creek about four miles the other side of Mesquite, but they were mere trickles and were often dry; and Trinity River was ten miles away, even as the crow flies.

Two of these early neighbors of the Shirleys, both elderly gentlewomen of Dallas, independently testified as to this inconsiderateness of the Shirleys about the well. Their remembering this local water shortage, caused by the selfishness of the Shirleys, over a period of nearly three-quarters of a century, is sufficient proof, at least, that the water problem was no trivial one to the Shirley neighbors around Scyene.

Our informants said that the neighbors of the Shirleys were the McCommases (the head of the McCommas family was Elder Amon McCommas, a preacher of the Christian or Campbellite Church, who had eight children, two of them, Rosa and Armilda, about Myra Shirley's age), the Ross Bradfields, the Johnsons, the Whites, the Millers and the Pooles. They did not recall the type of dwelling the Shirleys at first lived in, but said that dugouts, sod and clapboard houses were the common type; that the Shirleys were regarded as "rather common" because they had no slaves, although the well-liked Elder McCommas had no slaves either but was a preacher and, moreover, a northerner by birth; that Myra attended, for a time, the local community school, which was conducted by Mrs. Poole, but she was irregular in attendance and was regarded as "rather wild"; that, as a girl, Myra was of medium height, fairly pretty, fair-skinned but with black hair and eyes; that there was "something peculiar" about the Shirleys, not at all cordial or open, but secretive or furtive in demeanor and that, because of this, they were generally feared and shunned.

In regard to this characterization of the Shirleys as having something peculiar about them, the testimony of our informants in this case is not to be taken as a characterization colored by knowledge of later events; for we must remember that these Shirleys were from the Ozarks of Missouri; and that the Ozark people are clannish, taciturn, dead-set against changing their ways to conform with the ways of others and prone to regard all those outside of their immediate clan or "people" as "furriners"; that to them, a native of Kansas, Iowa, Louisiana, or Mississippi is as much of a "foreigner" as a Bengalese or a Lett. Ordinarily, the Ozarkans just don't mix with other people, and even when they try to, they don't mix well or relish the experience. The significance of this trait among the Ozark people should become more apparent as we go along.

From subsequent events, it would appear that the Shirleys did not prosper well in Texas; and one of the reasons may have to do with that difficulty the Ozarkan has in conforming to, much less profiting by, the experience, or success, of others.

Emigrants from the cotton states of the South, who began to trickle into Texas at the beginning of the Civil War and to grow into a stream as the devastation of war began more profoundly to affect them, were not long in discovering that the black bottom land, flat and treeless and therefore not requiring clearing, was about the best cotton-growing land imaginable; and soon they were making handsome cash crops in cotton—and impoverishing the soil by not rotating their crops sufficiently.

It is to be guessed that John and Preston Shirley, being Ozarkans, continued to use their Texas prairie soil in precisely the same way they had used their hilly and timbered Missouri land; that is, they made corn their principal crop, and used it for corn pone, "roastin' ears," and hominy for their own table and as feed for their horses and cattle. They raised hogs as their principal meat diet—aside from wild game— planted some sorghum cane perhaps and, in general, used their farm for their own subsistence rather than in expectation of selling their produce in town. Whatever cash they required, they would be likely to get by other means, such as horse raising and horse "trading," keeping a blooded stud to stand for a fee, and ways more devious.

I am not quite sure that the Shirleys were true Ozarkans; they seem to have traits of the "valley" people in them; but the fact that "Bud" Shirley seems to have been a bushwhacker of the sort who didn't take any interest in the social or political issues in the war at all and only used the occasion to gratify his personal grudges and carry on his clan's personal feuds seems to indicate that they had a lot of the Ozarks in them.

Myra Belle Shirley's earliest romance can be considered only in terms of conjecture—a conjecture based upon certain deductions from known facts and known dates, upon an alibi letter of Cole Younger to his old friend, August C. Appler, editor of the Osceola, Missouri, *Democrat,* while Cole was at large and accused of various robberies, and upon the most persistent and most credible story of the old-timers who lived in the neighborhood of Belle Starr during the years she spent in the old Indian Territory.

This conjecture is based upon my belief that the story of the old-timers of Haskell, MacIntosh, Muskogee and Latimer Counties of the present state of

Belle Starr

Oklahoma—that Pearl Younger, Belle Starr's first child, was the daughter of Cole Younger—is true.

In some of the old-timers' versions of this affair, they insist that Cole was Belle's first *husband*. In the only authenticated interview Belle Starr ever gave, that of May 30, 1886, to the editor of the Fort Smith, Arkansas, *Elevator,* Belle said that the first man she ever fell in love with and the first man she married was "a noted guerrilla," but she didn't give his name. The Richard K. Fox writer's story, published three years after Belle's interview, and after her death, makes this "noted guerrilla" the outlaw Jim Reed, to whom Belle may have been married, even according to the legends, as early as 1869.

Belle's known second child went by the name of Ed Reed, whereas, at no time did Belle, or anyone else, refer to her daughter as Pearl Reed, but always as Pearl Younger, or in some instances, Pearl Starr—after Belle had married Sam Starr.

Even when Belle's children took the stand to testify in their mother's behalf in her trials for larceny, their names were given as Pearl Younger and Ed Reed, after Belle's marriage to Sam Starr.

Strengthening our conjecture is the fact that after Belle had married the Cherokee Indian, Sam Starr, and had thereby acquired dower rights to Sam Starr's share in the communal lands of the Cherokee Nation, she named the place "Younger's Bend." This would seem to be a token of a woman's sentimental remembrances of her first lover.

It would appear that Cole, Bob, Jim and John Younger went to Texas in 1866, and possibly, a year or two earlier, stayed for a while with friends on a farm near Scyene, and that they were in the neighborhood of Scyene and Dallas off and on through 1871, Bob clerking for a while in a store at Scyene, and Jim serving as a deputy sheriff in Dallas during the year 1870.

The legends about Belle's romantic elopement with Jim Reed vary. Some say that it took place during the war, before the Shirleys left Carthage, which, of course, is preposterous; and some say that it occurred while the Shirleys were living in either Scyene or Dallas in 1869.

But the reminiscences of the old-timers in Texas about Belle, published after her death in 1889, jibe pretty well with the records which show that James H. (Jim) Reed, of Vernon County, Missouri, first came to Texas and bought a piece of land at Coon Creek, Bosque County, near Dallas, in 1872, sold the property shortly thereafter, and moved to Scyene. The records seem to show that Jim wasn't even around when some of the legends say he was married to Belle, for he had not reached Texas until five years after the alleged date of his marriage.

Also, legendary accounts uniformly give the year of Pearl's birth as 1869, whereas the same accounts give the year of Belle's alleged marriage to Jim Reed as 1867, which would make a lapse of two years after this marriage before a child is born, which would be a very unusual occurrence in those days, even granting that Jim was there.

It is my belief that Myra Belle Shirley had a love affair with Cole Younger in Scyene when she was about twenty and he was about twenty-four, that the child who was always called Pearl Younger was the illegitimate offspring of this love affair, that Cole Younger deserted Belle and child and went on the scout, and that a year or two later Jim Reed took Belle as his mistress and so lived with her until the time of his death in 1874, and that while Jim Reed and Belle were living together as man and wife, the boy, named Ed Reed, was born to Belle as the son of Jim Reed.

The Belle Shirley-Cole Younger romance may well have been a deep and passionate affair on both sides; and if Cole had soon to be on his way, so did Aeneas after he had begot Telemachus on the beautiful Carthaginian queen, Dido, in the nuptials so sweetly sung by Virgil. Aeneas had to be getting along because, according to the legend, he had to found Rome; Cole had to be getting along because the sheriffs were after him. Maybe the sheriffs were after Aeneas, too.

Hell and/or Texas

A clue to the enigma concerning Belle's first love affair was the equivocal statement made by Cole Younger in Stillwater prison, when news was brought to him that Belle Starr had been murdered. One of the dispatches from Fort Smith, Arkansas, telling of the murder, had included an obituary briefly outlining Belle's career. Inasmuch as this obituary stated that Belle had once been married to Cole, the local newspapers of Stillwater sent reporters to interview him about Belle and ask him whether it was true or not that Belle was his wife. Cole made the simple, but carefully worded, statement: "I have never been married, so it can't be true that the lady who has been murdered was my wife." He added, when pressed further: "I knew the lady slightly some years ago; but it has been many years since I have seen her." He declined to make further comment.

In spite of his record of outlawry, Cole Younger was a religious and extremely conventional man. Just as in his account of the details of the Northfield robbery, written during his imprisonment but while Frank and Jesse James were still at large, he presented the names of both men under their aliases of Howard and Wood, so would he never disclose any intimacy he had had with any woman, especially of a woman just murdered who had two living children. Least of all would he have admitted a "marriage," the records of which he could not produce, and thus risk the chance that Pearl's illegitimacy might come to light.

Then I found the following obituary in the files of the Fort Smith Weekly *Elevator* of the week after Belle's death. It was written by the one newspaper man who had known Belle over a period of years, and in whom Belle had reposed her confidence. She was highly inimical to other newsmen, and on two occasions publicly humiliated one reporter who had written stories telling of her numerous lovers and reflecting upon her morals. J. W. Weaver, editor of the *Elevator,* said that Belle gave him confidential information about herself on condition that he would not publish what she told him until after her death. Weaver says he kept the promise; that for two years his notes on her disclosures to him were kept in his desk until news of Belle's murder gave him freedom to release them. Even then his obituary was a model of restraint. Not only does most of it check with verifiable facts in Belle's career, but, perhaps even in a manner that Weaver was not aware of, it solves several difficult problems that had arisen for the biographer out of the contradictory nature of much that was written, even contemporaneously, about Belle.

This was Weaver's obituary:

Belle Starr, who was killed in the Indian Territory, was the most remarkable woman who ever figured in the history of border outlawry. Married in girlhood to a dashing captain of Quantrill's cut-throat band, and associated all her life with bandits, she became a governing power on the border that made her a terror to officers. For the past twelve years Belle Starr has lived at Younger's Bend, near this place. The house was all this time the headquarters of the most desperate criminals. Jesse James spent six weeks there while officers were on his trail. Besides looking out after the needs of the outlaws, Belle Starr often took part in many of the famous raids in which the James and Younger boys were concerned.

Belle always dressed gaudily, and wherever she went her dashing appearance in the saddle attracted much attention. Belle never courted notoriety, and had a holy terror of reporters, who, she claimed, often misrepresented her. After Quantrill's murderers surrendered, Belle, who was then about eighteen years of age, fell in love with Cole Younger, who was one of the most daring of the guerrillas, and, though her father objected to the courtship, she ran away with the desperado, and was married to him on horseback. John Fisher, a famous Texas stage robber, held her horse while the ceremony was performed.

Less than six months after the marriage Younger became mixed up in a gun fight which ended in four men losing their lives, and he had to run away to Missouri, leaving his bride behind in Texas. She prepared to follow him, but her father sent her a message to the effect that her mother was dangerously ill. Belle returned home as quickly as her horse could carry her, and found that her mother had not been ill. She made preparations to rejoin her lover, but her father, who was violently opposed to the scheme, thrust her into a closet and kept her in close confinement for two weeks. He then gave her the choice of entering a small school in Parker

Belle Starr

County or a seminary in San Antonio. She chose the former. Cole Younger returned to Texas while his bride was still pursuing her studies in the schoolhouse, and, learning of her whereabouts, put spurs to his horse and dashed off into the school district. Belle, by this time, had lost much of her love for the good-looking outlaw, and when they met she refused to accompany him. But Younger was so persistent in his attentions that the girl finally consented to run away with him again. Borrowing a horse from a young man at the school one day, she mounted the animal and rode away to join Younger and his companions, who were waiting to escort her out of Texas.

The party consisted of Jesse James, Frank James and both Youngers. Cole Younger bought a farm in Missouri and tried to lead a better life. One day a posse killed Cole's seventeen-year-old brother while he was returning to his father's farm from Sedalia. As soon as the news of the tragedy reached the Younger farm, Cole set out to wreak vengeance. He killed four of the assassins in as many weeks, and wounded five others. He then joined Jesse James, and participated in all the great crimes of that band until he was shot while attempting to rob the Northfield, Minn., bank. He was then captured and is now serving a life sentence in the Stillwater Penitentiary. Belle Starr was true to Cole until the iron gates of the prison closed behind him. She spent a large amount of money for his defense, and accompanied him to Stillwater in the vain hope that she might effect his escape. Failing in this, she returned to the border to resume the career which her husband tried in vain to shun. She spent most of her time among the Indians, and finally married a worthless fellow named Sam Starr, a cousin of Jim's, who was shot down by her side about two years ago.

Hell and/or Texas

Dressed in men's clothes, riding in a good saddle and armed with a brace of formidable pistols, Belle Starr has raided, caroused and participated in every known form of outlawry prevalent in the Nation. She rode at a pace and with a grace that knew no equal, shot with great skill, and with it all she was a well-educated and accomplished woman. Many citizens of Fort Smith have heard her play on the piano in this city, and she was generally recognized as thoroughly well posted in various other accomplishments. She has one daughter named Pearl Younger, a beautiful girl, possessing her mother's fire and her father's reckless criminality.

It must be borne in mind that outlaws, when captured, never admit their identity until the evidence of that identity has been so fully established that it is useless any longer to deny it. And they never disclose the right names of the companions who are still at large; but, on the contrary, often invent aliases for them on the spur of the moment instead of employing the aliases these companions have formerly used. Thus, after the famous Coffeyville raid, in which the Dalton gang was practically wiped out, Emmett Dalton, who was riddled with bullets but captured alive, at first steadfastly denied his own identity as well as the identity of his two brothers, Grat and Bob, and of Dick Broadwell and Bill Power, who were killed in the raid. He gave false names and plausible accounts of himself and his companions, until he was forced to confess by being faced with persons who had known him for years.

When one bears in mind that the names which figure in newspaper accounts of outlaws, and which are too likely to be the ones used in later writings, are not necessarily the right names of the persons involved, the problem of disentangling the facts becomes somewhat easier.

The fight at Baxter Springs, Missouri, in May, 1864, cost Quantrill his leadership. Hitherto, this murderous chieftain had directed his raids against undefended towns and the loot had been heavy, without danger to the guerrillas. Moreover, Quantrill had divided his band into squads, each under a lieutenant of his own choosing; and it was his technique to deploy his squads over the whole countryside, each squad to rob single farmhouses and all return at an appointed place to divide the loot.

There had been jealousies and even bad blood among these lieutenants, arising as much from quarrels over the spoils as in the hope in each lieutenant's breast that, in the event that Quantrill weakened or was killed, he would become the leader of the band.

These rival animosities became so apparent that it was reflected in the men under his various subordinates; they began to show a loyalty to their squad commanders that spelled danger to Quantrill's leadership.

Quantrill had augmented his following and kept his leadership by a continuous display of utter ruthlessness and bravado. He resolved upon a stratagem to put his men to a test and at the same time to unite them the more firmly under his generalship. He announced his intention of seizing the Federal fort at Baxter Springs. The decision met with opposition and open expressions of disapproval. In a body of regulars, of course, such insubordination would be unthought of; but members of a guerrilla outfit had a different status from regularly enlisted soldiers. Each guerrilla was an individualist; he could desert at any time he wished —if he could escape without detection—and he had no fear of court martial. He received no salary from the Government, no supplies, no uniforms. His pay was in the loot of the gang as a whole. On joining, he furnished his own horse and firearms; or if he had none, he was furnished a horse and firearms out of the general loot. His overcoat, rifle and cartridge belt might have been those robbed from the dead body of a Federal soldier.

Enjoying such an individual status, the irregulars felt free to gripe against any proposal that met their disapproval, even though in the end they acceded to the will of the majority or the will of the strongest leader. And gripe they did at the prospect of attacking a fort. It involved considerable risk of life. More-over, the loot, even if the attack were successful, would be small. That would be the real reason for the dissension; but the words used in voicing disapproval would be that there was no military advantage to them in taking a fort, except for mere butchery, be-cause their work demanded that they always be on the move.

The will of Quantrill prevailed. The attack was launched, but it was so half-hearted that the Federals beat it off so effectively that the band retired even before any of them got within rifle range of the fort.

But as they were riding down the road in reas-sembled cavalry formation, they unexpectedly came in sight of General Blunt, riding in a buggy, and escorted by his bodyguard of eighty cavalrymen, in-cluding the band, marching to the fort. Through his field glasses General Blunt had descried the blue over-coats in Quantrill's nondescript outfit, and, mistaking them for Federals, ordered the band to strike up. Quantrill quickly perceived Blunt's mistake and or-dered his men in salute formation. When Blunt's men marched proudly into range, Quantrill ordered his men to open fire.

Blunt leaped out of the buggy, mounted his saddle horse which was tied behind the buggy, and escaped. But his men were taken so completely by surprise that they hadn't time to unlimber their rifles. They were slaughtered, nearly eighty of them. Only two or three succeeded in whirling their horses in time to flee for their lives. Strangely enough, the players in the band were the only ones who returned the fire. They killed one of the men in Cole Younger's squad. But all except one of the musicians were killed in the next guerrilla volley, and that one threw up his arms in surrender.

Here was Quantrill's opportunity to display his bravado and ruthlessness. He went up to the man, took his sidearms, and in full voice to reach the ears of his men said, "Tell Old God that the last man you saw on earth was Quantrill!" Then he shot his captive in the head and rode off with his outfit. (Although shot in the head, the Federal musician soldier miraculously survived to recount his experience.)

The death of one of Quantrill's own men, however, was what ended Quantrill's leadership and broke up the gang. Recriminations followed at bivouac that night, at one point of which Quantrill announced his intention of taking the band into Kentucky, because the Federal forces were too numerous in Missouri for comfort.

George Shepherd, who had been one of Anderson's guerrillas, as well as Quantrill's most expert marksmen and coolest killers, announced flatly that he wouldn't go. Quantrill called for volunteers, and fifty or sixty men responded, including Frank James. Jesse

Belle Starr

James was one of the revolters, and so were the Younger brothers, Bob, Cole, Jim and John.

The gang split up the following day. Shepherd proposed to lead a group into Indian Territory in an effort to join Stand Watie, the leader of the Cherokee irregulars.

They didn't find Watie, but they did find Old Tom Starr, a Cherokee who had been carrying on a one-man war against the Union forces, as represented by the Ross faction of the Cherokees, not because his sympathies were with the South—he had no slaves and wasn't interested in the white men's quarrels— but because he and his eight or ten brothers had an undying hatred for all Ross-faction Cherokees.

Members of the Ross faction had assassinated Tom's father, James Starr, a member of the Ridge, or Treaty, faction, in a dispute that had split the Cherokees into a bitter and tragic civil war. Tom Starr had been outlawed by his tribal leaders, the chiefs of the Ross faction, who were in the majority and whose autonomous government of the Cherokee Nation had been recognized by the Government in Washington long before the War between the States began. During the war, Tom welcomed outlaws of Confederate persuasion and began showing his guests some tricks of his own.

Besides carrying on his personal hobby of slitting the throats of every Ross-faction Cherokee he could waylay on lonely roads—and he knew every one of them by sight, having attended councils with them— Tom Starr carried on a lively business of cattle-and-horse thievery and robbery.

This was right up the alley of Shepherd, Cole Younger and their following. Tom had a domain near the Canadian River east of Eufaula, where he was entirely surrounded by his numerous sons and daughters and sons-in-law and daughters-in-law, all of whom gave him fealty. They were his subjects, his bodyguards, his secret service and his police. The Starrs were as clannish as they were numerous.

Of Tom and his brood more anon.

Meanwhile, Shepherd, Younger, et al., had observed what a marvelous hideout Tom Starr's place was. They had known, as members of Quantrill's gang, canyons and caves and secret retreats in Missouri and Arkansas, but none so nearly perfect as this one.

They hid away there for some time, no doubt participating in some of the frequent looting excursions and horse-and-cattle thievery of the notorious Starr boys. The Starrs sold their stolen cattle and horses to white ''fences'' on the Texas and Arkansas borders. On the trail south to Texas, they had another hideout two miles north of what is now Wilburton—a hideout that is marked on most of the automobile maps as ''Robbers' Cave.'' It is one of the most marvelous natural fortifications in the country. Entrance to it is through two huge boulders just wide enough to let a wagon pass. Other boulders form a natural wall around the base of the hill, on the side of which the vast, dry cave is located. The top of the hill is a flat plateau of many layers of sandstone, forming a roof over the cave and serving as a point of vantage for a lookout, commanding a view of the rolling prairie for miles around this freak of nature produced in the glacial period. There are walls of boulders within the outer wall, including a perfect, natural corral, with cliffs thirty or forty feet high, which would hold one hundred horses. At the foot of the cliff in which the cave is located, there is a perfect spring of crystal-clear water which bubbles into a rapid stream and never runs dry. Amply provisioned and with enough ammunition, a dozen men within the walls of this natural fort could hold off an infantry regiment indefinitely.

The cave was used by the Starrs and later by the Youngers and other outlaws, and by Belle and Sam Starr as a halting place and a retreat en route to and from Texas while driving stolen cattle and horses to sell in Texas.

When they left Indian Territory, Shepherd and his gang went to Texas, taking with them cattle to be disposed of across the Red River border, including stolen animals to be sold on commission for Tom Starr. Cole Younger, who was an inveterate, voluminous and sanctimonious writer of letters to newspaper editors to establish alibis when he was on the scout, said some years later in one of them that he and his brothers went to Ellis County "to gather cattle." He didn't explain how or where he "gathered" them; but we may presume he "gathered" them and disposed of them somewhere, possibly in Fort Worth or Dallas, for cash.

Ellis County lies south of these cities.

Cattle and horse theft in 1864, 1865 and 1866 was fairly easy in that part of the country, which is East Texas, and not the extremely dangerous occupation it was later to become.

For one thing, the cattle industry had not been developed, and for another, Texas was almost untouched by the Civil War, after the unsuccessful attempt of the Federal troops to invade Texas through Galveston, and as a result, Texas was a haven for refugees from the other Southern States. Beef was needed, not for export, as it was later, to the Omaha, Kansas City and St. Louis packing houses, but by the local slaughterhouses to feed these refugees. Horses and mules, too, were in demand for breaking the ground and for other farm needs. Inquiry was not made by the butchers as to where the cattle came from, nor did settlers ask for previous bills of sale for horses.

Although the war itself had left Texas prosperous

and undisturbed, its end was the beginning of Texas'
troubles, for scarcely had the rebellion officially ended
on May 26, 1865, with the surrender of Kirby Smith
in Texas, than the carpetbaggers from the North, like
a plague of locusts, began to swarm into the State and
take over.

First, they paralyzed farm production in the State
by deluding the Negroes, most of whom were paid
workmen and not slaves, to leave the farms and flood
the towns, with the understanding that the Government was going to give forty acres of land and a
small fortune to each.

The purpose of this was to get the Negroes to the
polls to sway the elections in behalf of the carpetbaggers. This was easy to do, because in the South,
after the war, most of the whites were disfranchised
at the same time that the Negroes were enfranchised.
In most States, not only were all the white voters required to take the oath of allegiance to the United
States, to be exempt from prosecution and free to vote,
but they were by law deprived of their vote if it could
be proved that, even as civilians and non-combatants,
they had given aid and comfort to the "enemy." Inasmuch as all those in the South who kept their Southern
sympathies must have given "aid and comfort to the
enemy" at some time during the war, the carpetbaggers and their minions had things all their own way.
Citizens of towns like Dallas and Fort Worth were

stricken with fear when Negroes invaded the town, demanding or expecting what the carpetbaggers had promised them. The Negroes became public charges and the care for them devolved upon the citizenry, whether they willed it or not.

The times were certainly not propitious for bandits to reform, or for outlaws to walk in the paths of law and order. The Younger brothers and other deserters from the ranks of Quantrill were prevented from returning to their homes in Missouri and from taking up peaceful pursuits, even if they had wanted to do so, by the fact that they were proclaimed outlaws by name, and within the State, they were subject to arrest, trial and punishment for any crimes they might have been accused of having committed during the war years. And conditions in Texas favored what was probably their natural inclination and aptitude for the dangerous life.

The outlawing of these Confederate guerrillas would have been perfectly justified if Federal guerrillas, guilty of high crimes, had been outlawed also. But general amnesty was proclaimed for all outlaws, pillagers, arsonists and murderers among the Federal guerrillas, for all crimes committed before May 26, 1865.

This amnesty was granted in spite of the fact that the outrages of the Jayhawker Jennison and his men were so barbaric that they moved a large number of

Belle Starr

Federal officers, on November 16, 1864, to sign a statement addressed to Jennison, whose cutthroats had been incorporated in the Federal Army as the Fifteenth Kansas Regiment, as follows:

The undersigned officers with this command respectfully protest against the indiscriminate pilfering and robbing of private citizens, especially of defenceless women and children, that has marked the line of march of this division of the army of the border from the Arkansas River to this point. While we are all in favor of the complete destruction of the property of bushwhackers and of those who harbor them, we think that no property should be taken or destroyed without the express order of the officer commanding. If soldiers are permitted to rob and plunder without discrimination the result would be demoralization of the men and disgrace to the officers and the service in which we are unwilling to share.

When the protest of these officers was fruitless, Captain Stotts addressed himself thus to General Sanborn:

Jennison has just passed through this vicinity on his return from the Arkansas River. The night of the 19th he stayed at Newtonia, the 20th at Sarcoxie, and the 21st on Dry Fork. Where he passed the people are almost ruined, as their houses were robbed of the beds and bedding. In many cases every blanket and quilt was taken; also their clothing and every valuable that could be found or the citizens forced to discover. All the horses, stock, cattle, sheep, oxen and wagons were driven off. What the people are to do it is difficult to see. Many of them have once sympathized with the rebellion, but nearly all of them have been quiet and cultivated their farms during the last year, expecting the protection of U. S. troops. Jennison crossed Coon Creek with as many as 200 head of stock cattle, half of them fit for good beef, 200 sheep, 40 or 50 yoke of work oxen, 20 or 30 wagons, and a large number of horses, jacks and jennets, say 100, as they were leading their broken down horses and riding fresh ones. The Fifteenth Kansas had nearly all this property and the men said they had taken it in Missouri. Threatening to burn houses in order to get money is the common practice. They acted worse than guerrillas. Can the stock be returned to this department so that the owners can get their property !

Jennison was finally relieved of his command, but there is no record of any recovery on the part of citizens, Federal or Confederate, for the theft and destruction of their property by Jennison and his men.

One day in July, 1866, six horsemen rode up to the front gate of John Shirley's house at Scyene, and the leader hallooed. That was part of the etiquette of Ozarkans in calling upon friends or in the preliminaries of asking a farmer for a night's lodging. One didn't unlatch the front gate, walk up to the front door and knock; one hallooed from afar, even if there were no fence or gate. It was an unwarranted intrusion upon one's privacy to come too close to the house without making oneself known and receiving a welcome. And, it was also a little dangerous.

The six horsemen were on excellent mounts. Their

saddles were of the Texas kind, modeled upon the Mexican saddle but not so ornate. The pommel was high and shaped like the top third of a baby spreading-adder poised for a strike. There was no bolster effect at the base of the pommel, as there was in a Mexican saddle. Hanging from the left foreside of the saddle of each horse was a scabbard holding the latest model single-barrel shotgun. The horsemen had considered the points of the "buffalo rifle," with its long-range, in comparison with the points of the single-barrel shotgun, with its wide-range effectiveness, and had adopted the latter. So, above their pistol-holster belts with their leather loops to hold pistol cartridges, they wore canvas belts, hung from the shoulders, with canvas loops to hold their shotgun shells. Their stirrup guards were shaped like the prow of a boat and were of leather reinforced by a bent sheet of steel to glance away bullets that might strike the feet. One had a chance at hobbling away if struck in the leg, but not much chance if struck in the foot.

The man who hallooed was five feet, eleven and one-half inches tall in his stocking feet. He had very light brown hair, fine in texture and wavy—curly rather. It was in swirls on his head and thinning out above the temples and at the crown, as fine-textured, wavy hair on men has a tendency to do. He wore side-burns very low. At least, it looked as though he did. The fact was that he hadn't shaved in a long time and, although he had chin-whiskers, the hair grew heavier at his temples than it did on his face, which was of that bluish-pink blond cast which tends to become florid instead of tanned or leathery under the impact of sun and wind. He also had something of a mustache, though not much. The mustache was brownish, too, and a little sandier than the whiskers; he had shaved it oftener and it was coarser. His eyes were steel-blue; the gray in them was glistening.

I am not imagining all these descriptive details. They are strictly from the identification data in the offers for the arrest of this man and in the commitment papers when he was entered for a life term at the Stillwater penitentiary in Rice County, Minnesota, District Court.

He was twenty-two years old. His full name was Thomas Coleman Younger. Everybody then, and since, called him Cole.

John Shirley, who was slopping the pigs out near the barn, squinted his eyes and looked toward the road. When he couldn't recognize any of the dim figures at that distance, he yelled out: "Hold on thar! I'll be out in a minute."

Then he went to the house, told the women to get their rifles and ammunition ready and stand look-out at the windows. He buckled on his cartridge belt, took each revolver out of its holster, spun the cylinder, broke each of the guns in turn to see that there were cartridges in the six cylinders. Holding a gun in each hand, he walked out the front door and down the pebble-filled path to the front gate. As he walked, he squinted. Among the six men on horseback he recognized not one, and he was too used to conditions in Missouri and Texas to trust anybody. Still, robbers didn't halloo; they waylaid, or rushed and took you unawares. If they hallooed, it was only to make sure there was nobody home or concealed out in the brush or behind a woodpile to take a pot shot at them if they started to raid a home. This gang had seen him in plain sight, out there slopping the pigs. They wouldn't be hallooing if they weren't friendly. John Shirley walked with greater ease as he reasoned these things out.

"How . . . do . . . you . . . do . . . Judge!" called Cole Younger, sweeping off his broad-brimmed black felt hat, with a bow, hastily dismounting, throwing the reins over his horse's head and going forward to meet the old man.

"Well, if it ain't Cole Younger! Hy-yah be, son? My, you've growed up since I last seed yer. Who're yore friends there? . . . Don't matter; don't matter at-tall; anybody's a friend of Cole Younger is a friend of mine. . . . Maaah! Myra!" Cupping his hands, John

Shirley megaphoned toward the house: "Come on out! Friends here!"

"You know that'un thar, don't you, Judge?" asked Cole, pointing to Jim Younger. "That's Jim. He's younger'n me."

"Haw! A Younger that's younger'n you! That's good! Get it? A Younger tha's younger than you!! Hah, hah!"

Cole Younger didn't see anything funny about it. He never had seen anything funny about it. His name was Younger and he couldn't see anything comical about his having a brother younger than he was. He was deficient in that sort of humor.

He went on, solemnly: "But you must'ave remembered seein' Jim around Carthage. The next'un thar, that's John, and the next'un's Bob."

Each of these adult-looking but very young men acknowledged their older brother's introduction with a nod and a hearty but grave "Glad to know you, Judge."

"I don't know whether you remember that feller or not," continued Cole, nodding toward Jesse James, "but he was a member of our outfit. His name is Jesse. He's one of the James boys from up in Clay County."

"Don't seem to recolleck you, son, but it don't make a blame bit o' diffrunce. . . . Nev'mind, Cole, all them thar introducings. We'll git acquainted later. Untie yoreselves and make yoreselves to home.''

Mrs. Shirley and Myra had come down the gravel pathway to the gate and had stood regarding the outfit comprehensively but not too pointedly looking at each member of it.

''Tha's my ole woman,'' said John Shirley with a sweep of his hand toward Mrs. Shirley, ''and that's my daughter, Myra, gents.''

Mrs. Shirley nodded and Myra curtsied slightly. Then they turned abruptly and went toward the house.

''I'm not goin' to stand fer it! I ain't goin' to stand for it attall! Them's six men thar and yore pappy's askin' 'em fer to stay here fer supper and maybe overnight. It ain't like we'uns was back thar in the hotel in Carthage and I an' you had to do all the fixin's. We got paid fer what we cooked and sarved then. Here we don't get nothin' and I'm allus slavin' myself fer a no-account passel of trash like what we'uns just seen. I tell yuh, I ain't goin' to stand fer it.''

Myra said nothing. She was thinking about the wink that the man who had hallooed had given her. He had acted like she was just a kid. She was twenty years old, going on twenty-one. She hadn't winked back at him. Maybe if she had, he'd have seen she wasn't so wet behind the ears as he thought.

They reached the front door.

Mrs. Shirley threw her right hand in a convulsive movement to her brow, palm over the right temple. She began to stagger. Myra recognized the old dodge. Her mother was going to pretend a sick headache to get out of doing something that had been forced on her. Myra wondered if this time her mother had invented a sick headache to center attention on herself. And she wondered, too, if there was any special person in that outfit whom her mother wanted to make very solicitous about her sick headaches. Myra was thinking about the man who hallooed and she was suddenly jealous of her mother. In fact, she hated her at the moment.

"Come in and lay down, Ma," said Myra, taking her mother by the arm. She led her to her bed and spread a quilt over her.

John Shirley came in.

"What's the matter with your ma?" he asked.

Mrs. Shirley moaned.

"She's got an attack of another one of her sick headaches," said Myra. "Them fellers goin' to be here for supper?"

"I reckon so. Why?"

"Well, they'll just have to fix their own supper!" said Mrs. Shirley.

Myra's father had opened the driveway gate to let the horsemen ride in and had gone to the stable yard to watch them, help them and offer advice if they needed any. He showed them where to stow their saddles and saddle blankets; told them they'd have to fill the trough with water dipped with buckets from the water barrels; and he had unlocked the door to the corncrib.

The corncrib was constructed of six-inch notched logs without chinking. It was about twelve feet long by ten feet wide and was set upon large oak stump cylinders about three feet off the ground and covered with a thatch of dried cornstalks laid over a criss-cross of sapling bows. The corncrib was thus raised to keep the corn from dampness and rot and also to save it from invasion by rats.

Mr. Shirley climbed into the crib and, sitting cross-legged on the floor, began to shuck corn, tearing the husks back, but not off, so they looked like the flanges of a modern airplane bomb. Some of the horses would eat the husks as well as the kernels on the corncobs; but others wouldn't, and the husks would be saved for the hogs.

Cole Younger came up to Mr. Shirley at the crib after he had unsaddled and watered his horse and had turned him loose in the horse lot.

"Judge," began Cole, "I was wonderin' if us boys might impose on you for supper tonight and maybe bunk up here for a few days. We could all sleep in the hayloft and we could help out with whatever you have to do around here besides payin' for our keep."

"Shucks, Cole! You know better'n that! We hain't got much, but yore welcome to all we've got. You know that."

"But us'n's have been doin' pretty good, Judge," said Cole, pulling his hand out of his right pants pocket and showing a handful of twenty-dollar gold pieces. "We've sold some cattle and we're figurin' on locating around here. Leastways, I was. You know we hain't got much of a chance to raise any crops up in Clay County as things is now. Besides, it wa'n't much of any good as farmin' land in the fust place. This land 'round heayar looks pretty good."

"Son, there hain't no better black bottom soil in the country than they is right 'round here. You can raise anything on it. . . . How you all been makin' out?"

"You knowed Ma and Pa was dead, didn't you?"

"Yes. I been told about that," said Mr. Shirley, bending his head suddenly down over the corn he was husking, as if to concentrate on that.

"Things ain't so good back up in Missouri. . . . Never was much good, I guess," added Cole with a smile and attempt at good humor.

"That's what I figured. I've boughten myself a good piece of land 'round here and I'm buildin' myself up to open me a livery stable in Scyene or Dallas or some place."

"Not thinkin' about opening a hotel, was you, Judge?"

"No, son. There's more money, I figure, in having you a stud farm and running a livery stable. If I could only get some help around here, I could raise enough fodder so's it wouldn't cost me nothin' to feed my stock and we could all live well on the chickens, eggs, hogs and garden stuff we can raise on this place. But when you get old like me you cain't do much plowin', and nowadays you cain't git no nigger help, ner no white help neither fer love ner money."

"How's Preston doin'? I ain't seed him yet."

"Pres was doin' all right. Had him a nice piece o' land and was doin' right well on it until we had thet grasshopper plague last year that eaten up nearly eve'y speck of a crop he had. I hate to say it, 'bout my own boy, Cole, but Pres is gettin' to be plumb onery now. Know what he's doin'?"

"No. I was wonderin' why he wasn't around."

"He don't live here, nohow. This hain't his place. His place is about half a mile down yonder on the road toward Mesquite. . . . How'd you find this place, anyhow, son?"

"They told me in town."

"Guess they all know me there."

"Seems like they do."

"You didn't see Pres in town, then?"

"No."

Hell and/or Texas

"Pres hain't farmin' no more. He's dealin' faro at the Lone Star saloon and gamblin' place."

"Where'd Pres learn how to deal faro?"

"You cain't prove by me. And yet, you see, I lost track of Pres pretty much for a long time after he came down here to Texas before the war. Anyhow, he's dealin' faro instead of 'tendin' to his farm."

Inside the house, Myra Shirley, who ordinarily showed no disposition to help with the cooking, was almost frantically setting about the preparation of an evening's meal. She knew how to cook only a few things, having resisted her mother's attempts to instruct her. She peeled and put potatoes on to boil, peeled and dropped onions into the same kettle, threw in a four-inch slab of salt pork and about a pint of dried lima beans. She set a pot of coffee on to boil, dumping a measured pint of ground coffee into a half-gallon pot and then cracked an egg and threw it into the pot, shell and all. When the water boiled, she stirred it to keep it from boiling over, let it simmer about a minute and then set it aside to seep. She was working over a kitchen range that burned coal or wood, which had been the principal article of household goods the Shirleys had brought from their hotel in Carthage to Texas. They had also brought their kitchen and tableware, linen and cotton sheets, quilts, blankets and one wooden bedstead. They had sold the rest of their belongings at auction, getting very little for them.

The dining table of the Shirleys' was eight feet long and consisted of three sections of board joined together with hinges. It could be folded up altogether or, by utilizing only one wing as the top, it served as a card or reading table. Spread out its full length, it rested on three wooden saw-horses.

Myra was setting the table for seven (she and her mother wouldn't be eating until after the men had been served) when her mother appeared in the doorway.

"What do you think you are doing?" she asked.

"Fixing some supper for our guests, Mama."

"Oh, you are, are you?"

"Yes. And why not? You're sick. Leastways you was very sick a little while ago. Somebody has to fix supper and I can do it just as well as you."

"You think you can, do you? That's a pretty come-off. If you think you are sech a good cook, why is it you never want to do any cookin' except when there's some strange men around?"

"I was just trying to help. . . . Why don't you go lie down, Mama, until you feel better?"

Myra knew how to stir her mother into action.

"What 'ave you got in there?" asked Mrs. Shirley, indicating the pot of beans, potatoes, onions and salt pork.

"I just threw in what we had to make a kind of stew," Myra said.

Mrs. Shirley went over and sniffed the concoction. Then she tied an apron around her waist. She had lost her headache. From the kitchen window she could see the men lathering their hands, arms and faces with "yaller" soap and sloshing off the soap with cold water from a washing trough that had been hollowed out of a log and set up on pegs near one of the water barrels.

"Go ahead and pretty yourself up," said Mrs. Shirley. "Then come back and help me serve the supper."

After the men had washed up, Mr. Shirley produced a gallon jug of corn whiskey and a gourd dipper and offered the jug around. Cole Younger declined to drink, but his brother, Bob, and Jesse James poured whole dipperfuls for themselves. The others drank as though they were at a party where they were not sure how they should act. They were awkward and diffident.

Throughout supper, Myra's attention was centered upon Cole. He, on the other hand, addressed his conversation almost entirely to Mr. Shirley. He talked of Quantrill and of the gang's escapades. He said he and his men had some old scores to settle back in Missouri and that, inasmuch as the carpetbagger governments had made outlaws of the men who had served under Quantrill, he meant to live up to his reputation of outlawry.

"Most of my men here," said Cole, "are deadshots with a pistol up to 300 yards. Jesse, there, can pick off his man at 500 yards."

Myra looked at Jesse and then at Cole in wide-eyed admiration.

The foregoing scene and dialogue are, manifestly, improvised as an imaginative reconstruction based upon events and characters, as well as time and place and circumstances. There is no way of verifying how long the Younger boys stayed at Scyene or what they actually did there.

The evidence is strong enough, however, to establish belief that while they were there Myra Belle had a love affair with Cole Younger. At least one consequence of an intimacy was that she found herself pregnant with the child who was born into the world bearing the name Pearl Younger.

There is also evidence that Cole suddenly assumed a high moral attitude just as soon as he learned that he had begot a child on Belle. He regarded her as no better than a whore. He was a pious fellow, Cole was, a sanctimonious bandit whose favorite reading was theology. In his daydreams he wanted to be a preacher, and he was apt to add insult to injury during a hold-up by quoting a Biblical aphorism, giving chapter and verse. To solace himself for having been thwarted in his life's ambition to save souls, he sent his victims to hell in a hurry. He preferred to do his evangelical work with his six-shooters among the unarmed and defenseless.

Cole Younger, however, had a great and egotistically sentimental sense of honor about himself and about anyone connected with him. He tells, in one of his alibi letters, that he challenged a man in Louisiana, Captain James White, to a duel because the man had made disparaging remarks about the girl with whom Bob Younger was in love. But it would appear, even from Cole Younger's own letter to a newspaper editor on the subject, that the shooting affray was not over a woman's honor but because Cole didn't want to pay a gambling debt. He was winged in that duel. This goes to show he wasn't such a deadshot as he himself and the legends try to make out. He once boasted that he and all the members of his gang in the Northfield, Minnesota, bank robbery were deadshots at 500 yards, and that they could have taken more lives than they did if they hadn't been such humanitarians, but Cole, at only twenty paces, shot so wildly that he merely wounded Captain White in the right shoulder.

At any rate, Cole and his gang left Scyene, and the next time we hear of them is in connection with the invention of bank robbery.

It disposes of Cole's contention—that he led the sort of life he did because of circumstances which forced him to it—to recall that the first bank robbery ever perpetrated in the United States was a hold-up of the Clay County Savings Association Bank on St. Valentine's Day, 1866. Clay County was the home of the James and Younger brothers. The depositors in the bank were their friends and acquaintances, and even, some of them, their relatives. The officers and employees of the bank were also men known to the James and Younger families. They were not enemies of the Jameses and Youngers. In holding up such a bank, the Youngers and the Jameses were not only not carrying out any justifiable act of revenge, but were stealing from and endangering the lives of people close to them in ties of sentiment or personal relationship. Their task in robbing this little bank was very easy, and the work, one would say, of men who were essentially cowards.

Liberty was a small town. The Clay County Savings Association Bank, which was the only banking institution in the village, was a one-story brick building facing the town square. Even so, it was the most impressive building in the village of Liberty; the others were all of frame construction. The village was quiet on that St. Valentine's morning until shortly after nine o'clock. A gang of ruffians, headed by Cole Younger and Jesse James, rode into the town, shooting off their revolvers and shouting the blood-curdling rebel yell in an effort to scare the wits out of everybody, and make their task easy. As these lily-livered desperadoes rode into the peaceful village, they shot at every person, man, woman or child, who did not seek cover. But the only casualty of this escapade resulted when a nineteen-year-old boy, George Wymore, hesitated as to where to go and crossed the street immediately in front of the bank. He was shot dead by one of the desperadoes.

The robbery of the bank was effected in record time. There was no resistance within the bank or outside. The only one hurt in the raid was the boy who was killed. Yet, the robbery established a record, in that the gang got away with more than sixty thousand dollars, of which fifteen thousand dollars was in gold currency, and the balance in United States bonds. The bonds were not negotiable, and were, in effect, only so much worthless paper on their hands. The gold, too, was an incriminating bit of evidence against anyone of the gang who tried to pass it; not because gold was not recognized currency, but because so few people had gold for use as money, that the mere possession of it, except in bank transactions, was incriminating evidence against the possessor. Out of the sixty thousand dollars they had robbed from the bank at Liberty, the Younger and James gang probably had only a few hundred dollars they could exchange for food, lodging and provisions, without exciting suspicion. The nearest exchange broker for their stolen gold was a Mexican named Gonzales, in San Antonio, Texas, who accepted stolen gold in exchange for any designated kind of currency, at a forty per cent discount. Gonzales was three hundred miles away.

Meanwhile, to augment their store of passable cash, the Younger-James gang descended on May 31, 1867, upon the Hughes and Mason Bank in Richmond, Ray County, the next county east of Clay, and using the same tactics of terrorism as they had used in the town of Liberty, they frightened this unoffending village into yielding its wealth. But the resistance in Richmond was brave, though fatal. Seven men and boys—including the mayor of the town, who had heard the gang's rebel yell from afar and who had rushed out with rifles, shotguns and pistols to defend the village against invasion—were shot down and killed. The bank was easily robbed of its available currency, which happened to be only four thousand dollars.

These two robberies, so quickly and so daringly consummated, aroused not only the State, but the whole country. Having been perpetrated in Clay and Ray Counties, the Younger brothers and Jesse James had been recognized by the victims, and rewards for their apprehension were immediately set upon their heads.

Moreover, these two crimes, with their attendant publicity, seem to have set the vogue for a succession of robberies attributed to the Younger and James gangs, which they could not have committed because of the physical inability of anybody to be in two places at the same time.

It would appear that with the comparatively little negotiable loot the Younger brothers and Jesse James had been able to get out of these two robberies, they had gone to Texas, first, to see Gonzales and turn what gold they had into greenbacks and silver, and later, to buy—or, at least, Cole Younger was to buy—a farm near Scyene, Texas, which was to be a hangout for the gang, and a home, after a fashion, for Belle and Cole.

In this, however, Cole had reckoned without Myra Belle Shirley's independent spirit. If he expected her to be a mere slavey to his gang, he was profoundly mistaken. Belle had already suffered from family and local opprobrium for having borne his child, and she had broken definitely with Scyene and Dallas society, and with all their conventions. Leaving her child, Pearl, with her parents, she had entered the saloon life of Dallas as a woman on man's terms, but asking no quarter from men. Throughout her career, she was to be theatric, dramatic and even melodramatic in her personal showmanship. After a brief interlude as a singer or entertainer in one of the Dallas dance halls, we find her dealing poker and faro as a professional gambler, and doing very well financially. She dressed spectacularly, but entirely within the conventions. She wore a high-collared bodice jacket and long flowing skirts, which she knew how to drape prettily over a side-saddle made especially for her at a cost of one hundred dollars. She was much more definitely a personage in Dallas and Dallas County than were the pious Cole Younger and his punks. When Cole returned to Dallas, his notion of doing right by Belle was to ask her to become a kitchen slavey to his outfit. He had to abandon the project, under the eloquent cussing-out she gave him. Then he asked his much-imposed-upon sister to come down from Missouri and be cook and menial to himself and his gang.

Thereafter, and not until Cole Younger was caught up by the law and was imprisoned at the Minnesota State Penitentiary at Stillwater, we have no information that Belle entertained any romantic feeling for her first lover, except to name her Pearl after him, and sentimentally to call the farm she finally acquired "Younger's Bend."

Her interests were concentrated upon that man among her immediate acquaintances who showed the utmost daring and recklessness in outlawry. At her time and in her neighborhood, there was no more appealing—or appalling—scoundrel than Jim Reed. He was from Vernon County, Missouri, and thus he and his family were known to the Shirleys. He had taken no part in the War between the States.

After the murder of Belle on February 3, 1889, newspaper reporters seeking information about her past, located F. M. Reed, a farmer near Metz, Missouri, a town nine miles southwest of Rich Hill, where the Reeds had lived before the War between the States, and where the widowed mother of the Reed boys still lived in 1889. F. M. Reed's memory was hazy and even erroneous as to dates, but the interview he gave regarding his brother checks up fairly well with the other testimony we have concerning Jim. He said:

"Our family resided here before the war. Brother Scott and I—the oldest boys—cast our fate with the Southern cause in 1861. Soon afterwards, the Jayhawkers made things so interesting around here, that mother and the children moved to Carthage and rented a house from John Shirley, who was Belle Starr's father. Brother Jim, who was then about thirteen years of age, and Myra Belle Shirley were children together."

From there on, F. M. Reed gets badly mixed up in his dates, or, the newspaper reporter was careless in setting the dates down; for he says that fate drew

Belle and Jim together in Dallas, Texas, in 1877, where, he says, he witnessed their marriage.

If what he says is true, disregarding the date, F. M. Reed, who had retired to a farm sometime before 1889, was himself at one time a member of the outlaw band of which Jim Reed was a ringleader.

The "marriage" of Jim and Belle was undoubtedly a mock one, even on Belle's and others' accounts of it, and a travesty of convention.

The story is that Reed and about twenty other outlaws, including the notorious John Fischer, rode up to the Shirley place at Scyene, and hung out there for several days. During this time most of the men in the outfit made love to Belle. She, however, favored Jim Reed.

Belle was bored with the life she was leading in Dallas and Scyene and wanted to join the outfit of desperadoes on their own terms as a member of the gang. This decision had met with violent opposition from John Shirley, whose family's social standing in the community had already been hurt by Belle's having given birth to an illegitimate child. John Shirley had ordered the desperadoes off his place.

This display of conventional behavior inspired the whole troop to indulge in a little melodrama of their own. They staged a rescue for Belle from the second-floor bedroom of the Shirley house. It was there that she had been imprisoned. Jim Reed was to run up a ladder and abduct her. Then a marriage ceremony was to be performed while they were all on horseback, the officiating "preacher" to be none other than John Fischer himself.

Just how the members of this outfit supported themselves for the next several years is not definitely known. F. M. Reed says that Jim and Belle returned to their old home in Rich Hill, Missouri. Just to show the hiatus in his narrative, I quote his statement:

In 1868, brother Scott was assassinated by some Shannon boys, between whom and a family of Fischers there had previously been some killing done. Brother Jim went immediately to this scene of Scott's murder and allied himself with the Fischers and participated in the killing of two of the Shannons in retaliation. After this, the Arkansas officials hunted him until he moved to California, and from there he went to Texas, where his outlawry became so notorious that the State offered a reward of one thousand dollars for his body, dead or alive, and private corporations offered three times that amount for his conviction for special acts.

This induced Morris, who lived near McKinney, Texas, to murder him. I knew Morris well, as he was our neighbor when we lived in Texas. He only got the State reward, the private corporations claiming that they did not offer a reward for assassination. Morris ingratiated himself into Jim's favor as a hunted outlaw and pretended to be his friend. They stopped at a house near Paris, Texas, for dinner. Morris prevailed on him to leave their revolvers on their saddles, as it might create suspicion to go in armed. While they were eating, Morris feigned to swallow a fly and, sickening, went outdoors. There he procured the revolvers and, returning to the door, shot brother Jim as he was eating with his back to the door.

In the April 17, 1874, issue of the Dallas *Democratic Statesman,* Major Purnell, United States Marshal, had a slightly different explanation, twenty-five years before F. M. Reed's. Major Purnell, at the time, was an officer in search of the three men who had committed the robbery of the San Antonio-Austin stage on Tuesday evening, April 7, 1874. In the Dallas *Democratic Statesman* of April 17, 1874, Major Purnell gave this statement:

It is now definitely settled that the robbery was perpetrated by three men from Missouri, as follows: James H. Reed, alias "Bill Jones," from Vernon county, Missouri, where all the family now live, consisting of mother, brother and two sisters.

He came to Texas in 1872 and settled in Bosque county and bought a piece of land, which he soon afterwards sold, and removed to Scyene, Dallas county, where he now lives.

At this place he seduced a girl, named Rosa McComus, whom he carried to San Antonio with him when he went, promising to marry her there. He is five feet eight inches high, twenty-eight years old, Roman nose and sandy hair. Cal H. Carter, also from Bates County, Missouri, about the same height, black hair, aged twenty-eight years, weighs about one hundred and thirty-five pounds, mustache and whiskers lighter than his hair.

Nelson, alias Jack Rogers, large young man, about six feet

Hell and/or Texas

high, fleshy and very awkward, and J. M. Dickens from Vernon County and his wife, making in all a party of six persons, who went to San Antonio about the last of February, and rented a house; and all lived together, having and paying for everything in common, and living happy as one household.

On the first day of April, Dickens, his wife and Rosa McComus came to San Marcos, and on the next day, they were joined by the other three men, and they all camped together on the banks of the beautiful San Marcos, having already, as it is supposed, concocted their villainy, and were only looking for a suitable place in which to transact it.

Here Reed, who seems to be an enterprising cuss, traded horses with a citizen by the name of Woolfork, he agreeing to pay Reed twenty-five dollars to boot in cash for his wife.

On Monday, the women and Dickens moved to Woolfork's, and in the evening the three other men left town, and on the next evening the San Antonio stage was robbed two miles this side of the Blanco. The horses which the parties rode from San Marcos returned there the next day, as the robbers had turned them loose, preferring the spirited animals belonging to S. T. Scott & Co.'s stages to their jaded ponies.

Dickens, his wife and the girl McComus are still in San Marcos, Dickens having rented a farm and gone to work; but a strict surveillance is kept over them, and they will be brought to this city today, to be examined before the United States Commissioner to elicit further facts, if possible.

As well as is possible to divine, the robbers are traveling in a northwestern direction, keeping between the settlements and the Indian country. They have told some parties whom they met that they were going to Arizona and others that they were going to the Indian Territory.

❧ 159 ☙

Belle Starr

Reed has a friend in the Territory, to whose house he goes whenever he gets into trouble, and it may be that he is making for that place now, but he is said to be very fond of the girl whom he seduced, and it may be the lodestone that will draw him back to Texas.

At any rate, this much is now certain, and though it may be some time before they are overtaken, yet it is only a question of time. The amount which they got was too small to keep them in idleness long, and they will seek some other place, where a National bank is about to be started, with the hope of making a larger haul next time.

The president of the First National Bank of Austin will doubtless give them a wide berth hereafter, for it will doubtless be some time before the adventure is erased from his memory.

The description of "Nelson, alias Jack Rogers, large young man, about six feet high, fleshy and very awkward" is strangely indicative of Cole Younger.

When Major Purnell says that he, Jim Reed, "seduced a girl named Rosa McComus," the chances are that Major Purnell was, in this instance, a victim of the wily wit of our Belle.

A Rosa McCommas, not McComus, was a schoolmate of Belle's at Scyene. Moreover, Rosa was the daughter of the Elder Amon McComma., a preacher in the Campbellite Church, whom Belle had cause to dislike. Rosa was of Belle's own age, and because of her superior position as the daughter of a preacher in the Texas of carpetbagger rule, she would have given Belle much cause for envy. Added to this, the evidence is that while Belle was little more than plain, though forceful and interesting, Rosa was a very beautiful and quite conventional girl, who became, in time, the legitimate wife of Jesse Cox. The McCommases had an exemplary reputation in Texas. Belle, one may assume, decided to use Rosa's name among the many aliases she used at the time. She would do this for the same reason that, when caught, other outlaws were in the habit of giving the names of the most prominent persons trying to institute law and order in the three States of Missouri, Arkansas and Texas.

CHAPTER FOUR

INDIAN TERRITORY OUTLAWRY

Jim Reed took Belle back to Rich Hill, Missouri. He got her safely settled on a farm, so that he could go out to execute a slight mission of retaliation. Apparently, Scott Reed, Jim's brother, was mistaken by some Shannon boys for the John Fischer who had "married" Jim and Belle. The Shannon boys had killed Scott Reed, thinking he was Fischer, firing upon him from ambush.

There follows a pretty story, invented by Richard K. Fox's resourceful writer. The story was borrowed by Harman, who retailed it thus:

When Jim heard of it, the lines of his face contracted, and taking Belle and her baby down by a large oak tree that grew on the bank of a creek coursing through his father's farm, he said to her:

"Be here with our baby, twenty-one days from today, at 1 o'clock and I will meet you." Then kissing her and the baby, he disappeared.

Belle counted the days, and an hour before the appointed time was at the bank of the creek, wondering whether her husband were dead or alive. The time drew on, minutes seemed hours, and just as the hands of her watch announced the hour she heard a smothered laugh, and the next moment her husband reached over her shoulder and taking the baby from her arms tossed it in the air, then kissed the baby and her. He was accompanied by a young man whom Belle had never seen.

The "young man" was Sam Starr, son of Tom Starr, according to the legend.

This legend indicates that Jim Reed had already allied himself with the Starr brothers in the relentless feud which had been stirred up prior to the War between the States as the result of the effort of the Ross faction of the Cherokees to dominate the affairs of the Cherokee Nation.

James Starr, grandfather of Belle's future husband, had been murdered in 1845, by a posse of Cherokee Nation citizens in the civil war that had resulted when the Treaty Party and the Ross faction had taken up arms against each other. The killing of the elder Starr by this posse had started James Starr's sons, Tom, Washington, Ellis and James, Jr., and Ellis Starr, a cousin, Suel Rider and Ellis West, also cousins, on an outburst of murder and robbery against all members of the Ross faction.

Tom Starr, the eldest of James Starr's sons, was six feet five inches in height, straight as an arrow, well built, with black hair and gray eyes, generally with the eyelashes plucked, of great muscular strength, large feet and a habit of smiling when he was engaged in peculiarly murderous occupations.

Because Tom's father, James Starr, was murdered by henchmen of the Ross faction, Tom had never forgiven any of the Ross party members. Although he had been granted amnesty for past crimes by special treaty with the Cherokee Nation in 1846, this had not deterred him from outlawry, especially against his enemies. He considered the Ross members legitimate prey on all occasions, and, as the Starr family was very numerous, he had many brothers and other kin who acted as spies and informants for him and who, themselves, did not hesitate to decimate the Rosses, steal their horses and cattle or burn their houses.

Tom's and his kin's blood-revenge was relentless and without quarter, and was continued by his sons, of whom there were at least eight, including Sam, Ellis, Cooper, Molsie, Tuxie, William, Jack, Ellis and Washington, and two daughters, Nettie and Sophie Starr—together with their in-laws and cousins, the Toneys, Phillipses, McClures, Mabrys, Wests and Rosses. They all had land and homes around that bend in the Canadian River between Briartown and Eufaula, which was a wild remote region, rarely traveled by people who did not know their way about in those parts, or who were not known to be friendly with the inhabitants.

The Starr brothers began so to terrorize the Chero-

kee Nation that standing rewards were offered for
the capture of any one of the Starr gang. People who
were suspected of ''harboring'' the Starrs were outlawed, too, both by the Cherokees and by the Governor of Arkansas. After the burning of the large brick
house of one R. J. Meigs, a squatter and profiteer near
Park Hill, whites who had no business in the Indian
Territory began to flee into Arkansas and demand
protection from State and Federal troops.

We do not know how Jim Reed had ingratiated
himself with Tom Starr and the Starr boys, or
how he had been on the scout with Tom, after having
recognized Tom's place as an admirable hideout for
outlaws, but Jim's acquaintance with the Starrs had
probably sprung up at about the same time the
Youngers made old Tom's place a retreat after the
breakup of Quantrill's gang.

After Jim Reed had chalked up two murders in
his feud with the Shannon clan, a price was set upon
his head. He was obliged to go with Belle and Pearl
to California, where they resided two years. During
this time Belle's second child, Ed Reed, was born in
Los Angeles. How Jim earned a living on the Pacific
Coast is not explained. It seems safe to guess that he
was up to his old tricks of plain and fancy robbery.
At any rate, he was forced to leave California because

of pressure brought upon him by the local constabulary.

About the same time that Jim and his family were living in Los Angeles (that is, in 1869-1870), at least three of the Younger brothers, Cole, Bob and Jim, and Frank and Jesse James, were supposed to have been "operating" out there, too, and were named as participants in a stage robbery near San Diego. It is possible that Jim Reed had gone out there with his old bandit friends in search of fresh fields for outlawry. After the robbery of the Russellville, Kentucky, bank on March 20, 1868—a robbery that had netted the six participants about $14,000—Frank James had gone by boat around the Horn to San Francisco. He had been advised by his physician to take a boat trip to recover from an old lung wound he had suffered during the war. Jesse had gone overland to join Frank, and they both were guests of their uncle, Dr. Woodson James, who was the head of a sanitarium at Paso Robles.

Many connecting threads in the James-Younger-Belle Starr narratives lead to the conclusion that Jim Reed participated in the Russellville, Liberty and Gallatin robberies, and that he was the man, whose name in the warrants was given as James White, sought in connection with these crimes.

Upon his return from California, Jim Reed bought a farm near Scyene, close to the ranch of his father-in-law, John Shirley, who had become reconciled to Belle's "marriage" to Jim after the birth of the boy named Ed.

Meanwhile, the James and Younger gangs, sometimes operating as a unit and sometimes as two or three separate squads, had established various hideouts, retreats and meeting places. One of these was known as Rest Ranch and was in Collin County, Texas, northwest of Dallas and less than a day's ride from Scyene. Another was certainly Tom Starr's place in the Indian Territory. Another may have been John Shirley's ranch or stock farm near Scyene, for in 1869 we have a record of a warrant having been issued for his arrest on a charge of harboring criminals. Inasmuch as there is no record of Shirley's having been arrested or convicted on this charge, it is possible that the complaint was withdrawn under intimidation. It would take a courageous, naïve or reckless person to swear out a warrant for the arrest of any of the James-Younger-Reed gang of outlaws or of any of their friends, as subsequent events will show.

John Younger, youngest of the Younger clan, had killed a man in Independence, Missouri, when he was only fifteen years old. His older brothers, Bob, Cole and Jim, had spirited him out of the country and had hid him at Rest Ranch in Collin County. With some of the sentimental solicitude sometimes found in criminals for a youngest brother, the other Younger boys would not allow John to join their gang, or, indeed, any other gang. They kept pretty close watch on him to make him "go straight." They even supplied him with funds so that he would not have lack of money as an excuse for banditry.

Thus indulged, John Younger became a frequenter of the saloons, dance halls and gambling dens of Dallas, always wearing two guns, displaying his marksmanship and swashing the buckle, no doubt, as a brother of the robbers whose names were beginning to be bywords throughout the land because of their sensational robberies.

Late in January, 1871, John Younger and some of the boys were whooping it up in Joe Krueger's saloon in Dallas. In the saloon at the time there was an old drunkard who hung around the bar cadging drinks. John Younger, well along on a toot himself, bought several rounds of drinks for the house, including the old barfly. Bragging about how good a shot he was with a pistol, he offered to buy the old fellow drinks for the rest of the night if he would let him shoot the pipe out of his mouth at ten paces. He stood the old codger in profile near a wall, backed off ten paces, drew his revolver and fired several shots in rapid succession.

What damage was done to the pipe is of little importance. But the injury to the tip of the old fellow's nose did have fatal consequences. After his nose was bandaged, the victim of John Younger's bad marksmanship went to the sheriff's office and swore out a warrant for the arrest of John Younger, charging attempted homicide.

The duty of serving this warrant for the arrest of John Younger fell upon Colonel Charles H. Nichols, deputy sheriff of Dallas County.

It may account for some of the immunity enjoyed by the Youngers and the Jameses in Dallas and Collin Counties to mention the fact that most of the peace officers were either former Confederate Army officers from Missouri or members of the same Quantrill, Anderson and Todd guerrilla outfits in which the James and Younger brothers had served. Deputy Sheriff Nichols had achieved the rank of lieutenant colonel under General Joe Shelby's command, formerly a Missouri guerrilla band, but later incorporated into the Confederate Army.

With some reluctance, Colonel Nichols went out to Scyene to serve what he considered an unwarranted warrant.

Indicative of the nonchalance with which murder was regarded in Dallas of the period, and also of the general ignorance of Dallas citizens of their neighbors in Scyene, is this news account in the Dallas *Weekly Herald* for February 4, 1871. The story was headed simply, "Obituary."

Belle Starr

Col. Charles H. Nichols is dead! He was Deputy Sheriff of Dallas County, Texas, and went out to Scyene on Monday morning to arrest a young man by the name of John Younger, who had been guilty of some offense against the good order of society. Col. Nichols saw Mr. Younger and informed him he had a writ for him in Dallas. Younger readily consented, but asked permission to eat his breakfast first, to which Col. Nichols consented. Having known Younger in Missouri and confiding in his honor, he sent some men to watch the stable where were the horses of Younger and a friend of his, recently from Missouri, named Porter. On going toward the stable for their horses and seeing it was guarded, they hurried to the store where were Col. Nichols and a gentleman he had summoned to aid in the arrest of Younger.

They entered the house and commenced shooting at Col. Nichols and his friend. The latter was instantly killed, and the former mortally wounded, but not until he had wounded Younger in the arm.

Younger then mounted on the horse of Col. Nichols and hastened his escape—his friend with him.

Col. Nichols lingered until Friday, the 20th ult., when at 7:30 o'clock, A.M., he fell quietly asleep, aged 28 years. He was buried in Dallas the next day with Masonic honors, followed to his last resting place by his weeping wife and a long train of sympathizing mourners.

The *Weekly Herald* reporter did not think it was necessary to learn the nature of the complaint against John Younger or to give the name of the "gentleman" who was suddenly deputized by Colonel Nichols and who was instantly killed. However, later accounts mention only the killing of Colonel Nichols, so possibly the *Weekly Herald* was in error in stating that another deputy was killed. The later accounts also state that John Younger and his companion had been pursued by a posse "into the Indian country where the trail was lost," and that the Governor of Texas had offered a reward of $500 for the arrest of John Younger.

All of these accounts, including that of the *Weekly Herald* indicate that when Colonel Nichols went out to arrest John Younger he knew enough about the Youngers to take a posse along with him and that he knew where John Younger was staying. The men he set to guard the stables while John Younger was eating breakfast could scarcely have been men he had found on the place, but help he had brought with him. The *Weekly Herald* also speaks of a store, so the attempted arrest and shooting must have taken place in the town of Scyene. Inasmuch as some of the later accounts speak of Colonel Nichols' having gone to Younger's *hotel in Dallas* in the early morning to make the arrest, it seems probable that John Younger had been staying at a small hotel in Scyene, and that it was here that he asked to eat breakfast.

From this we might infer that John Shirley had opened up a small hotel in Scyene. We do know that on June 14, 1867, he had bought from Emily and

W. M. McCormick for $1,200 some lots in the town of Scyene.

But whether or not John Shirley built a hotel on this property can only be conjectured. If he did, it was unquestionably a rendezvous for the James and Younger gangs.

Three years after slaying Colonel Nichols, John Younger was to be killed in a fight with two Pinkerton detectives in St. Clair County, Missouri.

The first robbery in which Belle herself was alleged to have participated was that of Walt or Watt Grayson, a wealthy Creek Indian, who lived on the North Canadian River, a few miles west of Eufaula, and not far from Tom Starr's home, on the evening of November 20, 1873. Contemporary newspaper accounts in the Texas and Arkansas weeklies say that Grayson was tortured by the robbers until he revealed the hiding place of $30,000 in gold.

Some accounts of this crime insist that there were four persons in the party of robbers and that one of these was a woman dressed as a man. Later legends have it that this member of the party was Belle. It may well have been.

The Fox Publications biographer accepts the legend and makes his heroine very fiendish in quoting from what he alleged was Belle's diary:

Outlawry

When we reached the Grayson house it was decided that I should tap at the door, and when the old man came to it that the others should enter by force if he refused to come out. The door was thrown open, however, and there was no difficulty in securing the proprietor, who was completely taken by surprise. The old lady screamed with terror, but I placed the cold muzzle of my pistol against her brow, and that silenced her. Two men—a white man and a negro—who were sleeping in the place, entered from the rear. The former was armed, but Read struck him from behind with his revolver, and he fell like a beef. The negro was placed upon his knees, hands up. Meanwhile, old Grayson was secured, but he deliberately refused to divulge the whereabouts of his treasure. A rope was then produced and one end of it placed around his neck, and the other thrown across a rafter. I was chosen as hangman, and bore down on the old Creek until he gasped for breath. Grayson was grit from away back and stood it like a stoic until he had to cave in. At last, consenting to reveal the whereabouts of the treasure, he walked over to a table, which he removed from where it was standing. Beneath this table was a wolf-skin rug. This he raised, and— behold!—a trap door was brought to light. Raising the trap, he descended, Roberts following him with a lantern. They returned from the cellar with two oyster cans full of gold pieces. The second trip developed a rusty kettle full of gold coin, which took the efforts of all hands to raise from the cellar. The third and last trip resulted in three large bundles of notes, which added greatly to the spoils. When all was over Watt Grayson walked back to the spot where the rope was hanging. He caught the noose in his hand and said:

"You white men kille me now; no more money."

The old man was right. We had completely gutted the

establishment. Next morning in the Younger Bend we counted out $34,000, but found to our disappointment that $12,000 of that sum was in Confederate greenbacks.

In the confused and confusing Fox narrative, there is one sequel to the Grayson robbery which gives one pause. The Fox writer says:

According to a treaty at one time entered into between the United States and the Creek Indians, the former contracted to be accountable for any damages committed by white men upon that tribe, and to pay all just claims made by the Creeks against citizens of the United States. Therefore, ten years after the Grayson robbery, his sons, G. W. Grayson, delegate for the tribe, and Samuel Grayson, a merchant of Eufaula, made claim for $34,000 upon the treasury of the United States. To justify this claim it was necessary to have a witness, as it might be assumed by Uncle Sam that the old Creek Indian had not quite so large a sum in his possession. In fact, the enormity of the claim astounded the authorities at Washington, and the robbery by many was looked upon as a farce. Bella, hearing of all these things, concluded to make a treaty with the Creeks, and sent word to the Graysons that she was willing to turn State's evidence in consideration of a complete pardon for any and all acts she may have committed within the limits of the Creek territory. This was granted, and accordingly the Bandit Queen made testimony that she and her husband had robbed old Watt Grayson of $34,000. Nothing, however, was said about the $12,000 Confederate "shinplasters" which was part of the claim made against the United States.

Nothing was said by the Fox writer about whether this claim or any part of it was granted by the United

States Government. Yet there is much that is strangely circumstantial about this story. The figure $34,000 may have been derived from the fact that the annuity to the Creeks was $34,500. Of this amount, the Creek agent, John Logan, in his report as far back as September 20, 1845, states that the whole amount of the annuity, instead of being distributed per capita to all the members of the tribe, was appropriated in its entirety by two or three of the principal chiefs. As a sub-chief, Watt Grayson could easily have accumulated a fortune in gold even greater than $34,000. Moreover, he would have buried or hidden it, for there were no banking facilities within the Indian Nations.

Still, another point is that Belle, ten years after the Grayson robbery, *could* have made just such a treaty with the Creeks. By that time she was a citizen of the Cherokee Nation as the wife of Sam Starr, and, as such, was subject not to the laws of the United States, but only to the tribal laws of the Cherokees in all crimes excluding murder. Murderers who were citizens of the Indian Nations within the territory were subject to apprehension by Federal marshals and to trial in the Federal court at Fort Smith. This peculiarity of jurisdictions made the Indian country an especially inviting haven for murderous white outlaws, inasmuch as the Indian tribal police could not touch white murderers within the Indian Nation—

nor could they even arrest a white man—unless the white man was a citizen of the Nation by adoption within a tribe.

On September 3, 1875, a notable event in the annals of crime and justice took place in the jailyard of the Federal court of the Western District of Arkansas, in Fort Smith. Six men were executed simultaneously. By one springing of the trap door, six convicted murderers dropped to their deaths at the end of ropes hung from the same scaffold.

Of these six whose hanging made history, only one need concern us here. His name was Dan Evans. He was hanged for the murder of a nineteen-year-old boy named Seabolt. Evans was convicted on the testimony of the boy's father and by reason of the fact that he was still wearing at the trial a pair of boots taken from the dead body of the boy. The father had testified that Evans and his son had left Texas for the Indian Territory, and that before he left, he had given his son a pair of boots; that he had bought himself a pair exactly like those he bought his son; that just before his son left with Evans, one of the heels of the boy's left boot had come off and that he had repaired the boot by driving three horseshoe nails into the heel. The prisoner's left boot was found to be repaired with horseshoe nails and his boots were found to be the same kind as those worn into court by the elder Sea-bolt.

But the real point of interest to us here is that before he was hanged, this Dan Evans said he was one of Jim Reed's partners in the Grayson robbery. At the time he made this confession, Reed was already dead, and although Evans said that others were in the robbery, he named only Reed, and a man named Wilder, who was already serving a penitentiary sentence for his participation in the Grayson robbery. Evans, like Wilder, boasted of the thrill they enjoyed when they ran their fingers through the glittering gold coins.

After the Grayson robbery, Jim Reed and Belle went to Dallas, where Belle stayed at the Planters' Hotel while Jim kept on the scout and in hiding at his place near Scyene.

During her stay in Dallas, Belle dressed and behaved in a spectacular manner. She purchased a horse and buggy, a riding horse and a stud which she kept in the stables back of the hotel, hiring a Negro as her special hostler and groom. She dressed in black velvet, with long flowing skirts when she rode side-saddle, and wore white chiffon waists, a tight black jacket, high-topped boots and a man's Stetson hat turned up in front and decorated with an ostrich plume. The only peculiarity about this costume was that around her waist she wore a cartridge belt from which two revolvers were suspended in holsters. She attended the races, the circus and the county fair. She would enter bars and drink like a man or take her place at gaming tables for a try of her luck at dice, cards or roulette.

When the mood struck her, she shocked the women and more respectable citizens of Dallas by changing into beaded and fringed buckskin costumes like those worn by Buffalo Bill, and riding at breakneck speed through the streets of the town, scattering everyone to the sidewalk. The constabulary and the whole town was afraid of her; and she gloried in being pointed out as the Bandit Queen. She had nothing to fear as long as there was no warrant out for her arrest. Not even the knowledge that her husband had a price of $1,500 on his head was any legal reason for molesting her.

But Jim and Belle were soon implicated in an affair that set all Texas by the ears. Stagecoach robberies had been prevalent in California, Wyoming, Arizona and even in Kansas, but the hobby hadn't yet taken hold in Texas. Cattle rustling had been the chief occupation of outlaws in that State after the rapid development of the cattle industry. Although railroads hadn't penetrated to Texas until 1870, the establishment of railheads as far west as Fort Dodge, Kansas, had made cattle raising in Texas a prosperous industry. But stagecoaches were still the only regular means of communication between Austin and San Antonio or Galveston, until after 1881.

When the San Antonio-Austin stage was robbed, therefore, there was a great to-do about it. The account of the robbery by the Austin *Weekly Democratic Statesman* of April 9, 1874, is as follows:

On Tuesday evening (April 7), a most daring and outrageous robbery was committed on the passengers on the stage coming from San Antonio and this place, and on the United States mail. About sunset when the stage was nearly two miles on this side of the Blanco, three men approached and drawing their six-shooters on the driver, Bill Anderson, well known in this city, ordered him to stop, which he immediately did.

The stage had on board nine passengers, viz.: Messrs. McLemore, O'Neal, Waters, Brackenridge, Frazier, McDonald, Wells, Munroe and one lady, Mrs. Lloyd. As soon as the stage stopped, all the passengers were ordered to alight and seat themselves in a row; as none of them had any arms, resistance was useless, and they obeyed. After seating themselves, two of the robbers stood before them, each having a six-shooter in each hand cocked, and ordering them to give up their money, watches and other valuables.

After having collected all they could from the persons of the passengers, they proceeded to cut open and rifle their trunks, taking such articles of value as they could get away with speedily; and lastly came the United States mails; after cutting open the sacks and rifling them of their contents, they left them lying scattered around, with the exception of one, which they took away with them. After this they proceeded to cut the horses loose from the stage, and rode off, leaving the bewildered and frightened passengers to proceed on their journey as best they could.

The driver returned to the nearest stand, about three miles back (Joseph Vanis), and getting fresh horses proceeded on his way to this city, where he arrived about daylight Wednesday morning. No violence was offered to any of the passengers, and they all conceded that the robbers went to work like men who knew their business.

The amount taken from the passengers was about $2,500, and four gold watches. As soon as the Legislature met yesterday, a joint resolution was passed authorizing the Governor to offer $3,000 for the apprehension of the robbers; to this the U. S. mail agent offered $3,000 more, and Sam Scott, manager of the stage added $1,000 more. At dark, parties left Austin in pursuit of the robbers.

Missing from this report, but prominently featured in later accounts, was the fact that one of the passengers was Bishop Gregg from San Antonio. In the diary the Fox writer invented for Belle, he attributes to her an account of the robbery, stating that the whole thing was planned and executed by her and Jim and that, as a gesture of respect for the cloth, they had returned Bishop Gregg's purse and watch. The trouble with this invention is that Bishop Gregg's purse and watch, according to the contemporary newspaper accounts, were not returned.

But the activity of the Austin, San Antonio and Dallas constabulary was at the fever-heat of zeal. The Dallas *Daily Herald* for April 28, 1874, nearly three weeks after the robbery, announced arrests:

Outlawry

The officers of Dallas county are masters of the situation. They have struck the keynote of swift and stern punishment to the violators of the law, and they are meting it out with a mailed hand. Not a day, scarcely an hour passes but the trap is sprung and a vengeance certain as lightning strikes the culprit.

On Saturday evening, Marshal Peak, in making his rounds, chanced to stop in the hotel on Main Street, east of the Central road, kept by Mr. Rollins.

A face in the crowd seated around attracted his attention, and quick as thought it suddenly flashed on him that the man who had fixed his gaze, was none other than one of the bandits who had robbed the United States mail on its way to San Antonio some weeks ago, photographs of those "gentlemen of the road" having been furnished the sheriff of this county.

Satisfied that one of the men was before him, he quietly informed him that he was his prisoner and at once lodged him in jail. He gave his name as W. D. Wilder, but from papers found upon his person there can be no doubt that Wilder is an assumed name and that he is the notorious outlaw and mail robber, William (Jim) Reed.

Later in the evening, Marshal Peak arrested another suspicious character, who gave his name as Bidwell, and who answered in part to another photograph in the possession of the marshal, but he was released in about an hour afterwards by that officer, he not thinking that there was sufficient grounds for detaining him.

Subsequent developments disproved the judgment of the marshal, and he at once dispatched officer Crabb and ex-officer Phares in search of him. With the usual success which attends the efforts of these gentlemen, they found Bidwell three miles this side of Scyene, fast asleep or feigning slumber, in a grove of timber near the public road. Taking him in custody, they brought him to this city and placed him in jail.

There seems to be no question in the minds of the sheriff and marshal that they have got the right "birds." Everything found upon them, papers, books, letters and many other things, form almost flawless links in the chain of evidence against them. Immediately on their arrest, Sheriff Barkley telegraphed to the U. S. marshal at Austin and received a reply that he would be in this city today.

Not only the people of the city of Dallas and county, but every citizen of the state, aye, even those of the whole union, owe unbounded thanks to Sheriff Barkley, Marshal Peak, Officer Crabb and ex-Officer Phares for this splendid stroke of executive shrewdness, promptitude and courage.

Alas, evidence was not sufficient to keep the prisoners, "Wilder" and "Bidwell," in custody pending a grand jury hearing. They were released on the order of U. S. Marshal Purnell from the Dallas jail. This action aroused some criticism of both Sheriff Barkley and Major Purnell on the part of the press.

Subsequently a curious note comes into the *Herald* story which stated that, upon the request of Marshal Purnell, Wilder, on his release, accompanied the Marshal "as far as Scyene, where the wife of the brother of Reed, the principal in the robbery, resides, and from whom, it is thought, some light may be obtained as to the whereabouts of the bandit chief."

Outlawry

Why would a marshal go with a man just released as a suspect in a robbery to the lair of a bandit chief to question the wife, Belle, as to the whereabouts of her husband?

It appears that this "Wilder" may have made a deal with Major Purnell.

At all events, about three months later, Jim Reed was shot and killed by *Deputy* Sheriff John T. Morris of Collin County, Texas. Two dispatches from Paris and McKinney, to the principal Texas newspapers tell the story succinctly:

Paris, Texas, Aug. 6.—Jim Reed, the San Antonio stage robber, was shot and killed by J. Morris, of McKinney, Texas, this evening, about fifteen miles northwest of this city.

Morris has followed Reed for three months, and had succeeded in capturing him once, but he escaped. They were traveling together and were stopping at a farmhouse for dinner. Morris asked Reed to surrender, and he said he would; Morris told Reed to get up, but instead of doing so he ran under the table and raised it up between him and Morris and started out of the door with it. Morris shot two balls through the table. The third shot killed Reed almost instantly. Morris then brought the body to Paris.

McKinney, Aug. 8.—Last night the remains of Jim Reed, the mail robber, arrived here from Paris, near which place he had been apprehended and shot; and were buried today after having been fully identified by those who knew him. He was a noted but desperate character, and the citizens are truly glad at the riddance. Many horses were stolen, and citizens killed and robbed, by the band to which he belonged.

Morris, who captured, and then had to kill him, is, I learn, in hot pursuit after Cal. Carter and John Boswell, Reed's desperate companions in the robbery on April 7 of the San Antonio and Austin mail coach. It will be remembered that this party stopped the stage, robbed the passengers, gutted the mail bags and took off the stage horses at the mouth of six-shooters in regular highwayman style. Since this occurred, they have been in this county, and in efforts to apprehend them at the time, one of the deputy U.S. marshals was killed through misapprehension. At this they fled to the Indian Nation, and then were surrounded by a posse of U.S. deputies and sheriffs at the house of an Indian named Star, a short distance from Muskogee, but they managed to again escape.

Much praise is bestowed on Morris for his bold and successful undertaking, and he is justly entitled to the pro rata reward, of which there has been $8,000 offered for the three, besides various other rewards having been offered by the Governors of Missouri and Arkansas.

Reed's body had become very much decomposed, particularly about the head, having been shot just between the nose and right eye. The drayman, in carrying him to the potter's field mistook the place, and in returning, with the breeze to the windward of the corpse, he took sick, and was compelled to abandon it on the roadside. It was, however, taken charge of by the sheriff, and finally interred. It is hoped that the others may be taken and dealt with in like manner.

It is my deduction and firm conviction that the "Wilder" who was released by Purnell was in reality

Outlawry

John T. Morris, a former member of Reed's outlaw gang. On his own confession, Morris pretended to rejoin Reed and was with him constantly for three months, waiting for an opportunity to arrest Reed before he was forced to kill him. One of the clues to this deduction is that the real Wilder, given name W. D., was arrested at Reed's old place on Coon Creek, Bosque County, put in irons and taken to Fort Smith, where he was tried and given a penitentiary sentence for participating in the Watt Grayson robbery.

If the first-mentioned "Wilder" were John T. Morris, that would explain why Belle's mother described him as a traitor, and it would also give rise to the false legend about Belle's refusal to identify Reed's body, thus cheating Morris out of the reward. On that ride of Marshal Purnell to Scyene, it looks as though the two had made a deal whereby Morris or "Wilder," who had been let out of a rap by Marshal Purnell on a promise to get in with Reed and bring Reed in dead or alive, would share the reward.

According to the Fox biographer, Belle spent the year following Jim Reed's death living very quietly with her daughter Pearl in Dallas, "going for occasional rides into the country on one of her thoroughbreds." The boy, Ed, she left in care of Mrs. Shirley. In Dallas, Belle's scarcely suppressed theatrical instincts found vicarious expression in having Pearl trained in music and dancing for appearance on the stage. Pearl, then fourteen, made her debut on the stage in Dallas in a vaudeville show. The child suffered a hemorrhage of the brain and collapsed on the stage. Belle was warned by her physician not to permit her daughter to go on again, lest a second collapse prove fatal.

Before the accident to Pearl, however, we have what appears to be an authentic letter of Belle's addressed to her brother-in-law in Missouri. Harman says that he copied it from the original on October 4, 1898, at Fort Smith. The letter was written on the stationery of Sheriff James E. Barkley of Dallas. The envelope bore the date August 19, 1876, and was addressed to F. M. Reed, Metz Post Office, Vernon County, Missouri, but meant for all Belle's in-laws.

Dear Mother and Brothers and Sisters: I write you after so long a time to let you know that I am still living. Time has made many changes, and some very sad ones indeed. My poor old father has left this world of care and trouble. He died two months ago today. It seems as if I have more trouble than any person. "Shug" got into trouble here and had to leave; poor Ma is left alone with the exception of little Eddie. She is going to move away from here in a few days and then I'll be left alone. Eddie will go with her, and I don't know that I shall ever see him again. He is a fine, manly looking boy as you ever seen and is said to resemble Jimmie very much; he is very quick motioned, and I don't think there is a more intelligent boy living. I am going to

Outlawry

have his picture taken before he leaves and I will send you one; would like for you to see and know him. I know you would love him for the sake of the dear one that's gone. Eddie has been very sick and looks pale and wan, but I think my boy will soon mend up. Rosie is here in Dallas going to school; she has the reputation of being the prettiest girl in Dallas. She is learning very fast. She has been playing on the stage here in the Dallas theatre and gained a world-wide reputation for her prize performance. My people were very much opposed to it but I wanted her to be able to make a living of her own without depending on any one. She is constantly talking of you all, and wanting to visit you, which I intend she shall some time.

Jno. L. Morris is still in McKinney, at large. It seems as if justice will never be meted out to him. Pete Fisher is in Colin City, where he has always lived. Solly hasn't the pluck (Rondo) yet; I was offered $2,000 for him the other day. If Sol had come to Texas, freely would I have given the horse to him if he had sought revenge.

I think Brocks are in Montague county. I will realize nothing from my farm this year. Brock rented it out in little pieces to first one and another, and none of them tended it well, so I made nothing. I am going to sell it this fall if I can.

I am far from well. I am so nervous this evening from the headache that I can scarcely write.

(NO SIGNATURE)

Harman says that the letter was unsigned but that it was a "most peculiar trait of this peculiar woman" that she never signed her name to a letter, never recorded the date thereon, and never gave the address.

Belle Starr

Harman says that "Shug" was a "younger brother." But "Shug" was Preston, an older brother. The Pete Fisher was the man whose death the Shannon brothers intended when they murdered Scott Reed. The John L. Morris was the former comrade in outlawry with Jim Reed who became a deputy sheriff, captured and killed Reed and got a reward for putting the bandit out of the way. Belle is here reproaching Jim Reed's younger brother "Solly," for failing to murder Morris in revenge; and she promises him a horse if he will come to Texas for that purpose.

The letter disposes of the legends that Belle herself was a killer. If she were, she would have disposed of Morris herself. There is no authentic story that Belle ever even shot at any one, much less killed a great many people. The melodramatic story of how she killed Colonel Nichols on the streets of Dallas and how she continued to go her way unmolested in the town is a fabrication because we know that Colonel Nichols was killed by John Younger.

According to Harman, Mrs. Shirley "removed from her home after the death of Judge Shirley." Mrs. Shirley was living in Dallas as late as 1889, having moved there from Scyene. Harman says that Belle took her boy, Ed Reed, to Rich Hill, Missouri, and there placed him under the care of his grandmother Reed until he was twelve years old, and that she shipped her daughter to relatives, with whom Pearl stayed for two years.

Having got rid of her children, Belle returned to Dallas and "began to exhibit her former roving disposition," and roved herself right into an arson charge. As Harman tells it, "She was out on a reckless ride with another girl as wild as herself, Emma Jones, by name, between whom and Belle a strong intimacy had sprung up. The day was windy, and their route lay through a small prairie village. In a spirit of bravado, the Jones girl attempted to build a fire at a back corner of a small building occupied by a merchant, with a stock of goods. The wind blew the matches out and prevented her attempts. Belle came upon her and said, 'You can't build a fire; let me.' Belle did and the store was consumed."

Emma snitched, and Belle was brought to trial for arson. A wealthy stockman, named Patterson, was in court one day during the trial and immediately fell in love with Belle. He "secured her release and gave her a large sum of money." That is as far as Harman carries us in the episode involving the stockman. There is no way of determining what Patterson received in return for his benefaction. Harman merely goes on to say that Belle went to Conway, "took Pearl out to a stretch of timberland, and seated on the bank of a little stream, counted out a large roll of paper money remaining from the wealthy Patterson's gift. Kissing her child, she said: 'Baby, here is $——,' stating the amount; 'enough so you and I will never want again. Mama will go into the Territory and fix up a nice home and have lots of music and nice horses and then come and get her baby and we will always be happy.' "

Apparently none of the generous stockman's money was ever used in fixing up a nice home, as Mama promised. Pretty soon after the mother-and-child idyll in the Arkansas woods, Mama was arrested in Dallas on a charge of horse stealing.

The Fox biographer embellishes upon the tale of the "wealthy stockman named Patterson" in quite a different connection. He says that at about the time that Jim Reed was in jail for the San Antonio mail robbery (Reed was never in jail and never under arrest until the time he was killed), "one Patterson, a stockman residing in Jack County, who had just shipped a carload of beef cattle to St. Louis, came to board at the Planters' Hotel. Before two days he had fallen desperately in love with Bella, who beheld in him a first-class subject for dissection."

The ingenious biographer goes on to invent one of the most fantastic yarns in the annals of Belle Starr whoppers. He says that on leaving for a trip to Jacksborough, Patterson told Belle that, since the banks were closed, he wanted her to keep $2,500 in cash for him until his return and gave the money to her. On his return, Patterson "could not possibly recover his money."

There follows a courtroom scene that does more credit to fancy than to fact:

Bella showed him her diamonds and told him she had utilized his loan and would pay him back when she got rich. The stockman became angry and swore out a warrant for Bella's arrest. She gave bonds and appeared before the county judge on the appointed day. The prosecution was heard, and there being no defense, the judge said he was sorry for the lady, but he was afraid he would have to consign the case to a higher court, as Mrs. Reed was evidently guilty of a serious breach of trust. Patterson, who by this time was much excited from the effects of occasional potations of whiskey, cried out:

"Don't do it, Judge. It's all a lie. Myra h'aint got a nickel of my money, and if she had she's welcome to it anyhow."

The judge frowned and lost his temper.

"Then, sir," he said, "how dare you dishonor and belittle our court by playing practical jokes of this kind? I'll show you whether or not you can frolic around a court of justice! Sheriff, arrest that man for contempt and bring him right here! Now, sir, you are guilty of perjury as well as contempt of court and I fine you one hundred dollars."

Poor Patterson was crestfallen. He had only five dollars in his pockets, and as he shook his head he looked the very picture of woe. He had done the best he could or knew how to do, and Bella was sorry for him. The thought struck her and she walked up to the judge's bench and laid $100 before him, saying: "Your honor is perhaps ignorant of the fact that Mr. Patterson is hopelessly insane, which will account for the trouble which he has not only given me but the whole court. Please overlook the matter and I will take my cousin back to his hotel.''

She did so, and that evening refused an offer of marriage from the Jack County stockman, who in his turn refused to take back more than $1,000 of the money he had reposed in her keeping.

Aikman accepts Harman's version and elaborates upon it, saying that Patterson, falling in love with Belle while she was standing trial for arson and malicious mischief, sought Belle out and asked her how much it would cost to pay all legal expenses and get the charges dismissed.

''Belle, without batting an eye or making a promise, told him that by the most conservative estimates it would cost $2,500. The philanthropic Patterson finally sold cows and delivered the wad in cash. A day or two later the arson charge was withdrawn as had been all along a foregone conclusion, and Mrs. Reed was released on the payment of a nominal fine for malicious mischief, approximately $2,490 to the good.

''Mr. Patterson,'' continues Aikman, ''enjoyed her company and one or two innocuous hotel dinners and was put off in his collection efforts with a plea of stupendous legal expenses. Then he sought advice from his friends and of course was urged to file fraud charges and prosecute. But here, one regrets to say, his very excess of doting chivalry led him to blast a lady's reputation.

" 'Hell, leave her keep it,' was his epigram. 'I reckon after what she's had to put up with, she's earned every cent of it.'

"Dallas promptly assumed with snickers and some indignation that what the widow had 'put up with' referred to the uncomely and notoriously amorous Patterson's advances, and cheerfully condemned its former parlor heroine to the ostracism of loose women. Belle had finished with relying on caste to countenance indiscretions.''

One of the fanciful yarns about Belle has it that while she was in jail in Dallas for horse stealing, she prevailed upon the turnkey to let her out on a promise to elope with him; and that the warder's discomfiture was great when Belle sent him back with a note sewed inside his coat, reading, "Returned because found unsatisfactory." The jailer's explanation was that Belle had snatched his pistol, forced him to open the jail and let her out and had also compelled him to go with her and act as escort, cook, dishwasher, horse wrangler, and general utility servant—at the point of his own gun. He managed to escape from Belle only by great watchfulness and ingenuity.

This yarn, no doubt, emphasizes a point that is undoubtedly the truth. It is that in about her thirtieth year Belle became not merely an associate of outlaws but a directing mind for them; that she kept men under her subjection by her imperious will, scathing tongue, superior intelligence and her sex appeal. She changed lovers with great rapidity, choosing them by caprice and dropping them by caprice. Her lovers were said to include the outlaws Jack Spaniard, Jim French, Sam Starr, John Middleton, Jim July, and the white man among the notorious Indian Territory horse thieves and desperadoes who went under the appalling alias "Blue Duck."

Belle cherished a sentimental memory of Cole Younger all her life. Her *open* identification with outlaws and outlawry coincides quite pointedly with the end of Cole Younger's career as a free agent when he was incarcerated in the Stillwater, Minnesota, penitentiary under life sentence—together with his brothers, Bob and Jim—after their capture and trial following the disastrous attempt of the Younger-James gang to rob the First National Bank of Northfield, Minnesota, on September 7, 1876.

J. W. Weaver, pioneer newsman in Western Arkansas, for many years reporter and editorial writer for the Fort Smith *Independent* and correspondent for the New York *Herald,* who published his reminiscences in the early nineties in the Fort Smith *Elevator* and who was, perhaps, the only person outside of her outlaw companions in whom Belle reposed confidence, stated after Belle's death that, until the time she was murdered, Belle was unremitting in her efforts to secure a pardon for Cole and that she secretly supplied money for Cole's legal defense. It will be remembered that, although the grand jury indicted all three of the Younger brothers and they all pleaded guilty to escape the death sentence, the grand jury hung the severest rap on Cole, indicting him as a principal in one murder and as an accessory in the murder of cashier Heywood, but indicting Bob and Jim only as accessories in both murders and in robbing the bank. It was Jesse James, who escaped, who killed Heywood.

Of Belle's lovers, her first, Cole Younger, was the only one to die with his boots off. Cole died at his home at Lee's Summit, Missouri, on March 21, 1916, after a year's illness of heart disease and dyspepsia, after having served twenty-five years in the penitentiary, aged 72. The necrology of the others is:

Jim Reed, killed by Deputy Sheriff Morris, August 6, 1874.

John Middleton, drowned May 3, 1885.

Blue Duck, killed by unknown party, Indian Territory, July, 1886.

Sam Starr, killed by Frank West, December 18, 1886.

Jack Spaniard, hanged August 30, 1889, for murder.

Jim July, alias Jim Starr, killed resisting arrest, January 6, 1890.

Jim French, killed robbing a store, autumn, 1895.

Belle was, in the parlance of the modern criminal underworld, a "fix," that is, some one who had the

Belle Starr

knack and intelligence and cash to get at the right persons among the administrators of the law and arrange nolle prosses, paroles, releases, pardons, verdicts and suspended or light sentences. As the "brains" of cattle and horse thieves, burglars, hold-up men and other outlaws, it was her function to secure the quickest possible release of any member of the gang who got entangled with the law.

In a fairly long career of intimate association with outlaws and outlawry, she served only one prison term. She was quickly released on the few other charges of larceny brought against her. This indicates that she not only had a knack of escaping the clutches of the law in operations in which she was an accessory, but that she possessed the powers of dictatorial leadership, and she exercised them over the bandits she harbored at Younger's Bend.

Most of her ruffianly crew, indeed, probably looked upon her as a magician because she could read and write. Much is made of her devotion to literature. To be sure, the only books specifically mentioned as among those in Belle's library were Mark Twain's *A Tramp Abroad,* which she is depicted as writing about in her alleged diary eight years before the book was published, and the Bible. Still, if she could make out the words on a warrant for arrest, it would probably seem like witchcraft to Jim French, Jack Spaniard and Sam Starr.

Outlawry

The Fox biographer invents a "motivation" idea to explain Belle's espousing outlawry as a revolt against, and a revenge upon, the Dallas society that had snubbed her. There may be an item of truth in it; but the difficulty in swallowing it whole is that there is very little evidence in the contemporary records of the period that Dallas "society" was any more high-toned than Belle was. Every general store had a whiskey barrel and a tin cup for free drinks for the customers until the saloonkeepers, resenting this unfair competition, ganged up on the storekeepers and had a town ordinance passed stopping the practice as contrary to morals and decency. There were preachers and preachers' wives in the town, of course. Undoubtedly there were some women of obtrusive and even offensive refinement and delicacy, having brought the hauteur they had cultivated in their native hamlets into this bustling, wild and woolly pioneer town. With Belle's father on the law in 1876 on a charge of harboring criminals, her alleged husband proclaimed a notorious criminal in every weekly edition of the newspapers and killed while resisting arrest on charges of murder and robbery, her daughter the child of one of the two most publicized bank and train robbers, and herself a "widow" with two children on her hands in a Southern society where any work outside the home except school-teaching was considered a little more socially degrading than prostitution—all this should be explanation enough for Belle's practice of the profession she knew best— horse and cattle thievery.

In company with various rustlers, highwaymen, Indian halfbreeds and cowboys, Belle seems, during the four years between 1876 and 1880 to have familiarized herself with all the finer phases of the dangerous life. She learned when and where to cut out mavericks, what trails to take through the Indian country, to pick up Indian ponies along the way and how best to avoid both the Indian Nations' police and the Federal marshals, where and how to run corn liquor, where to dispose of stolen property at the best price and how to get herds of stolen cattle through to Abilene or Fort Dodge for sale on the hoof to the cattle-buyers who would ship them East by rail to the packing houses. And, most important of all, Belle learned how to live on the scout with a minimum of inconvenience in a life that meant days and nights in the saddle, sleeping in the open, going without food in dangerous territory, and avoiding anyone who might represent the law.

The tales tell that Belle became familiar with Dodge City, Kansas, which for a long time disputed Virginia City's (Nevada) reputation as being the wickedest city in the world. It is quite possible that, in the company of some of her cattle-rustling companions, Belle did visit the town to dispose of stolen cattle. One of the legends about Belle and Dodge City sounds incredible but piquant.

The story is that "Blue Duck," her current lover, borrowed $2,000 from Belle when they were in Dodge City after having disposed of a herd of stolen cattle in 1877, and lost the entire amount in a Dodge City gambling joint. When Belle heard "Blue Duck's" sad story, she buckled on her revolvers, took "Blue Duck" along and told him to wait outside the gambling house with their horses in readiness. She walked through the saloon and upstairs to the gambling room, drew her revolvers and commanded the whole house to stick-'em-up. Then she sauntered over to where there was a card game in progress around a large table, with large stakes piled up in front of the dealer and the customers. While still covering the crowd with one of her revolvers, she swept all the money into a bag and backed out of the room with $7,000, saying: "Gentlemen, there is a little change due you. I haven't time to give it to you now. If you want it, come down into the Territory and visit me some time."

Long after Belle's death and long after this little conceit first appeared in the Fox biography and even after it reappeared in Harman's *Hell on the Border*, an old-timer in Dodge City "remembered" the episode and explained how it was possible for Belle to get away with such a feat in a room full of armed men, all of whom it would have been impossible to keep covered. His testimony was: "Well, we wuz so blamed flabbergasted at seeing a woman entering the place with two drawn revolvers that our minds couldn't take in the sitchyachion until it was all plumb over and she was gone."

If the incident had actually occurred, it is hardly likely that Robert M. Wright, one of the founders of Dodge City and its official historian, would have failed to recall it in *Dodge City, the Cowboy Capital,* which is a remarkably vivid and detailed account of the cowtown's untamed days, the days of Wild Bill Hickok, Wyatt Earp, Ben and Bill Thompson, Bat Masterson and Billy Tilghman. In fact, although Wright describes many slayings in gun-fights which resulted in the burial of more than thirty men in Boot Hill with their boots on and without coffins— because wood on that treeless prairie was too expensive—he recalls no stick-up of a gambling joint.

Gambling joints, indeed, were considered sacred precincts in all lawless towns, inclosed fields of honor for duels over questions of honesty, but immune from stick-ups. Come to think of it, I can recall no other instance in all bandit lore, of a hold-up in a gambling house, except, of course, Belle's unprecedented exploit.

CHAPTER FIVE

AT YOUNGER'S BEND

Some time in or about 1880, Belle married Sam Starr, son of old Tom Starr, and took up residence in the log cabin at Younger's Bend, which was to be her home the rest of her life. Marriage, under the Cherokee tribal laws, was a simple matter, *if the contracting parties were Indians*. They were man and wife if they set up housekeeping under the same roof. They were divorced if one of the contracting parties decided to live with someone else.

But the marriage of a white man to an Indian woman or of a white woman to an Indian man was not so simple a process, because it involved the lands of the tribe which were held communally and not individually. A member of the tribe could choose a site and hold it as long as he lived on it; and he would own the improvements and could transfer title to the improvements and move somewhere else, but the land itself was the tribe's.

In 1880, Sam Starr was only twenty-eight while Belle was thirty-two years old. After the death of Jim

Reed, Belle's choice of lovers was among men who were progressively younger than she was. Her last husband, Jim July, who called himself Jim Starr after taking up with Belle, reputedly at Belle's demand, was only twenty-four years old, while Belle was thirty-eight.

Sam Starr had about sixty-two acres of land on the north side of the bend of the Canadian River, near Briartown. His immediate neighbors were all members of the Starr clan, either as direct descendants of James Starr or by marriage into the Starr family.

Only a mile east of Sam Starr's place began the boundaries of the lands of the West clan, of whom, Frank West, just before Christmas in 1896, was to engage Sam Starr in a gun fight in which both were killed.

To the north, across broad fields, rises Hi-Early Mountain, a peak in whose boulder-guarded caves the bandits who made Belle's place their rendezvous hid out when the grapevine brought them word that United States marshals were about to make one of their periodic calls on Belle in search of criminals.

Approach to Sam and Belle Starr's place was possible only over a narrow trail along a canyon and through the uplands off the old Briartown-Eufaula trail, now obliterated. The spot is even wilder and more inaccessible now than it was when the populous

At Younger's Bend

Starrs cultivated their meager crops and their villainy.

Belle built two other cabins on the place during her lifetime for the housing of her outlaw guests. These and the original cabin have now disappeared. The place is desolate, and almost nothing remains of the tomb which Pearl Younger caused to be erected out of slabs of native rock over the grave of her mother.

Steele Kennedy of the Tulsa *World* visited the place in the fall of 1933 in company with Charles G. Still, a widely known Arkansas peace officer. One of the old nesters in the neighborhood of Belle Starr canyon contributed a poetic gem to their collection. He said: "When night settles down over that canyon yonder you can hear the sounds of guns firing along the river, the clanking of chains like prisoners marching to their cells. All through the night, Belle Starr's favorite mare can be heard pawing at the ground near her grave, and if a gun is fired into the ground near Belle's grave, the sod will flare up and pop like the pistols of bandits a-firin' from the hip."

There is an oft-repeated story that when Belle Starr first returned to "Uncle Tom" Starr's refuge for outlaws after the death of Jim Reed and proposed to take up permanent residence there, "Uncle Tom" was advised by an old chief of the tribe to kill Belle as he would a snake. The old chief is alleged to have spoken somewhat in this manner: "Uncle Tom, I'm warning you that this woman will be the ruin of your boys. If you don't kill her, she will ensnare them and bring them to destruction. She is wicked and poisonous. She will make them do her bidding and will lead them into outlawry. When that happens it is only a short way to Judge Parker and to Hangman Maledon with his rope at Fort Smith." Uncle Tom shook his head and said that he could not harm a woman.

One of the Fox biographer's fanciful inventions describes Belle as having set down in her diary the details of the Austin-San Antonio mail robbery and as having written that, after they had counted the swag in the mail pouch, she amused herself by reading the letters they had opened in search of money—"one hundred and fifty letters from lover to lover, husband to wife, brother to sister, and so on." Then Belle came across her own name in one of the letters: "It was dated from Nevada, Missouri, and was addressed to the sheriff of Bastrop County. One of the sentences struck me forcibly: 'Get this woman out of the way and you have Reed, Younger, Roberts and the others under your thumb. I believe she will take a bribe, if you make it big enough. Without her aid the boys will soon go under.' My loud, scornful laugh attracted my husband, but I tore the letter into shreds and opened a conversation with regard to our next act on the program of life."

At Younger's Bend

Both stories are designed to point the dominating qualities of Belle Starr. The sentimental flourish to the first tale, to the effect that Tom Starr refrained from taking the old chief's advice about killing Belle, "because he couldn't harm a woman," is ludicrous in the light of the known facts of Tom Starr's career. Only one instance is enough to illustrate Tom's lack of tender sentiments. It was related by R. P. Vann, the grandson of Joseph Vann, one of the most famous and, for a long time, the richest of all Cherokees.

Mr. R. P. Vann's testimony can be trusted implicitly. At one point he said: "Tom Starr killed Israel Vore and his wife and burned them up in their house about 1843 before I was born. A little boy about five years old was burned up at the same time. One time I bought forty or fifty head of cattle from Tom Starr and when I went after them I stayed all night at his house. My brother liked to whipped me for doing that. Tom Starr talked to me all night. He told me about the Vores and their house and told me that while it was burning a little boy about five years old came running out and begged him not to kill him and Tom said he just picked him up and threw him in the fire. He said he didn't think God would ever forgive him for that and I said I didn't think He would either." (*Chronicles of Oklahoma,* June, 1933.)

Mr. Vann was talking not about some other Tom Starr, but about the "Uncle Tom" of this history. He knew Tom and all the Starr kin, including Sam. He knew Belle, too. When he says he knew her "very well" you can trust that, too, for Mr. Vann was, by nature and temperament, a master of understatement. He was brought up with Sam; and he lived within less than ten miles of Sam and Belle as long as they were alive at Younger's Bend. I shall recur to some testimony Mr. Vann gave about Belle and Sam later on. It will be a surprise, for it differs from nearly all the versions that have appeared in print, but bears out the version given to me by old Cherokees and Choctaws in the region of Belle Starr's operations.

When Belle took up permanent residence at Younger's Bend as the wife of Sam Starr, the countryside had entirely recovered from the desolation by incendiarism perpetrated during the War between the States and by the civil war within the Cherokee Nation. There were regions within the Nation after the war that were like the results of Sheridan's total warfare in the Shenandoah Valley which, he said, he had left in such a state that a crow flying over it would have to carry its own rations. But after fifteen years, new homes had been built, fences had been mended, crops had been planted, the forests were thick again, and wild turkeys and prairie chickens were plentiful. The Canadian, Arkansas, Illinois and

Verdigris Rivers and their tributaries were filled with bass, perch, eels and crappies, and with catfish weighing ten and fifteen pounds.

White outlaws disturbed the serenity of the Nation; bootleggers smuggled whiskey into the Territory on boats plying up the Arkansas, to debauch the Indians; some of the Cherokees were still carrying on the ancient feuds; the Creeks had stirred a minor civil war of their own over the election of a chief—yet comparative peace had been restored.

The United States Government had begun to supply the members of the Five Civilized Tribes with family allotments of beef on the hoof and rations of flour, bacon, coffee, beans and jean clothing. The Cherokees held stomp dances at seasonal intervals, at which there was much dancing, chanting, fornication and merriment. There were horse races, ball games—a kind of murderous lacrosse in which a half-dozen players would be knocked out completely and fatalities were frequent—and, among the converts to Christianity, camp meetings, revivals and baptisms.

Tulsa, in 1880, was still called Tulsey Town and had a population of 300. It had grown up around a trading post that had been erected on an old Creek tribal council grounds, on which ashes from their former council grounds in Alabama had been brought at the time of the sorrowful Removal. The town had one hotel of clapboards nailed on to two-by-fours.

It was two stories high and had eight rooms. The windows of this hotel were shot out regularly and its façade riddled with bullets by drunken cowboys hurrahing the village. Tulsey Town and Claremore were bad towns; but Catoosa, in the Cherokee Nation, on a branch of the Frisco railroad running from Monett, Missouri, to Sapulpa, was the hell hole of the whole Territory in the early eighties.

Catoosa is a backward but peaceful little village of of about 300 population now, eighteen miles east of Tulsa on Route 66 to Vinita; but in the eighties it had a record of filthy vice, drunkenness and murder that would make Dodge City seem like a Quaker town. It was just a mean place, without the excuse of being a cattle-shipping point, like Fort Dodge or Abilene, where cowboys who had been driving herd from Texas for three or four months might be excused for going on sprees and whooping it up at the end of their dismal chores.

Especial attention is called to Catoosa because it was in this town that one of Belle's sweethearts, Jim French, met his timely end.

After Belle gave him his walking papers, he became a member of the notorious Cook gang, an outfit so tough that it caused the railroad between Fort Smith and Coffeyville, Kansas, to change its schedule for six months, cancelling its night train runs and going through, heavily guarded, only in the daytime. After the break-up of the Cook gang, Jim French turned to petty burglary. He and a companion tried to rob the general store of Reynolds & Co., in Catoosa one night, but found, too late, that the manager and a night-watchman, heavily armed, were within. The night-watchman blew French's companion's face off with a shotgun and the manager, though badly wounded himself by French, raised himself from the floor with one arm and shot French through the base of the skull. Belle must have been familiar with Catoosa during the period of its worst reputation, because it was at the crossroads of two important cattle trails, one east and west and the other north and south. Her stolen horses and cattle could have been more easily disposed of there than at any point within the Terri-tory, for the town was largely made up of "fences" for stolen chattels. Moreover, it was an excellent out-let for the moonshine liquor which was made at Younger's Bend. In Catoosa, also, Belle could in-dulge her passion for gambling in the company of the sort of characters she boasted she liked to be with—the hard-living, hard-riding gunmen and des-peradoes.

Belle and Sam had scarcely got themselves or-ganized in the marital state when an old friend of Belle's, but a stranger to Sam, dropped in on them and made himself at home for several weeks. Belle introduced the visitor as "Mr. Williams from Texas."

He was Jesse James. Jesse was in the toughest spot of his life, until the moment he climbed up on a chair to fix a picture in his home in St. Joseph, Missouri, when Bob Ford took advantage of the occasion to blow Jesse's brains out.

Having lived quietly for four years after the North-field, Minnesota, bank robbery, in which he and Frank escaped but the three Younger brothers were caught, Jesse had run out of money, had reorganized his gang and just committed the last of a series of robberies—and the last of all his robberies. The papers were full of his pictures and details of his latest exploits. The *National Police Gazette* had run a serial on the *Life of the James Brothers, Jesse and Frank,* as though they were already dead, and this serial had been made into a twenty-five-cent book that was selling like peanuts at a circus. The nickel—erroneously called the dime—novel writers were turning out new works of fiction about the notorious James boys every week. Governor Crittenden had just added another $5,000 to the rewards outstanding for Frank and Jesse James dead or alive. Every Pinkerton detective, every peace officer, every town constable in the country—except in Clay and Jackson Counties, Missouri —scanned every stranger's face for resemblance to Frank or Jesse James. The country was loud in demanding that the Jameses be brought to justice.

Frank had not joined with Jesse in any of these later robberies. He, under the name of Woodson, and Jesse, under the name of J. D. (or David) Howard, had kept low and quiet with their wives in Nashville, Tennessee. Frank had refused to take up the old life any more, especially because he was in very bad health. Instead, he began bombarding Governor Crittenden and the newspapers with mawkish letters, picturing himself and Jesse as maligned and saintly souls who were being hounded for crimes they had not committed, and whiningly begging either amnesty or clemency in return for surrender.

Jesse had got an old gang—Ed Miller, Bob Hite, Bill Ryan, Jim Liddel and Dan Bassman—together, and they had pulled three express-train robberies in succession. The first was in the heart of Jesse's own native bailiwick, Glendale, in Jackson County, Missouri; he and his gang had robbed the Chicago and Alton passenger train there on October 7, 1879. Then, on July 15, 1881, they had robbed the Chicago, Rock Island and Pacific express at Winston, Davies County, Missouri, and murdered the conductor and a trainman. Finally, they held up a Chicago and Alton express train at Blue Cut, Jackson County, on September 7, 1881. Then the gang disbanded, and Jesse lit out for Younger's Bend, which he must have learned about from the Youngers.

Belle Starr

Jesse was unprepared for any display of domestic felicity, for he had no way of knowing that Belle had married Starr. He appears, however, to have taken the news in his stride. It is quite certain that he was prepared and able to pay for board and room. He was badly in need of quiet and seclusion for quite a while.

Belle could not have cared much for Jesse James for three reasons: First, he was at liberty and Cole Younger was in the penitentiary. Second, Cole and Jesse never got along together because they were too much alike in their wanton cruelty, murderous instincts and desire to dominate. Third, Cole, in an account of the Northfield robbery, written for the press in prison, had not only openly accused Jesse of drinking heavily for Dutch courage and thus bungling the plans, but of being the one who had senselessly pulled a knife, tried to cut Cashier Heywood's throat and then had shot at Heywood.

So, it is likely that Belle's and Jesse's relations while he was at Younger's Bend were on a cool and meretricious basis. Belle, no doubt, demanded a heavy price for the protection Younger's Bend offered. She said, in the biographical sketch she is alleged to have written for Weaver, that in coming to Younger's Bend, she had intended giving up the hectic life she had led. She wrote:

At Younger's Bend

After a more adventurous life than generally falls to the lot of woman, I settled permanently in the Indian Territory, selecting a place of picturesque beauty on the Canadian River. There, far from society, I hoped to pass the remainder of my life in peace and quietude. So long had I been estranged from the society of women (whom I thoroughly detest), that I thought I would find it irksome to live in their midst.

So I selected a place that few have ever had the gratification of gossiping around. For a short time I lived very happily in the society of my little girl and husband, a Cherokee Indian, a son of the noted Tom Starr. But it soon became noised around that I was a woman of some notoriety from Texas, and from that time on my home and actions have been severely criticized.

My home became famous as an outlaw's ranch long before I was visited by any of the boys who were friends of mine. Indeed, I never corresponded with any of my old associates and was desirous my whereabouts should be unknown to them. Through rumor they learned of it.

Jesse James first came in and remained several weeks. He was unknown to my husband, and he never knew till long afterwards that our home had been honored by James' presence. I introduced Jesse as one Mr. Williams from Texas.

But few outlaws have visited my home, notwithstanding so much has been said. The best people in the country are friends of mine. I have considerable ignorance to cope with, consequently my troubles originate mostly in that quarter. Surrounded by a lowdown class of shoddy whites who have made the Indian Territory their home to evade paying tax on their dogs, and who I will not permit to hunt on my premises, I am the constant theme of their slanderous tongues. In all the world there is no woman more persecuted than I.

Weaver did not publish this sketch until after Belle's death, and he said he had kept it in his desk for two years. If Weaver had had the manuscript in his desk for two years, that would date Belle's statement in the late winter or spring of 1887. During this period she had, for a third time within a year, cleared herself on a charge of larceny. She was beginning to be a familiar figure on the streets of Fort Smith, as a defendant and co-defendant, with Sam, for horse-stealing, as a witness for "Blue Duck" when he was charged with murder and simply as a visitor with plenty of money to spend. She rode a fine black mare named "Venus," owned an expensive and highly decorative side-saddle, wore a brace of ivory-handled Colt .45 revolvers in holsters especially made for her. She liked to drop into barrooms, drink with the men and play the accompaniment on the piano for the popular cowboy and sentimental songs of the period.

From 1880 to 1882, however, Belle appears to have confined herself pretty much to acting as the "brains" of outlaw gangs from her citadel at Younger's Bend. At least she was ingenious enough to keep out of the clutches of the law. In February, 1883, she made her first appearance before "Hanging" Judge Parker in the Federal Court of the Western District of Arkansas, on the charge of stealing two horses on April

At Younger's Bend

20th, the year before. She and Sam had been arrested at Younger's Bend and had been brought into Fort Smith, where they were arraigned and the date of their trial was set. They gave bond for their appearance and left Fort Smith without attracting attention.

But when they appeared for trial, the incident was a sensation. It was the first time a woman had been brought before the Federal Court at Fort Smith on such a charge. Moreover, the indictment read that she was "the leader of a band of horse thieves." Reports of the indictment and the progress of the trial went out over the telegraph wires to the newspapers. Belle was taken up by the rewrite men in distant metropolitan journals and promptly labeled "The Queen of the Bandits," "The Petticoat Terror of the Plains" and "The Lady Desperado."

Fame, of a sort, had at last reached her.

CHAPTER SIX

"HANGING" JUDGE PARKER

AND HIS COURT

Sam and Belle came up for trial on February 15, 1883. They had pleaded not guilty and had requested a trial by jury. The prosecutor in the case was the brilliant and relentless W. H. H. Clayton, a man who should share with "Hanging" Judge Parker the fame and honor of sending eighty-eight men to the gallows in the Fort Smith Federal jail yard.

The trial lasted four days. The jury's verdict was guilty, after only an hour's deliberation.

Belle was convicted on two counts, Sam on only one. Judge Parker reserved sentence until March 8, and on the appointed day they were in court. Although conviction on two counts normally would have meant that Belle would have to serve two years to Sam's one, Judge Parker gave her six months on each count and Sam a full year. Before the day was out, the pair were on the way to the Federal penitentiary in Detroit.

"Hanging" Judge Parker

The sensation which Belle's trial caused in Fort Smith is best reflected in this account in the Feb. 22, 1883, issue of the Fort Smith *New Era,* a weekly:

In the U. S. district court last week the case of Sam Starr and Belle Starr, his wife, of the Cherokee Nation, charged with the larceny of two horses on the 20th of April, 1882, was one of the most interesting that has engaged the attention of this court for a long time.

The very idea of a woman being charged with an offense of this kind and that she was the leader of a band of horse thieves and wielding a power over them as their queen and guiding spirit, was sufficient to fill the courtroom with spectators during the trial, which lasted four days, the jury finding a verdict of guilty against them.

From the evidence, it appears that on the date mentioned, Belle and her husband penned the horses in the lot of John West, and after securing them, carried them off, since which time they have never been seen but once, and that was when Belle and a man named Childs crossed the North Fork of the Canadian River a few days after the larceny.

The line of defense put forward by the attorneys for the defendants was an alibi and endeavored to prove that John West, the only eyewitness to the larceny, was the guilty party, who, in order to save himself from the clutches of the law, filed the information against the defendants and had them arrested, but after a full hearing of all the evidence in the case, the jury, after an absence from the court of about one hour, returned a verdict as above stated.

During the trial, Belle, who is a ready writer, would frequently hand notes to her attorneys, and it was a subject of remark that they paid strict attention to the contents. A devil-may-care expression rested on her countenance during the entire trial, and at no time did she give sign of weakening before the mass of testimony that was raised against her. Once, when allusion was made to Jim Reed, her former husband and the father of her child, tears welled up in her eyes and trickled down her cheeks, but they were quickly wiped away and the countenance resumed its wonted appearance.

As an equestrienne, Belle Starr is without rival, is said to be an expert marksman with the pistol, and it is claimed that she was at one time the wife of Bruce (sic) Younger, the notorious horse thief and desperado, and while she could not be considered even a good-looking woman, her appearance is of that kind as would be sure to attract the attention of wild and desperate characters.

It was undoubtedly from this story, which was sent out over the press wires, that the Fox writer got the name "Bruce" Younger as one of Belle's early suitors. The Fox writer knew the outlaw Younger brothers were Bob, Cole, Jim and John, and that there was no brother named Bruce. So he made this mythical Younger a cousin.

This case marks the beginning of the feud between Sam Starr and his cousin, John West, whose land was transversed by the Eufaula-Briartown trail and lay only a mile northwest of Sam and Belle's place.

Harman quotes the following letter, which he alleges he copied from the original in Fort Smith, as one written by Belle to her daughter, Pearl Younger, on the eve of Belle's departure for Detroit:

"Hanging" Judge Parker

Pandemonium, Feb. —, 1883.

Baby Pearl,

My dear little one: It is useless to attempt to conceal my trouble from you and though you are nothing but a child I have confidence that my darling will bear with fortitude what I now write.

I shall be away from you a few months, baby, and have only this consolation to offer you, that never again will I be placed in such humiliating circumstances and that in the future your little tender heart shall never more ache, or a blush called to your cheek on your mother's account. Sam and I were tried here, John West the main witness against us. We were found guilty and sentenced to nine months [Belle's sentence was for one year] at the house of correction, Detroit, Michigan, for which place we start in the morning. Now Pearl there is a vast difference in that place and a penitentiary; you must bear that in mind, and not think of mama being shut up in a gloomy prison. It is said to be one of the finest institutions in the United States, surrounded by beautiful grounds, with fountains and everything nice. There I can have my education renewed, and I stand sadly in need of it. Sam will have to attend school and I think it is the best thing ever happened for him, and now you must not be unhappy and brood over our absence. It wont take the time long to glide by and as we come home we will get you and then we will have such a nice time.

We will get your horse up and I will break him and you can ride John while I am gentling Loco. We will have Eddie with us and will be as gay and happy as the birds we claim at home. Now baby you can either stay with grandma or your Mama Mc, just as you like and do the best you can until I come back, which won't be long. Tell Eddie that he can go down home with us and have a good time hunting and though I wish not to deprive Marion and ma of him for any length of time yet I must keep him a while. Love to ma and Marion.

Uncle Tom has stood by me nobly in our trouble, done everything that one *could* do. Now, baby, I will write to you often. You must write to your grandma but don't tell her of this; and to your Aunt Ellen, Mama Mc., but to no one else. Remember, I don't care who writes to you, you must not answer. I say this because I do not want you to correspond with anyone in the Indian Territory, my baby, my sweet little one, and you must mind me. Except auntie; if you wish to hear from me auntie will let you know. If you should write me, ma would find out where I am and, Pearl, you must never let her know. Her head is overburdened with care now and therefore you must keep this carefully guarded from her.

Destroy this letter as soon as read. As I told you before, if you wish to stay a while with your Mama Mc., I am willing. But you must devote your time to your studies. Bye bye, sweet baby mine.

BELLE STARR

In Detroit penitentiary Belle was employed in the weaving of chair bottoms out of split cane, while Sam was put to hard labor. Their record must have been good, for they were released at the end of nine months, having earned three months off for good behavior.

Nothing further is reported of the pair until May, 1885. Legend has it that they attended the county fair in Fort Smith which was held in October, 1884, and that Belle took part in the Wild West show in a realistic exhibition of a hold-up of a stagecoach, Belle playing the role of a female bandit—a lone road agent, at that—and Judge Parker acting as one of the passengers in the stagecoach.

Contemporary newspaper accounts describe the fair and tell of the part Judge Parker played as a passenger in the stagecoach, but they make no mention of Belle. This does not necessarily indicate that Belle did *not* play a role assigned to her; but it seems curious that the newspapers would have failed to make a great deal of an event in which a Federal judge who had sentenced a woman to the penitentiary for horse stealing would invite her to join him as one of the actors in a public exhibition.

We can discard without any compunction Harman's story of the sequel to this joint play-acting of stern Judge Parker and "The Bandit Queen." The story runs that Belle was exceedingly angry at Prosecutor Clayton, not for sending her and Sam to the penitentiary, but for ridiculing Sam on the stand during the trial because of Sam's lack of education. The reason for her anger was that she had accepted Judge Parker's invitation to take part in the exhibition on the understanding that Prosecutor Clayton was to be one of the passengers in the stagecoach. Her plans failed to materialize because Clayton could not attend the fair and Belle was thwarted in her design to kill him by inserting one real cartridge among the blanks.

On second thought, Belle certainly would have dismissed such a fantastic idea, for she was too shrewd a woman to commit a murder in the presence of a thousand witnesses.

Judge Isaac C. Parker, before whom Belle appeared for sentence and before whom she was to appear a number of times afterwards, held a unique position in the annals of jurisprudence. For fourteen years of his twenty-one on the bench as Federal Judge of the U.S. District court in Fort Smith, his decisions were absolute and irrevocable; there was no appeal from them.

During his long term in office, 13,000 cases were tried by him, and he pronounced the fatal words "I find the defendant guilty as charged" no fewer than 9,500 times. He sentenced 172 men to death, and of these, 88 were hanged while he was on the bench; the others had their sentences commuted to life imprisonment, or the court's decisions were lost on appeal, during the seven years after Judge Parker had lost final jurisdiction over the cases tried before him.

Judge Parker's enormous record for pronouncing the death sentence earned him an undeserved reputation for cruelty among those who considered only the words "he hanged eighty-eight men." His jurisdiction was over the whole of Indian Territory, as well as Western Arkansas, in all cases involving Federal offenses, and he had the scum of the Southwest to deal with.

Judge Parker, who had never been ill a day in his life, became seriously ill immediately upon being notified that his court was to be abolished. His court expired on September 1, 1896. He died on November 17 of the same year, never having left his bed after his sudden and inexplicable illness.

Famous, too, in Judge Parker's court was wispy, long-whiskered George Maledon, official hangman of the court, who once performed the feat of hanging six men at the same moment from the same scaffold.

Almost equally famous in the court were Prosecutor W. H. H. Clayton, who has been mentioned before, and who was later appointed judge of the Federal District court established at McAlester, Indian Territory, and J. Warren Reed, the criminal lawyer who, in spite of the reputation for the sternness of Judge Parker's decisions, ran up an imposing record of winning cases for his defendants. It was J. Warren Reed whom Belle retained to bring about the commutation of ''Blue Duck's'' death sentence to life imprisonment, and ''Blue Duck's'' pardon within a year.

In the spring of 1885, as Belle's love for Sam was growing cold it became enkindled for one John Middleton, a cousin of Jim Reed's, who had come to join

Belle Starr

Sam and Belle's gang of outlaws at Younger's Bend, after a very thorough apprenticeship in outlawry. He was wanted in Arkansas for larceny and arson; he was wanted in Texas for larceny, jail-breaking and murder. On November 16, 1884, he had gone to the home of Sheriff J. H. Black of Lamar County, called him to the door and shot him down in cold blood.

Middleton, with $1,500 in rewards offered for his arrest, was welcomed at Younger's Bend some time around Christmas, 1884. Meanwhile, Sam had been implicated in the robbery of the Creek Nation treasury with one Felix Griffin. They had been recognized, warrants were out for their arrest, and United States marshals, accompanied by many deputies and numbers of Indian police, had ridden up Belle Starr canyon too many times in search of Sam for him to stay in the neighborhood. He hid out with some kin above Webbers Falls. For some months, Belle was left alone with Middleton.

Finally, the pair decided to give Sam the slip.

The story Belle told later was that she wanted to get away for a while and go with Pearl to visit Pete Marshall and family, who lived near Chickala, Arkansas.

But it seems to have been understood between Belle and Middleton that he was to accompany her only as far as Keota, each going by a different route from there to a rendezvous in Arkansas at Middleton's mother's home in the mountains near Dardanelle in Logan County.

On May 5, 1885, Belle and Pearl climbed into a covered wagon which had been loaded with enough of their effects for a long stay. Driven by an odd-job boy and fugitive from justice named Frank Cook, they set out, taking the Whitefield route to Fort Smith. Middleton rode ahead on a saddle horse, from the pommel of which hung Belle's pistol and in his side holsters were two of his own. Belle took his Winchester in the wagon with her. Turning off at Keota, Middleton struck out southwest toward the pass between Sugar Loaf and Poteau Mountains on the Arkansas border to go thence by way of Booneville and Danville to Dardanelle. It was a lonely and circuitous route, but Fort Smith, or any other populous town, was a dangerous place for Middleton to be seen in, because of the number of warrants out for his arrest.

Unfortunately for Belle, the horse Middleton was riding belonged to A. G. McCarthy, a white man who had married a Choctaw woman and lived near Whitefield. The horse was most easily identifiable. It was a sorrel mare, about fifteen hands high, branded with a 31 inside a half circle on the neck and with an A on the shoulder, and it was blind in one eye.

Three days after Belle and Middleton parted, one H. Tally of Pocola in the Choctaw Nation found a horse tangled up in the brush on the bank of the

Poteau River, a few miles southwest of Pocola. The horse was bridled and saddled, and from the horn of the saddle hung a .45-caliber pistol. Tally reported the find to the local authorities and a search was begun on the theory that the rider of the horse had been drowned. Although there was a ford near the place where the horse was discovered, the river was up because of recent rains.

The same day the horse was found, the searchers came upon the dead body of a man washed up on the bank and half buried in mud, the body badly decomposed. The face appeared to have been eaten away by buzzards.

The body was clothed in dark cashmere pants and vest, a dress shirt and half boots. Around the body was a cartridge belt with holsters containing two .45 pistols. A silver watch, a ten-dollar bank note and eleven dollars in silver coin, two jackknives and a comb were found.

The remains were buried by the searchers, and a description of the horse and its trappings and of the body and the articles found on it was telegraphed to the Fort Smith *Elevator* and published therein.

Meanwhile, in April, before Belle and Middleton had left, Captain Gunn of Fannin County, Texas, Captain John Millsop of Paris, Texas, and John Duncan of Dallas, all of them bearing marshals' badges and credentials and warrants for the arrest of John

Middleton on a charge of murder, had descended upon Younger's Bend, guided there by John West, a captain of the Cherokee Nation's Indian police. (Although the Starrs and the Wests were neighbors and cousins, there had been bad blood between them ever since John West gave the testimony which sent Belle and Sam to the penitentiary.) They had found no one home except Belle, whom they disarmed and questioned. Then, giving back her pistol, they had departed, but had continued in search of Middleton. They had news that Belle and Middleton were eloping, and they had got on her trail, following it as far as Russellville, Arkansas, where they found her—but not Middleton. Relying upon their information that Belle was leaving Sam for Middleton, they were waiting around for Middleton to show up when they read the story of the drowned man in a copy of the *Elevator* that had reached Russellville. From the descriptions, they had a hunch that the body was that of the man they were waiting for. They went to Fort Smith to consult the editor of the *Elevator* for further news, and there they found McCarthy, who assured them that their surmise was correct, that the body was Middleton's and that he knew for a fact that the horse was his.

Marshals Duncan and Millsop, Captain John West, and O. D. Weldon, a reporter for the *Elevator*—to make sure—went immediately to Pocola, and exhumed the body. West's identification was positive; he knew the man well.

The officers took the pistols and other articles found on the dead body and, accompanied by John West, went to Belle's retreat in the mountains near Dardanelle and showed her the pistols. She did not believe their story that Middleton was drowned. Thinking they had killed him, or that it was a trick of some sort, she cursed them in the language of invective in which she had become a virtuosa. Then she packed and left at once for Pocola, where she had the body exhumed that she herself might identify it. Satisfied that the body was that of her lover, she had it buried properly in a coffin in another spot, with the grave carefully marked.

But the officers had not gone to Belle merely to bring bad news and her lover's personal effects; they had another job to perform. They arrested Frank Cook, the odd-job boy, on a warrant charging larceny. He was taken to Fort Smith, tried and sentenced to the penitentiary.

Belle returned to Younger's Bend. Whether or not she convinced Sam of her story, or, indeed, that she had any story to tell, or that she thought a story necessary, no one can know. The Indian is as inscrutable as the Chinese. Indians do not show their emotions or betray what they are thinking. It is quite possible that John Middleton's face and half of his head were not eaten away by buzzards, but that Sam Starr blew the face away with a shotgun, having trailed Middleton silently.

We hear no more of Belle until May, 1886, when she was arrested at Younger's Bend by United States Marshal Tyner Hughes, accompanied by Deputy Marshal Charles Barnhill, and brought to Fort Smith to answer two charges—one of them quite sensational.

It was charged that, dressed as a man, she led a party of three men who robbed an old Indian named Ferrell and his three sons at Cache, in the Choctaw Nation in March. The other charge against her was brought by A. G. McCarthy, who accused her of being an accessory in the theft of the horse which John Middleton was riding when he was supposedly drowned.

Marshal Hughes reported that although he also had a warrant for the arrest of Sam Starr, he had found no one at home at Younger's Bend except Belle, and that she had made neither resistance nor remonstrance, but had quickly mounted her horse and come in with him, chatting amiably on the way. Arraigned in court, she gave bond promptly, as usual, and spent the whole week in Fort Smith, shopping and taking in the sights and amusements.

The Dallas *News* for June 7, 1886, in a story carrying a Fort Smith date line for the week before, gives us this glimpse of Belle in Fort Worth on the occasion of her arrest on the charges just mentioned:

Fort Smith, Ark., May 30.—For the past week the noted Belle Starr has been quite an attraction on the streets of this city. She came to answer two indictments in the Federal Court and expected to have been tried in the present term, first for being implicated in the stealing of a fine mare, the one ridden by the notorious John Middleton when he was drowned in the Poteau River, twenty-five miles above this city, in May, 1885; and second, on a charge of robbery, in which it is claimed that Belle, dressed in male attire, led a party of three men who robbed an old man named Ferrell and his three sons, some forty miles north of here, in the Choctaw Nation, about three months ago. Court adjourned on Monday last, and her case went over until August next.

Monday night Belle swung her Winchester to her saddle, buckled her revolver around her, and, mounting her horse, set out for her home on the Canadian. Before leaving, she purchased a fine pair of 45-calibre revolvers, latest pattern, with black rubber handles and short barrel, for which she paid $29. She showed them to your correspondent, with the remark: "Next to a fine horse I admire a fine pistol. Don't you think these are beauties?"

Belle says she anticipates no trouble in establishing her innocence in the cases against her, but thinks it terribly annoying to have to spend her time and money coming down here to court five and six times a year.

Belle attracts considerable attention wherever she goes, being a dashing horsewoman, and exceedingly graceful in the saddle. She dresses plainly, and wears a broad-brimmed white man's hat, surmounted by a wide black plush band, with feathers and ornaments, which is very becoming to her. She is of medium size, well formed, a dark brunette, with bright and intelligent black eyes . . .

While here she kindly granted your correspondent a long interview concerning her past life, but made it plainly understood that she had but little use for newspaper reporters, who, she claims, at various times have done her great injustice. Being asked for a brief sketch of her career, she said in substance that she was born in Carthage, Mo., and was 32 years old last February.

In 1863, her father, being a Confederate, removed with his family to Texas, where he continued to reside after the close of the war. After the surrender, Quantrill's men came to the locality and were at all times welcome guests at her father's home.

When less than 15 years of age she fell in love with one of the dashing guerrillas, whose name she said it was not necessary for her to give. Her father objected to her marriage and she ran away with her lover, being married on horseback in the presence of about twenty of her husband's companions. John Fisher, one of the most noted outlaws in the State of Texas, held her horse while the ceremony was being performed, her wedding attire being a black velvet riding habit.

About six weeks after the marriage her husband, being an outlaw, was forced to flee from the country, and he went to Missouri, leaving her in Texas. Her father learned of his hasty departure, and in order to induce her to return home sent her a message that her mother was dangerously ill and her presence was requested in haste. She immediately went home, but found she had been duped, as her mother was not sick at all, and it was then she experienced her first captivity, for the old gentleman locked her up and kept her in confinement for about two weeks, after which he gave her choice of going to school in San Antonio or to a small place in Parker County. She was placed in school at the latter place and remained there for some time, but was not allowed to communicate with anyone outside of her family.

While there her husband came again to Texas, and after considerable trouble learned where she was and came after her.

By this time her admiration for him had become somewhat impaired, and at first she refused to go with him, but after considerable persuasion she borrowed a horse from a young fellow who was attending the same school, ostensibly to take a short ride, and meeting her husband after dark they struck out for Missouri, where her husband purchased a farm and made an effort to settle down and lead an upright life.

He was harassed by enemies to such an extent that he could not live in peace, and finally they killed his brother, and in return he killed two of them, after which they again fled to Texas, and from there went to Los Angeles, Cal., and remained in that State for some time. From there they again returned to Texas, and her husband was killed.

Having followed the fortunes of an outlaw thus far, she has since been true to his friends and comrades, and she has continued to associate with men of his calling, having lived among the Indians nearly ever since, with the exception of two years spent in Nebraska. She has spent some of the time among the wild tribes . . .

In relating her experience during the past three years, she says since the return of herself and her husband from Detroit, Mich., where they served one term, less than a year, for alleged horse stealing, her name has been coupled with every robbery or other depredation that has been committed in the Territory, and in a spirit of mirth she said:

"I am the best-guarded woman in the Indian country, for when the deputy marshals are not there somebody else is."

In speaking of her recent arrest by Deputy Tyner Hughes, she said she was never more dumbfounded in her life than when he rode boldly up to her house and informed her he had come to serve a writ. She was not used to that manner of approach, as the marshals generally came into the Bend with a crowd of from twenty-five to forty men and crawled upon their hands and knees in the darkness.

"And whenever you see a deputy marshal come in," said she, "with the knees of his pants worn out, you may be sure he has invaded Younger's Bend. Hughes is a brave man and acted the gentleman in every particular, but I hardly believe he realized his danger."

She says she never heard of the robbery of Ferrell until she was arrested as the leader of the party who committed it, her accusers asserting she was in male attire. She admits that her husband is at all times on the scout to avoid arrest, and there are several charges of larceny, robbery, etc., against him, which have been trumped up by his enemies, who would not hesitate to swear him into the penitentiary should he surrender and stand trial.

When at home her companions are her daughter, Pearl (whom she calls the "Canadian Lily"), her horse and her two trusty revolvers, which she calls her "babies." The horse she rides she has owned for nearly five years, and no one ever feeds or handles him but herself, and it would be risky business for anyone else to attempt to ride him. She says she has been offered $300 for him time and again, but that $500 would not get him. He is a small sorrel horse, and when in good condition is a beautiful animal, but looked rather the worse for hard riding when here last week. Belle is a crack shot, and handles her pistols with as much dexterity as any frontiersman. No man enters Younger's Bend without first giving a thorough account of himself before he gets out.

Belle related many incidents of her life that would be of interest, and says she has been offered big money by publishers for a complete history of it, but she does not desire to have it published just yet. She has a complete manuscript record, and when she dies she will give it to the public. She spends most of her time writing when at home.

In winding up our interview, she said:

"You can just say that I am a friend to any brave and gallant outlaw, but have no use for that sneaking, coward class of thieves who can be found in every locality, and who would betray a friend or comrade for the sake of their own gain. There are three or four jolly, good fellows on the dodge now in my section, and when they come to my home they are welcome, for they are my friends, would lay down their lives in my defense at any time the occasion demanded it, and go their full length to serve me in any way."

Sam Starr took the life of Frank West and lost his own life almost simultaneously in the same gun fight, as the result of a mistake in identity.

For two months prior to the fatal duel, Sam had been on the lookout for Frank. He wanted to kill him in revenge because he thought it was Frank who had shot him and had killed Belle's mare, Venus, which Sam was riding, while the Indian police were trying to arrest him. It was not Frank West who had shot Sam and killed Belle's horse, but Bill Vann, chief sheriff or captain of the Cherokee Indian police, although Frank West had been present at the shooting and, with a white deputy, had been delegated by Bill Vann to guard Sam after Sam had been taken prisoner.

It happened this way:

For two years, Sam had successfully eluded the United States marshals, who wanted him on charges of horse theft and of robbing a post office. He had also eluded the Choctaw and Cherokee Indian police, who wanted him on charges of robbing the treasury of the Creek Nation.

Late one evening in September 1886, Chief Bill Vann, his younger brother, R. P. Vann, Frank West and the white deputy, Robinson, an adopted citizen of the Cherokee Nation, caught sight of Sam Starr as he was riding three-quarters hidden between rows of corn in a field.

Bill Vann called to Sam to come out and surrender. Instead, Sam put spurs to his horse and tried to escape. Bill Vann thereupon shot several times in rapid succession, unseating Sam and killing the horse. What was later described as a fusillade of bullets and was believed by Sam to be such, was only Bill Vann firing his revolver. The Indian police rushed up to the wounded Sam, disarmed him and took him prisoner. They had to stay overnight at a near-by farmhouse, so that Sam's wounds might be dressed. They planned to make the long journey on horseback next day to the Choctaw Council. Bill Vann left Frank West and Robinson to guard Sam, and departed with his young brother for another farmhouse in the district, to seek accommodations for the night.

A gang of Sam's brothers and henchmen, having learned of the capture of Sam, surrounded the farmhouse in which he was held prisoner, and some of them broke into the cabin, overpowered West and Robinson, and took Sam away with them.

Belle learned that Vann was organizing a large posse of Cherokees to capture Sam again. She forthwith demonstrated her sagacity by persuading Sam that he would have a much better chance in defending the charges against him in the United States District court at Fort Smith than he would have in the Tribal court of the Choctaws. If he submitted to arrest by the Federal officers, he would be under the protection of the United States and could not be touched by the Indian officers.

That that *was* wise counsel may be seen from the fact that if Sam had been tried by either the Choctaw or the Cherokee Tribal courts, his chances would have been exceedingly slim. The Choctaw chiefs hated old Tom Starr and his sons as being responsible for much of the outlawry in their Nation. Then, too, if

Sam were brought before the Cherokee Tribal court, he would have had two strikes against him from the start because the Starrs were of the wrong, or minority, faction in the ancient feud that had split the Cherokees. Lastly, even the most extreme punishment that could be handed out to him in the United States Federal court would be mild in comparison to the verdict if he had been found guilty by either of the Indian Tribal courts. The Indians, in council, had a way of teaching malefactors a lesson by refined tortures, public whipping, hanging and burning while still alive.

Sam was persuaded. Belle had thought he would be, and had notified U. S. Marshal Tyner Hughes, her old friend who had arrested her once, that Sam wished to give himself up, and that with Sam, she would meet Hughes at a certain spot across the Canadian from Younger's Bend, as soon as Hughes could get there.

Thus, the citizens of Fort Smith, on October 11, 1886, were startled by the spectacle of the long-hunted Sam Starr, and the now infrequent visitor, Belle Starr, riding through the streets to the Federal court, unarmed and under the escort of Marshal Hughes.

Belle's hunch proved to be right. Sam was arraigned and released immediately under bail, as usual. In the meantime, the two remained in town while Belle easily beat the charges against her of leading the party that had robbed old man Ferrell and his three sons. Under that indictment, she was released on bail the previous May for an appearance which happily coincided with the time she persuaded Sam to go to court at Fort Smith.

On Friday night, the week before Christmas, there was a dance at the home of Mrs. (''Aunt'') Lucy Surratt adjoining Turk Brothers' store on the south side of the Canadian River near Whitefield. It was only a few miles from Belle's home. Belle, Sam and Belle's children, Pearl and Ed, now grown up, decided to attend the shindig. Sam buckled on his six-shooter— ''just in case'' he might run into Frank West.

They got to ''Aunt'' Lucy's after dark. Sam was half drunk and in a truculent mood by the time they arrived. There was a large bonfire in the center of the stomp-ground, at which guests warmed themselves. When the Starr family rode up, Frank West was sitting on his haunches before the fire, warming his hands. Sam spotted him. Belle walked in front of Sam toward Frank, who arose. Sam began calling Frank names for shooting him and killing Belle's horse. As Frank was denying that he had done either, Belle stepped quickly aside and Sam opened fire on Frank with his pistol, shooting Frank through the neck. Before collapsing, Frank managed to draw his revolver from his overcoat pocket and shoot Sam in the side, the bullet ranging through toward the heart.

"Hanging" Judge Parker

Sam staggered to a tree and, throwing his arms around it, held himself up for a minute and then fell over on his face. Both men were dead within less than five minutes of first seeing each other.

The same wagon which bore Sam's body home for burial in the yard of his father's place carried the body of Frank West to his home.

Shortly after Sam's death, Jim July, a handsome Creek Indian only twenty-four years old, well educated, who spoke nearly all the Indian languages fluently, took up residence at Belle's home and announced that he and she were married. Pearl Younger and Ed Reed, Belle's daughter and son, still lived with Belle in the one-room log cabin.

When Jim July moved in, he was already under indictment for horse theft and on the dodge.

All was seemingly quiet, however, at Younger's Bend until the evening of February 3, 1889. Pearl had given birth to an illegitimate daughter in Siloam Springs in April, 1887, whither Belle had sent her, refusing ever to see or have anything to do with the child. Pearl had left the child with relatives in Arkansas and had returned to Younger's Bend but had refused to disclose the name of the child's father. Ed Reed had begun his career in the footsteps of his mother and father and had been sentenced on July 12, 1888, to seven years in the Federal penitentiary at Columbus, Ohio, but had been released after serving only a few months and had returned to Belle's place.

All was seemingly quiet.

Even those among the neighboring women whom Belle had scorned or snubbed were not complaining. On July 6, 1887, Robert L. Owen, U.S. Indian Agent at Muskogee, had caused to be published in the Indian Territory papers a copy of a letter he had written Belle, reading:

Mrs. Belle Starr, Oklahoma, I.T.

Madam:—The complaint against you for harboring bad characters, has not, in *my* opinion, been established, and is now dismissed. I hope sincerely that you will faithfully carry out your promise to this office not to let such parties make your place a rendezvous.

ROBERT L. OWEN,
UNITED STATES INDIAN AGENT.

CHAPTER SEVEN

BELLE'S DEATH

On February 2, 1889, Jim July, who now called himself Jim Starr (Belle made him change his name to conform with her own), left for Fort Smith to answer a charge of larceny. Belle accompanied him on horseback as far as San Bois, about fifteen miles on the route.

On her return, she had stopped at the home of a farmer whose wife was a friend of Belle's.

Late next afternoon, Pearl Younger was frightened to see Belle's horse run into the yard, saddled, but without Belle. A few minutes later, Milo Hoyt, a neighbor, had come upon Belle's body lying face down in the mud of the road. She had been shot in the back with buckshot.

Friends wired Jim Starr in Fort Smith from Eufaula. The Fort Smith *Elevator* sent out the following story:

Fort Smith, Arkansas. Feb. 4.—A telegram was received in this city today by James Starr, the husband of the famous Belle Starr, announcing that she had been shot dead at Eufaula. No particulars were given and nothing to show who did the deed. . . .

James Starr was in the city yesterday when the telegram announcing her death was received. He is a tall, well-formed Indian, with long hair falling down over his shoulders. There was bad blood in his eye when he heard the news, and without delay he saddled his horse, provided himself with a quart of whiskey, struck out on a run for home, saying somebody was going to suffer.

The burial service for Belle was held on the Wednesday afternoon following the Sunday she was murdered. The day was clear; a bright sun made the air on the hilltop warm for February and almost like spring.

Women of the neighborhood had washed the body, anointed it with turpentine and oil of cinnamon and had dressed it in a black silk dress with a white waist and frilled collar. A carpenter in Briartown had fashioned a square coffin of finished pine boards. Some of the Starr brothers had taken turns digging a grave in the hard clay and rocky soil, about fifteen feet in front of the cabin. They had laid the body into the casket, with one of Belle's crossed hands clasping her favorite six-shooter, and had set the lid loosely. Only the members of the immediate family were seated around the remains in the living room of the house. The visitors gathered in the yard in silent rows, waiting for the burial ceremony to begin. Some had come out of curiosity, but most of them were

Belle's Death

Belle's friends—outlaws enjoying immunity of the Indian police and deputy sheriffs who lived in the vicinity, the men and women of the numerous Starr clan, white squatters, simple Cherokees, Choctaws and Creeks.

There was no religious service, either of the white man's or of the Indians' kind, no hymns, no ululations, no chanting of Cherokee dirges. Suddenly the Indian pallbearers, each heavily armed, came through the doorway bearing the coffin. They strode rapidly to a place beside the grave, set the coffin on the ground, removed the lid and withdrew behind the grave, where they stood watching those who passed in review.

Each Cherokee, as he or she passed by for a last look at Belle, placed a small piece of cornbread inside the coffin in compliance with an ancient tribal ritual for the dead.

The lid was nailed on and the coffin was lowered quickly into the grave. Most of the spectators departed from the rough hillside before the shovelers had finished their task. While they were patting the sod into a smooth mound, those whose backs were already turned in departure were suddenly startled to hear a loud shout, "Throw up your hands!"

They turned to see Jim Starr stand in front of Edgar Watson and his wife, with his Winchester pointed at Watson. Some women down the road screamed. They were in terror that a shooting was about to begin. But the Watsons remained calm. Watson held up his hands, said quietly that he was unarmed, and asked Starr (or July) what was the matter. Starr said, ''You are my prisoner. You murdered Mrs. Starr.''

Watson replied that he knew nothing about the murder. He said, ''If you kill me, you will kill the wrong man.''

Then he turned to ask some of the men near-by to stay with him and go with them to Fort Smith, adding that he was afraid he would be killed if he were left alone with Starr. They consented. Mrs. Watson joined some neighbors and went home. Watson permitted his hands to be secured by thongs; Starr had no handcuffs.

The small cavalcade, including Pearl and Ed, departed almost immediately for Fort Smith, traveling all night. They rested most of the next day at a farmhouse where they could procure meals, and then rode most of the night again, arriving at the marshal's office in Fort Smith early in the morning. Although Starr had already arrested Watson without the formality of a warrant, he swore out a charge against Watson, who was lodged in a cell.

A reporter for the Van Buren *Press* obtained statements from both Starr and Watson, which were published on February 16, 1889. Starr said:

Morton Harvey

STATUE OF BELLE STARR IN PONCA CITY, OKLAHOMA

BELLE STARR'S TOMBSTONE

Belle's Death

On last Saturday evening I started on horseback for this place, and Belle accompanied me about 15 miles to San Bois, where we stayed all night, and I left her the next morning. I came on to Fort Smith, and the next day I received a telegram stating that my wife had been shot. I mounted my horse and set out at once, and arrived at Younger's Bend in about nine hours. The distance is 75 miles. There I learned the following particulars:

Belle had remained in San Bois until the afternoon, and then started home. On the way she stopped at a house, where lived a man named Rowe, and there she met one E. A. Watson, a white man with whom she had a quarrel some time ago. Watson had that day made threats against her, and soon after she arrived at Rowe's, he, Watson left. About a half an hour by sun, as she was passing Milo Hoyt's farm she was shot from behind from the bush, three buckshot pierced her back, and she fell from her horse in the mud. The assassin then jumped over the fence and fired a second time at her as she lay in the road, this time with small shot, the load going into the left side of her face and arm. This was about one mile and a quarter from Younger's Bend. A woman living in a house at the end of a field heard the shots and saw the smoke. Shortly afterwards Milo Hoyt came along and saw her lying in the road. He was afraid to go to her and at once rode to Younger's Bend and told Pearl that he had seen her mother lying in the road. She got up behind him on his horse, and thus rode to the scene. She found her mother still alive and able to speak. What she told her, I am not ready to make public, but when I arrived she was dead, and I knew enough to satisfy me that Watson was the murderer. We buried Belle at Younger's Bend, and I went after Watson and got him. He tried to run, but showed no fight, or I would have killed him. He gave me no trouble, and he is now safely in jail. There is no doubt he is guilty.

The *Times* reporter visited the accused in jail and wrote that he found Watson to be "the very opposite of a man who would be supposed to commit such a murder"; that he "was of medium height, fair complexion, light sunburnt whiskers and blue eyes—he was decidedly good-looking and talked well."

Watson's statement as reported was:

I know nothing about the murder, and will have no trouble establishing my innocence. I knew very little of Belle Starr, though she for some reason, I know not what, has been prejudiced against me, and did not speak to me. I have lived near her about a year, and I made a crop in the Choctaw Nation last year. I am 32 years old, and have a wife who was living with me. I came to Franklin county, Arkansas two years ago from Florida, and from there moved about a year ago to where I now live, and I have never had any trouble there with anyone. I was at a man's named Rowe Sunday, when Belle Starr came along and stopped, and soon afterwards my wife came by and I left and went home with her and Belle Starr was shot by someone soon afterwards. I have no idea who killed her, but know that I did not, and had no reason to even feel hard toward her.

Watson was held in jail until the last week of April, when testimony was taken before Commissioner Brizzolara. The case against Watson was exceedingly weak, only Jim Starr seeming anxious to secure an indictment of murder. Belle's son, Ed Reed, refused to testify against Watson, saying he knew nothing against the man; and neighbors of the Watsons testified that the accused was a quiet, hard-working man of refinement and education, well liked, and never before in trouble of any kind. Starr (or July) asked for time to bring in more witnesses, and the Commissioner reserved decision for a week. When the case came up for hearing again in the first week of March, Starr had failed to procure any more damaging testimony than he had before, and Brizzolara released Watson, holding that the evidence was insufficient to bind the defendant over to the grand jury.

Some of the legends have it that it was Belle's custom to worm information out of her associates to use as a form of blackmail—which is very likely true; that Belle had been attracted by Mrs. Watson's culture and gentleness and the two had become fast friends; and that Belle had finally extracted the information that the couple had sought sanctuary in the Indian country to escape arrest for a murder Watson had committed. Then Watson had sought to lease a portion of Belle's lands but she had conceived a dislike for him and had leased the land to someone else. For this reason, Watson had killed her. Although many writers who have accepted the legend say there was no doubt that Watson was guilty, there seems to be every doubt. Not only was the evidence that was presented in Fort Smith considered insufficient to bind Watson to a hearing before the grand jury, but the motive for the murder seems trivial and absurd.

Harman, who says, "Suspicion could point to none other than Watson," and who tells the story of Watson and Belle as though it were such an open-and-shut case that it was a miscarriage of justice that Watson did not swing for the murder, nevertheless admits that there was another theory about the murder— an admission which most of the later writers who derive their stuff from Harman do not make. Harman puts it this way:

There were some who had another theory for the killing and who, for a time, believed that Belle Starr's assassin was none other than her son, Ed Reed, who was then nearing his eighteenth birthday. The grounds on which this theory was based were as follows:

Belle had a fine black horse which she prized very highly. Shortly before the killing Ed had asked permission to ride the horse to a dance several miles away. His request was denied and he stole the animal from its stable after dark and did not return until just before daybreak the next morning. Belle awoke at his return and on rising she went to the stable and discovered that her favorite had been badly mistreated and ill cared for. She grasped her quirt and stalked to the house and into the room where Ed lay in bed asleep, and gave him an unmerciful whipping. His punishment greatly angered the boy, and he left home and was not seen for two weeks; it was said that he threatened his mother's life in return for the chastisement, and there was talk of his arrest and trial by an Indian court, but the matter finally quieted and he was not arrested.

That, however, is the theory which R. P. Vann and many old settlers from Porum to Wilburton accepted. To me it is the more reasonable one, especially when we consider the fact that among the people in the Belle Starr country it is commonly accepted belief that there were incestuous relations between Belle and her son and that she complicated this with extreme sadism. The story of her whipping Ed because he used her horse is only an apocryphal allusion to her dark sins. They also say, with a perceptible lowering of the tone of their voices, that Ed hated his mother's domination and yet was jealous of Jim July.

That, at least, is a credible motive for Belle's murder, whereas the motive attributed to Watson is not.

Belle was, whatever her crimes and misdemeanors, a personality and a sort of freak of energy in her time; and, from being a woman known locally only as horse thief and harborer of criminals, her eccentricity of conduct, when women were meekly under the tyranny of men, has immortalized her in the folk legend of the Southwest. The fabulous stories of her intransigent wild spirit remain part of the romantic heritage of the humble, humdrum and unexciting lives of the people throughout the region with which her name is associated.

Belle Starr

Not long after Belle's death, her daughter Pearl caused to be erected over the grave a tomb from slabs of native stone. The headstone was carved by a local stonecutter named Joseph Dailey. At the top was an image of Belle's favorite horse, ''Venus,'' with a B-S brand on its shoulder; a star was above to the right, and below, to the left, was a bell. At the bottom was a clasped hand filled with flowers, and on the stone was this inscription:

BELLE STARR

Born In Carthage Mo. Feb. 5, 1848
Died Feb. 3, 1889
"Shed not for her the bitter tear,
Nor give the heart to vain regret;
'Tis but the casket that lies here,
The gem that filled it sparkles yet."

The work of ghouls had already begun within a year after Belle's death, as this dispatch to the Dallas *News* in 1890 testifies:

Talequah, I.T. March 20.—From Dr. H. Lindsley, who has just returned from Canadian district, we learn that the grave of Belle Starr, the noted female outlaw, who was assassinated in that country a short time ago, was robbed a few nights ago. It is supposed to have been done to obtain a very fine pistol that was once the property of Cole Younger, which was buried with her. All her jewelry was buried with her also. The fact has created considerable excitement in the neighborhood. No clew as to the perpetrators.

Belle's Death

It will be recalled that when Jim Starr went in to Fort Smith, just before Belle was murdered, it was to answer a charge of larceny. When he received the telegram announcing Belle's death, he asked for a continuance that he might go home to attend the funeral, and got it.

Although he returned to Fort Smith with Edgar Watson in an attempt to pin the charge of murdering Belle on Watson, he did not reappear in Fort Smith at the appointed time of his trial on the date that had been set when he got the continuance. And he was out on bail supplied by a local bondsman. The bondsman offered a reward of $150 for his arrest.

On January 23, 1890, Deputy Marshal Heck Thomas brought Jim into Fort Smith, badly wounded. He had been shot by Deputy Marshals Bud Trainor and Bob Hutchins near Ardmore, while trying to escape from their attempts to arrest him. He died in jail four days after he was brought in, and was buried in the potter's field on January 27, 1890.

Thus the curtain rings down on Belle and the last of her lovers. Her apotheosis was to begin with the publication of *Bella Starr, the Bandit Queen, or the Female Jesse James,* by an anonymous writer for the Richard K. Fox Publications in New York City, in a little paper-bound, twenty-five-cent book, that was published within a few months after Belle's death.

Belle Starr

She was to pass into American folklore and legend as one of the superwomen of our history—"Of all women of the Cleopatra type, since the days of the Egyptian queen herself, the universe has produced none more remarkable than Bella Starr, the Bandit Queen . . . more relentless than Pharaoh's daughter, and braver than Joan of Arc."

APPENDIX

———◆———

ONE

BAD MEN AND MARSHALS

There is one Bunyanism of the cattle country which American fictionists, however devoted to veracity they may be in other respects, will not let die. That is the Bunyanism of pistol shooting. And I refer, of course, not to straight-arm shooting with aim carefully taken, but to shooting from the hip or holster—the quick-as-lightning marksmanship without taking sight.

The tallest tale of the sort I have ever read or heard occurs in Miss Edna Ferber's novel, *Cimarron*.

In *Cimarron* Miss Ferber's hero is walking down the street in the new boom town of Osage with his wife in the old Sooner days of the Oklahoma land rush. She has already established her hero as a formidable and courageous fellow and as a man who is pretty handy with a gun. As the couple pass the Red Dog saloon a group of loafers is lounging on the porch. There is some conversation between the hero and his wife which would carry them, I should say, at least one hundred and fifty feet beyond the group. Somebody on the porch fires a pistol shot, knocking the hero's hat off.

The clearing between the top of his head and the crown of the Stetson hat is so small that, at that distance, the ruffian was taking a chance on murder in playing his little joke. Yet we may allow the plausibility of this marksmanship.

But our hero, perfectly nonchalant, takes a fine handkerchief out of his hip pocket (an action which sends members of the group scurrying), picks up his hat, dusts it off with his handkerchief, tosses the handkerchief to the ground and, with an action so quick that the wife could not follow it, whips out his gun, fires from the hip and cuts his own *sheep brand* into the ruffian's ear just as he is ducking into the saloon door!

Such a feat of marksmanship with a pistol could not be accomplished at that distance from an arm-rest, even if the victim had elephant's ears.

The movies and the pulp-paper Western thrillers are full of the sort of shooting that Miss Ferber gets into her book, but in the movies it is a trick of the camera and in the pulp-paper thrillers it is usually done by writers who wouldn't know a .32 from a .45.

Pistol shooting from the hip or from any position without aiming is like artillery firing: the range-finding and the determination of the gun elevation are done on the same mathematical principles, except that in pistol shooting from the hip the calculations must be made instantaneously and instinctively, and that is very hard to do.

Even when the distance is known and the target is stationary, and, by trial and error, the proper elevation of the gun is arrived at with some accuracy, it is very hard to hit, say, a tomato can at fifty feet. The kick-up of the gun must be taken into account, and other factors enter into making loose-arm shooting an exceedingly difficult sort of thing to do with precision.

From Marquis James, author of the Pulitzer Prize biography of Andrew Jackson, I learn that Bill Foster, an old-time peace officer and killer of killers now living on a farm near Stillwater, Oklahoma, knows of an instance where a bandit ''fanned the hammer'' and shot six bullets into a wall, all of them hitting a shot no bigger than a dollar, after a chair had been hurled at him to knock the pistol out of his hand. That is powerful shooting and it is the best Bill ever heard of. But the space covered was about twenty feet. And, moreover, the bandit did not hit the man he was aiming at.

At various times I have talked to old-time peace officers down in Oklahoma—tough men and good shots. I never heard any of them brag about their ability to shoot from the hip. When I would relate some incident of deadly precision somewhat like the incident in Miss Ferber's novel they would say, ''I've heerd uv sech shootin' but I ain't never seen none.''

A factitious glamor adheres to the bad men and marshals of the old West and Southwest—a glamor that is usually dispelled upon a close examination of the facts.

William MacLeod Raine in his *Guns of the Frontier,* which quite effectively debunks many of the legends about the bravery and the gun-shooting prowess of Western gun fighters, records only one authentic instance of a gun fighter who kept a record of his killings by filing a notch for each one on the handle of his revolver.

Not only would a man have to be short of memory not to recall how many men he had killed; but it is a known fact that whenever a hold-up man or murderer was brought to justice, he contended that he hadn't been near the place where the shooting was done. Knowing that he was liable to arrest almost any time, even the braggingest train-and-bank robber wouldn't be so stupid as to carry a record of his killings.

Needless to say, the stories of killings are greatly exaggerated.

Raine says that one old chronicler claims that Bat Masterson killed thirty-seven desperadoes in Dodge City alone while Bat was peace officer there; but the total number of deaths for which Bat was responsible is probably not more than five.

''Wild Bill'' Hickok, indeed, largely became a bad

man in order to live up to the reputation given him by
Colonel George W. Nichols, in an article which appeared in *Harper's* in 1867, that pictured Hickok as a
prodigious slayer and boaster of slayings. The article
quoted Hickok as saying that, in one fight, at Wilma
Creek, he killed fifty men single-handed with *fifty*
cartridges!

The truth is that Wild Bill was a cold-blooded murderer, and a coward to boot, who, even when he was a
peace officer, would shoot on suspicion without giving
his victims a chance at a fair fight. Of the two men
killed while Wild Bill was marshal at Abilene, Kansas,
one of them was his own assistant marshal, Mike Williams. Mike came running around a corner to Hickok's
assistance after a gun duel between Wild Bill and
Phil Coe, a gambler—a duel in which Coe was killed
before he had a chance to draw. Hickok whirled in his
fright and shot Williams dead without looking to see
who Williams was.

When the Daltons Rode, by Emmett Dalton, written
in collaboration with Jack Jungmeyer, provides further evidence of the tendency to exaggerate the gunmen's lethal powers.

Emmett Dalton was the only survivor of the famous
Dalton raid on the First National Bank of Coffeyville,
Kansas, October 5, 1892, in which eight men died and
four were wounded.

Of the eight who were killed there were Bob and Grat Dalton, Dick Broadwell and Bill Powers of the outlaw band; and the citizens, George Cubine, Charles Brown, Lucino M. Baldwin and City Marshal Charles T. Connelly.

Emmett says that, although more than one hundred shots were fired during the ten minutes of this famous street battle, not a single unarmed man was either killed or wounded; and that even then, the carnage was unusually great for affairs of this kind. Nearly everybody in town took part in the fracas. Emmett, or his collaborator, writes:

Personally I have met hundreds of bad men, hard men, shooting men, killers, both peace officer and outlaw. And I have yet to see the first notch on any of their six-shooters. I have, however, seen fake bad men ostentatiously file dummy notches.

Men who killed other men, I observed, did not boast of it. They did not advertise their prowess, aggressive or defensive, by cutting a notch on a gun. It is a fiction writer's elaboration.

Never did I see a man "fan" his six-shooter.

Never did I see any shooting from the hip.

Never did I see a man waste precious ammunition by using two guns simultaneously. Bob Dalton was accounted one of the best shots in the Southwest, with rifle, pistol or shotgun. Never once did he indulge any of the phony stunts attributed to so many "master" gunmen of the old border.

Most of these myths emanated from "professional Westerners." They were the fruits of so-called Wild West showmanship and ballyhoo, devised to play up to an already established fiction.

Indeed the six-shooter's deadliness has always been overrated. The number of shots fired, and the net results, in numerous historic frays with this weapon, make an almost ludicrous contrast. How often, in accurate accounts of the "carnage," does one come across the phrase, alibiing the short gun, "It was a miracle that so few were killed!"

Take some of the notorious killers. Read the extravagant death list claimed for them. Note how the narrators, after enumerating a few actual verifiable killings, fall back on ambiguous hearsay or surmise. As if the caliber of these notables depended upon the actual number of men they slew.

Many old-timers have a way of romancing about the things they saw or heard tell—like old soldiers' accounts of battles; the instinct for drama creeping in to embellish the bare and sometimes prosy fact.

I recollect one time in New Orleans when a venerable judge, undoubtedly accounted the personification of honesty among his friends, told me some very entertaining and luridly circumstantial tales of his encounters with Bob and Emmett Dalton in 1866. I was born in 1871. He didn't know he was talking to the very man he boasted of knowing. I didn't disillusion him. But I had never before seen or heard of him. He represents a type of fabricator whose "recollections" have colored much of Western lore.

If all the men who claimed to have known the Jameses and the Youngers and other outlaw notables, the Daltons included, were placed end to end they would reach well out toward the moon.

Not infrequently the circumstance of a noted outlaw's death has given him a sort of martyr's accolade. And this brings us another phase of popular reaction toward men of violence.

Witness the case of Jesse James, killed by Bob Ford's shot in the back of the head as he stood unarmed and unsuspecting. For this act Ford came to be more universally hated than even the lethal James. Perhaps Ford thought he would be acclaimed for his dangerous and almost miraculously successful venture. He was ridding the country of a "terror." But immediately, by that strange public revulsion, the terror became the martyr. And Ford became a reviled "assassin." If scores of folk sang the familiar ballad, "Jesse James went to rest with his hand on his breast: the devil will be on his knee," thousands chanted the lines about "the dirty little coward that killed Mr. Howard" (Jesse James's assumed name). Bitter must have been this strange tide of public opinion to Ford until he himself was laid away in a shroud of powder smoke.

"Big Bill" Tilghman, one of the finest and bravest of the old-time peace officers of Kansas and Oklahoma, was fired at, point blank, more than a hundred times at fairly close range by some of the most famous pistol-shots among the desperadoes of the period, and yet "Big Bill" was hurt by pistol fire only once in his entire fifty years of law enforcement, until he was shot to death by Wiley Lynn, a drunken Federal prohibition enforcement agent, when Big Bill was in his seventies, and a peace officer in the notorious oil boom town of Cromwell, Oklahoma.

According to E. A. Macdonald in *Hands Up!*, "Big

Bill'' told Fred Sutton something about pistol-shooting.

Never try to run a bluff with a six-gun. Many a man has been buried with his boots on because he foolishly tried to scare someone by reaching for his hardware. Always remember that a six-shooter is made to kill the other fellow with and for no other reason on earth. So always have your gun loaded and ready, and never reach for it unless you are in dead earnest and intend to kill the other fellow.

A lot of inexperienced fellows try to aim a six-shooter by sighting along the barrel, and they try to shoot the other man in the head. Never do that. If you have to stop a man with a gun, grab the stock of your six-shooter with a death grip that won't let it wobble, and try to hit him just where his belt buckle would be. That's the broadest target from head to heel.

If you point at something, you don't raise your finger to a level of the eye and sight along it; you simply point, by instinct, and your finger will always point straight. So you must learn to point the barrel of your six-shooter by instinct. If you haven't that direction-instinct born in you, you will never become an expert with the six-gun.

Fred Sutton died in Kansas City, Missouri, in September, 1937. He had been, in turn, cowpuncher, peace officer, Oklahoma homesteader, agent for Budweiser beer, oil promoter, banker (establishing the First State Bank of Oklahoma City) and later feature writer for the *Saturday Evening Post* and for many newspapers, as well as historian of the West in *Hands Up!*

As a historian, however, either he or his collaborator, tended to the ''tall'' tale; and he, probably as much as anyone else, was responsible for many of the fantastic stories of gun-play and Western heroics. In fact, *Hands Up!* is the source of Miss Ferber's strange fiction about how good at pistol shooting her hero of *Cimarron* was. Sutton and Macdonald didn't blush to write this, which, obviously, Miss Ferber accepted as the truth:

He (Ben Thompson) was elected marshal of Austin, Texas, and was a good one. While he was marshal a dude from the East, wearing a high silk hat, was walking down the street when a cowboy from San Saba County drew his six-shooter and drilled a bullet through the hat and sent it spinning. Thompson, hearing of it, borrowed a silk hat, hunted out the man from San Saba, struck a pose before him and invited him:

''Here, you're so good at shooting people's hats, shoot this one.''

The fellow drew his gun and dodged behind a post and tried to shoot at Ben from there, but, for some reason, could not get his gun to work. All that Ben could see of him was a little of one side of his face and the whole of one of his ears.

''I'll mark you, anyhow,'' said Ben, and he fired, putting a bullet hole through the man's ear as round and neat as if it had been punched out with a machine.

Ben Thompson has been generally acclaimed one of the best deadshots of the old-time gunmen; and it is said of him that the reason he was accurate in fire was that he was so cold and deliberate in aim, never getting flustered even while guns were popping all about him and always (or nearly always) holding his fire until he had such perfect aim that he couldn't miss.

But even Ben once got into a fight in a saloon where he had everything to his advantage. He was on a balcony, shooting down with an automatic Winchester rifle at his opponent. And yet he didn't hit anything except the glassware and furniture.

Ben's first demonstration of his marksmanship was when he was about eighteen years old. He persuaded a neighbor boy to squat down with his back bared while Ben stood off at about a hundred yards and emptied a shotgun filled with mustard shot at the kid's back to show what a good shot he was. He nearly killed the child, but not quite. He was found guilty of assault with a deadly weapon by the jury, but Governor Runnels of Kansas pardoned him.

With the downfall of the Southern Confederacy [writes William MacLeod Raine in *Guns of the Frontier*], Thompson slipped across the line and joined the forces of Maximilian, Archduke of Austria, who was trying to maintain himself as Emperor of Mexico against the will of the people. He served with General Mejia, and was at Queretaro when Maximilian made his last stand against Escobedo. Betrayed by Lopez, the Austrian was captured May 14, 1867. Along with Mejia and another general, Maximilian was executed a month later. Thompson had escaped and was safe with the forces of Marshal Bazaine, who was retiring from the country on orders from Napoleon III.

Belle Starr

His days of warfare over, Thompson spent the rest of his life as a professional gambler, except during the time when he was marshal of the city of Austin. The trail-end town of Abilene was just rising into its hectic hour of fame. With an army companion, Phil Coe, Ben started the Bull's Head gambling-house and saloon. It became the favorite resort of the Texans who came up the Chisholm Trail with the long-horn herds. Wild Bill Hickok was town marshal. It was his business to control the gamblers and the cowboys. The claim of those opposed to him was that he had an understanding with some of the houses by which tribute was paid him for protection. The Bull's Head was not one of those favored, and its owners were unfriendly to Hickok as he was to them.

The distinction between gunmen and marshals was frequently very fine indeed. Some were marshals one month and bandits the next, or vice versa.

TWO

THE JENNINGS GANG:

COMIC RELIEF

The career of Al and Frank Jennings and their gang is probably the shortest and funniest on record.

It lasted exactly one hundred and nine days—from August 18, 1897 to December 5, 1897.

It consisted of: (1) two attempts to hold up a passenger train, in each instance of which Al and Frank and the three other members of their gang got scared and ran away after the train had pulled to a stop; (2) an attempt to hold up a train by piling some cross-ties on the railroad track; the engineer speeded up when he saw the obstruction and knocked the ties off the track with the cowcatcher; (3) one actual train hold-up which netted the five of them $60 apiece and one good silver watch which they took away from the conductor.

They nearly starved to death during their hundred and nine days of banditry.

Four of the gang, including Al and Frank, were arrested by Deputy U. S. Marshal Bud Ledbetter, single-handed.

Frank served five years in the pen. His civil rights were restored, finally, and he returned to the quiet and useful pursuits of a decent citizen.

Al served five years. His civil rights were restored in 1907. He returned to the practice of law in Oklahoma. When people had about forgotten the meager details of his short and simple annals as a bandit, he wrote, with the aid of a ''ghost,'' a fantastically lurid story of his banditry and reform for the *Saturday Evening Post*. On the strength of that account and of the publicity given him in the yellow journals, he sought the Democratic nomination for the governorship of Oklahoma, but he was defeated—to put it mildly. Oklahomans have commonly preferred, in the matter of governors, bandits who have *not* reformed. Al took up lecturing and evangelism; he was held up in Brooklyn one night by a petty stick-up man and relieved of a dollar and a half in change. When last heard of, he was living a retired and peaceful life in Southern California.

The Jennings boys were brought up in Tecumseh, Oklahoma, then the county seat of Pottawatomie County. Their father, J. D. F. Jennings, practiced law there and served two terms as county judge, 1896-1898 and 1898-1900. The boys were trained enough in law in their father's office to pass their bar examinations, but only Ed, the eldest, seemed to have the stuff in him to succeed.

Ed hung out his shingle in Enid; Frank and Al loafed around Enid. Frank dealt cards in a gambling house for a living; Al just loafed. Ed, while arguing in court one day, in a dispute between two cowmen over pasture rent, had as his opponent Temple Houston.

Houston was a handsome, brilliant but eccentric grandson of General Sam ("Old Fuss and Feathers") Houston, father of the Texas Republic. Temple's mother and grandmother were full-blooded Cherokee Indians. Old-timers in Oklahoma say that Temple Houston was the most eloquent orator Oklahoma ever produced. He wore his blue-black hair to his shoulders, dressed in cowboy boots and white jeans, with cartridge belt and holstered pistols, but wore a black Prince Albert coat, a black broad-brimmed Stetson, a fancy vest and a tie made out of rattlesnake skin. He was also known as a deadshot, and so quick on the draw, that he once won a murder case for his client by demonstrating in court that an experienced man like himself could hand an inexperienced man like his client a pistol and draw and shoot before the inexperienced man could pull the trigger. He drew his gun so quickly and fired six shots in such rapid succession that he scared the daylights out of judge and jury.

When they got up off the floor and from behind desks, he explained that the cartridges were blanks.

In the argument with Ed Jennings in court over the pasture rent, the two lawyers got so worked up that one of them called the other a liar and then they tangled, until separated by court attendants.

That same night Houston went into the saloon where Frank Jennings was dealing poker for the house and Ed was sitting in at a game. Ed leaped to his feet and started to draw. Houston drew, fired one shot and killed him before Frank's gun was out of the holster. Houston was charged with murder but was acquitted on a plea of self-defense when competent witnesses testified that Ed had gone for his gun first.

Al and Frank, no doubt, had been reading too many dime novels about Jesse James, and reading them with incredible self-identification. Al had been palling around with a sawed-off, illiterate little moron named Richard West, alias "Little Dick," a survivor or cast-off of the Doolin gang. The night after Houston's acquittal, Frank and Al got drunk and started boasting around town about how they were going to kill Houston in revenge. When they woke up next morning with hangovers and recalled their boasts, they remembered, also, what a quick deadshot Houston was, and decided it was about time they left town. No use cluttering up the local graveyard with Jenningses.

They took Little Dick along and went down to their

father's place at Tecumseh. They hadn't any money. After mooching on Judge Jennings for a week or so, the judge let it be firmly known that he'd be damned if he was going to support three lazy, good-for-nothing loafers, one of them not even an in-law.

Plenty of farmers would have given the rummies jobs, but Al and Frank were temperamentally averse to doing any work. So they let Little Dick talk them, and a couple of Tecumseh plow-pushers, into the idea of being heroic bandits and holding up a train.

They knew just what to do; they had read it dozens of times in dime novels. First, you get yourself a piece of calico, cut two eye-holes in it, and you have a mask. Then you get yourself a cartridge belt and two pistols, not just one. Then you look up evening express passenger train schedules and figure out a local (not an express) stop. Then you sneak up on the night dispatcher at this local stop depot, and, just when the express is whistling for the nearest grade crossing, make the dispatcher go out on the track with a lantern and signal the train to halt. Then, with someone to hold the horses and keep the dispatcher under guard, you make the engineer and fireman climb down out of their cabs, line them up with the conductor at the point of a gun, then go ahead with your robbery. You overpower the express messenger and the railway mail clerk and take your swag out of mail pouches and the express company's money box. Next, you go through the coaches, demanding that the passengers stick up their hands while you go down the aisles and take what cash and jewelry each has on his or her person. Finally, you leap on your horses, fire a lot of shots into the air and ride away into the night.

It is all as easy as that—if you can do it.

Things went strictly according to plan for the "Jennings Gang" at the little local stop of Edmond, Oklahoma, sixteen miles north of Oklahoma City, about nine o'clock on the evening of August 18, 1897.

That is, all went according to plan until the conductor, a veteran in the service, about sixty-five years old, leaped off the train holding a lantern aloft so he could see, and came running toward the dispatcher demanding to know what the hell was the matter.

The bold bad bandits didn't even wait to hear the dispatcher's erroneous answer that it was a train robbery; they ran like jack rabbits, leaped on their horses and flew like bats out of hell. But they were as good as in the calaboose right then, for Edmond is only forty-five miles from Tecumseh. The dispatcher knew the Jennings boys; he'd have known them, by their voices, even if they had been dressed in a Ku Klux Klan fool's cap and nightshirt.

So the Jenningses were marked as bandits even if they hadn't earned the label.

Two weeks later, at eleven o'clock at night, they piled ties on the M. K. & T. tracks at Bond Switch, south of Muskogee, in the manner, and with the results, described above.

Next, they were going to hold up the Santa Fé express train when it pulled in at Purcell; but they saw a night watchman and heard a noise, so they galloped away again.

Night seemed to make them nervous. So they decided to try out their dime-novel technique in the daytime and see how it would work.

At eleven o'clock in the morning, October 1, 1897, the five of them rode up to a section gang on the Rock Island Railroad, eight miles north of Chickasha, and got the workers to flag the passenger train while they hid in the bushes alongside the tracks.

They actually held this train up, by golly! They ordered the passengers outside, made them stand with their backs to the coaches, pointed guns at the people and went down the line collecting contributions from all—netting about $300 and Conductor Dacy's watch. Then Al and Frank entered the mail and express car.

When the express-car messenger told them he didn't have a key for either of the two safes—a small and a large one—because both were safes billed straight through to Fort Worth, and showed the bandits all the keys he had, they were prepared for this emergency.

For emergencies of that kind you should always bring along some sticks of dynamite and a fuse.

But they didn't know how many sticks of dynamite you shot off to crack a safe. So they used all they had, putting the sticks on top of the big safe and then putting the little safe on top of the dynamite. Then they leaped out of the car, running the fuse outside, lighted the fuse, ran back and stuck their fingers in their ears.

The explosion blew out the whole side of the mail and express car and catapulted the small safe out into a grade ditch. But the explosion didn't crack, or even dent, either one of the safes. And that was all the dynamite the bandits had. The explosion, however, had dislodged Al Jennings' mask, and Conductor Dacy had recognized him. Trainmen knew Little Dick from the "Wanted-Reward-for-Robbery" notices stuck up in post offices, railroad stations and sheriffs' headquarters.

Marshal Ledbetter gave out the news that he was heading a posse to bring the bandits in "dead or alive." But he had no intention of wasting his time and the people's money like that. He just waited around until he knew the scared monkeys would be about starved to death, meanwhile keeping himself informed as to their movements. Then one day he rode out and got them, without firing a shot or drawing his pistol.

He had heard they were heading south from Muskogee in a wagon. He rode down to Rock Creek crossing, felled a tree across the road, and when the team halted there, he stepped out from behind some brush and told the boys they were under arrest. They didn't doubt it for a minute. They would have considered themselves under arrest if they had been confronted by a boy with a cap pistol. Bud took their guns and stacked them in the back of the wagon, sat down by them, and directed the one who was driving to turn around and go back to Muskogee, where he wanted to collect ten dollars. He had bet his deputies twenty to ten that he could capture *that* craven outfit single-handed, without firing a shot.

That was the end of the "Notorious Jennings Brothers' Gang." A lot of sensational stuff had been cooked up in the newspapers about "daring daylight train robberies" and "terrific battles in barricaded houses with peace officers and possemen" in which the Jennings gang was alleged to have participated heroically, until, I have no doubt, Al began to believe the junk himself by the time he got out of the penitentiary—otherwise he wouldn't have strutted around as a reformed killer and robber. Even nowadays I hear men, whose memories go vaguely back to the turn of the century, speak of the Jennings brothers as though they were cold-blooded murderers like those dementia-praecox victims, Frank and Jesse James.

Neither Al nor Frank Jennings ever shot anybody in his life. In fact, if either of them ever knew how to shoot a pistol, the fact wasn't demonstrated during their "bandit" career. There is no record of their having fired a shot. The true record is three attempted hold-ups, one burlesque train robbery, sixty bucks cash apiece and four and a half years in jail each, all for four and a half months' outlawry!

THREE

CHRONOLOGY AND NECROLOGY

1837 William Clarke Quantrill, alias Charley Quantrell, born Canal Dover, Ohio.

1838 Preston Shirley, Belle Starr's brother, born on farm
(?) near Carthage, Mo., or on a farm near Shirley, Mo. Did not participate in Civil War; emigrated to Texas in 1861.

1840 Bud Shirley, brother of Belle Starr, born on farm near
(?) Carthage, Mo., or on a farm near Shirley, Mo.

1843 Alexander Franklin (Frank) James, born Clay County, Mo., Jan. 10. Died a natural death on the "James Farm," Clay County, Mo., Feb. 18, 1915.

1844 Thomas Coleman (Cole) Younger, born Jackson County, Mo., January 15, son of Henry C. Younger, for a time County Judge and later member of State Legislature. Henry C. Younger murdered by Federal soldiers 1863.

1847 Jesse Woodson James, born Clay County, Mo., Sept. 5. Shot to death on April 3, 1882 by Bob Ford, in a house at 1381 Lafayette Street, St. Joseph, Mo., where he lived with his wife and two children.

1848 Belle Starr (née Myra Belle Shirley) born in or near Carthage, Mo., or on a farm near Shirley, Mo., Feb. 5,

1848; murdered Feb. 3, 1889 in the Cherokee Nation, Indian Territory.

1857 William Clarke Quantrill emigrates to Kansas, where he begins career as school-teacher, murderer, cattle thief, and hold-up man. Worked alone at first; later organized gang of cutthroats; and still later augmented his forces by enlisting Southern sympathizers to conduct guerrilla warfare against the North.

1863 Sacking of Lawrence, Kansas, Aug. 21, by Quantrill at the head of 450 guerrillas. Raiders murdered 182 men that day, burned and looted the town. Ostensible reason, given by Quantrill, was in retaliation for the burning of Osceola, Mo., by Gen. James H. Lane, U.S.A. Lane had burned stores and homes of Confederate sympathizers. Quantrill professed Southern sympathies but his raiders were a free-lance bunch of murderers and looters who did not hesitate to rob Southern sympathizers as well as Northerners. Cole, Bob and Jim Younger and Frank James were in this raid, but Jesse James, erroneously reported to be, was not.

1863 "Bud" Shirley, aged 22, Capt. James Petty, George Walker and eleven other Confederate bushwhackers attempted to capture six Federal militia in a home in Carthage Square, Carthage, Mo. Capt. Petty killed; others retreated; Walker wounded; no one else hurt.

1863 Carthage, Mo., Sept. 22, practically destroyed by guerrillas. Courthouse had already been burned and many records lost. Federal troops had constructed a fort out of the ruins; this was reduced to débris.

1863 Belle's brother, Edward or "Bud" Shirley, a bushwhacker, killed at Sarcoxie, Mo., by men of Co. C, Seventh Provisional Enrolled Militia.

Chronology and Necrology

1864 Centralia Massacre, September. "Bloody Bill" Anderson, with 84 guerrillas, among whom were Jesse James and Jim Younger, attacked a railroad train when it pulled in at the station in Centralia, Mo., and captured 84 Federal soldiers. The soldiers were lined up along the tracks and then Bloody Bill, Jim Younger and Jesse James walked along in front of them, shooting them down with revolvers at close range.

1864 Jesse James joins Quantrill's guerrillas.

1865 Quantrill shot in hayloft of farm near Louisville, Ky., in January by Capt. Ed. Terrill, head of a band of Union guerrillas, and Quantrill band was routed. Quantrill died of wounds later in February in Louisville hospital. Frank and Jesse James in Quantrill's guerrilla forces which disbanded after they were dispersed.

1865 John Younger, only 15 years old, tried for murder in Independence, Mo., acquitted on plea of self-defense.

1867 Belle's brother Preston Shirley killed at Spring Creek, Texas, by Joe Lynn. Cause of the fracas unknown.

1867 In the Dallas *Herald,* Sept. 21, 1867, appeared this advertisement: "Six yoke of oxen and a No. 1 wagon, may be had on reasonable terms, by applying to John Shirley, Scyene."

1867 In the issue of Oct. 5, 1867, the Dallas *Herald* asked editorially "Is Texas to be Africanized?" in vigorous protest against carpetbagger rule, which enfranchised the Negroes but disfranchised the whites—not only those who had served in the Confederate forces, but those who could be accused, falsely or otherwise, of having given aid and comfort to the Rebels during the War between the States.

1868 Cole, Jim and Bob Younger, according to Cole, went to Scyene, Dallas County, Texas, where their sister joined them and kept house for them. In 1870-71 Jim was Sheriff of Dallas City. "He and Bob sang in the church choir. At that time, Bob, who was only 17, fell in love with one of the young ladies of the village"— Cole Younger in a letter to Augustus C. Appler, editor, Osceola (Mo.), *Democrat,* undated.

1868 On April 19, the Dallas *Herald* reported that Dallas people assembled knee-deep in mud on Trinity bank to see the landing of the ''gob'' steamer from Trinidad Landing, Capt. I. H. McGarvey, commanding.

1868 Ku Klux Klan reported active during April and May in Dallas and adjacent counties.

1868 Frank James and Jesse James join their first cousins, the Younger brothers—Coleman, James, John and Bob —in forming a gang of robbers.

1868 Dallas third annual County Fair held in last week of October.

1869 Pearl Younger born to Myra Belle. (?)

1869 December. Cole Younger gets into duel with a Captain James White in Bastrop, Louisiana, because White ''circulated scandalous stories about the girl Bob was in love with,'' Cole shattering White's right arm with the first shot.

1866 The James-Younger gang invent bank robbery by holding up the Clay County Savings Association Bank, Liberty, Missouri, February 14, taking $15,000 in gold and $45,000 in non-negotiable U. S. bonds.

1869 Dec. 7, the James-Younger gang rob a bank at Gallatin, Davis Co., Mo. The cashier, Capt. John W. Sheets, counted out $1,000 and handed the money to Jesse James, who cold-bloodedly and without any excuse whatever shot Sheets dead and ran out of the bank.

1872 At 4 P.M. September 23, the treasurer of the Fair Grounds Association at Kansas City, Mo., reported he had been held up and robbed of $10,000 (the day's receipts) by three bandits who dashed up on horses and seized the tin box, containing the money, from a messenger boy who had been instructed to carry the money to a bank for deposit. This unlikely story of the Fair treasurer was accepted as another "bold robbery by the James-Younger gang"; but no other evidence than the Fair treasurer's say-so was forthcoming that there *was* a robbery by bandits.

1872 James H. (Jim) Reed of Vernon County, Mo., went to Texas, bought a piece of land in Bosque City. Sold out soon afterward and moved to Scyene, Dallas County. Seduced a girl giving her name as Rosa McCommas and took her to San Antonio. In San Marcos, he traded horses with a man named Woolfork and for $25 to boot threw in the girl, "Rosa," on the trade. Reed allegedly married to Myra Belle Shirley about this time; but my theory is that the "Rosa" was Myra Belle.

1873 May 21. Robbery of the Ste. Genevieve (Missouri) Savings Association Bank by five men believed to be the James-Younger band of outlaws. Loot: $4,000. No one hurt.

1873 Train robbery "invented" by Jesse James. First train robbery in the world, on July 21, when Frank and Jesse James, Cole and Jim Younger and three others held up the Chicago, Rock Island & Pacific passenger express near Adair, Iowa, getting $3,000 from the safe in the express car and several hundred dollars in cash and jewelry from the passengers.

1873 Henry Starr, son of George Starr who was a brother of Tom Starr, born Fort Gibson, I. T., December 2. Remotely kin to Belle Starr by marriage, he never met her. Killed Floyd Wilson, railroad detective, who was trying to arrest him for robbery, in 1893. Sentenced to hang April 2, 1895 by Judge Parker at Fort Smith. Sentence reversed; new trial; sent to penitentiary, Columbus, Ohio, for 15 years; pardoned by President Roosevelt. Entered real-estate business in Tulsa. Sentenced for bank robbery in Colorado Springs, Colorado; pardoned by Governor of Colorado. Severely wounded and captured while trying to hold up two banks the same day in Stroud, Oklahoma, on March 27, 1915, and sentenced to 25 years in the state penitentiary at McAlester, Oklahoma. Pardoned by Governor J. B. Robertson on March 15, 1919. Shot and killed in attempted bank robbery, Harrison, Arkansas, on February 18, 1921.

1874 John Younger killed in March near Monegaw Springs, St. Clair Co., Mo. by Captain Lull in duel with Pinkerton detectives.

1874 January 31, the Gadshill robbery in which Jim Reed, Belle Starr's husband is supposed to have participated as a member of the James-Younger gang. Robbery took place at Gadshill, a way-station in Wayne County, Southeastern Missouri, on the Iron Mountain Railroad. Loot: $2,000 from passengers; $1,000 from the express car safe, and $2,000 in cash in registered mail bag.

Chronology and Necrology

1874 On April 7, the San Antonio-Austin stage robbed two miles north of Blanco by three men. Ten passengers, besides driver Bill Anderson were: Bishop Gregg, President Brackenridge of the First National Bank of San Antonio, the Messrs. Waters, McLemore, Frazier, O'Neal, McDonald, Wells and Munroe and a Mrs. Lloyd. Took from passengers $2,500 and four gold watches. State award for capture, $3,000; U. S., $3,000 and Sam Scott, manager of stage, $1,000. Major Purnell, U. S. Marshal in Austin, accused Jim Reed (alias "Bill Jones," "Ross," "Wilder," etc.); Cal. H. Carter of Bates City, Mo. and Nelson Rogers (alias Jack); and named J. M. Dickson of Vernon City and his wife and Rosa McCommas as accessories to the robbery.

1874 M. P. Hunnicut, old citizen of Waco, Texas, on February 6, 1889, stated in special dispatch from Waco to the Fort Worth *Gazette* that he knew Belle Starr; that she was first married to Jim Reed who participated with the Younger brothers in the Gadshill robbery and that with his share of the boodle purchased a farm on Coon Creek, Bosque County, Texas. This is wrong because the Gadshill robbery took place in 1874 whereas Jim bought the Bosque County property in 1872.

1874 Jim Reed, Belle's "husband" shot and killed 15 miles northwest of Paris, Texas, by Deputy Sheriff John T. Morris of Collin City, Texas, on the evening of August 6th.

1874 D. W. Wilder shot and taken prisoner October 6 by Deputy Marshals W. H. Anderson and T. M. Wright on charge of Watt Grayson robbery. Caught at Coon Creek, Bosque County, Texas. With him was his mistress. This is undoubtedly the "J. H. Dickson" or

"Dickens" and wife named by Marshal Purnell on April 7th. They were caught on Reed's farm. Taken to Fort Smith. Wilder was tried and found guilty and hanged. Implicated Jim Reed and Dan Evans in the murder.

1874 John K. Fischer, noted outlaw who is alleged to have performed the marriage ceremony on horseback for Jim Reed and Belle Shirley, was killed in Waco, Texas, in fight with peace officers.

1875 On June 26, Dan Evans, who participated in the Watt Grayson robbery with Jim Reed and D. W. Wilder was hanged at Fort Smith for the murder of one Seabolt. Confessed that he, Wilder and Reed pulled the job.

1876 John Shirley of Scyene sought on charge of harboring criminals. No record of arrest or conviction.

1876 Northfield Bank Robbery. September 7, 1876. The eight bandits were: Frank and Jesse James; Cole, Jim and Bob Younger; Clell Miller, Samuel Wells (alias Charlie Pitts) and William Stiles (alias Bill Chadwell). Samuel Wells, Bob Younger and Jesse James were delegated to rob the bank; others in two divisions —one posted opposite the bank and other a rear guard. Two citizens killed; no money taken. Henry Miller, medical student, killed Clell Miller; Merchant A. B. Manning killed William Stiles and wounded Cole Younger. Joseph Lee Heywood, cashier, one of citizens killed. Three Youngers shot down and captured in thicket near Madelia by Capt. William W. Murphy, Sheriff James Glispin, Col. Thomas L. Bought, Benjamin M. Rice, George A. Bradford, Charles A. Pomeroy, S. J. Severson. On November 9th indictments by Grand Jury charged all three with being accessories to the murder of Heywood; with attacking Teller A. E. Baunker with intent to do bodily harm; and with robbing the First National Bank. A fourth count charged Cole as principal and two brothers as accessories, with the murder of Nicholas Gustavson, who not understanding English very well failed to "get in" when ordered to do so by one of the raiders and was shot and killed. Judge Samuel Lord presided; Prosecutor G. N. Baxter. Pleaded guilty, otherwise would have been sentenced to death. Lord gave three life imprisonment in the state prison at Stillwater. Robert died in prison September 16, 1889, of tuberculosis. Buried in the family plot in cemetery at Lee's Summit, Mo. Largely through service of Capt. Warren Carter Bronaugh over period of 25 years, Cole and Jim were released under parole on July 10, 1901, by pardon board. Both first worked for N. P. Peterson Granite Company of St. Paul and Stillwater as salesmen, at $60 a month and expenses. Jim committed suicide in the Reardon Hotel, St. Paul, July, 1902. Cole died at his home at Lee's Summit, March 21, 1916, after year's illness of heart disease and dyspepsia.

1880 Belle visited by Jesse James and Younger boys at Younger's Bend after her marriage same year to Sam Starr. The marriage was under Cherokee tribal laws. By marriage Belle received title to 80 acres of land, but for life tenure only, for the Indian lands, in those days, were held communally; allotments in severalty came only after action on the Dawes Commission Report.

1882 Jesse James killed by Bob Ford, St. Joseph, Mo. April 3rd.

Belle Starr

1883 Belle and Sam Starr convicted of horse theft in Judge Parker's Court, Fort Smith, February 19th, Sam on one count and Belle on two. Both sentenced March 8th to Federal penitentiary, Detroit, for one year. Prosecuted by Wm. H. H. Clayton, attorney for Western District. A jury trial.

1883 Jim Starr (real name Jim July) and Belle's last lover was sentenced at Fort Smith, July 20th to 30 days in jail for introducing liquor into Indian Territory and 30 days for selling liquor without a license. Acquitted of assault charge same day, charge brought February 9th.

1884 Saturday, October 18th, the Sebastian County Fair opened in Fort Smith, Arkansas, the principal event being a Wild West show starting at 2 P.M. A feature of the show was a mail stagecoach robbery by band of Pawnee Indians. Taking part in the show as stage-coach passengers were Judge Isaac C. Parker, Mrs. John S. Park, Mrs. L. W. Marks and Mrs. Lita Humbea. The Fort Smith *Tribune* critic described the Wild West show as "exciting and popular." Repeated next day, but in this second version of a stage robbery a child was seized and was being carried off by the Indians when the cowboy rescuers arrived. No mention of Belle's having taken part in the show. Judge Parker was president of the Fair Association.

1884 Legends say that Belle took part in Crawford County Fair at Van Buren, October 17-18, and in a stage robbery, a feature of the Wild West show, Belle was the lone robber who held up the stage; Judge Parker a passenger; Belle took his gold watch. Belle allegedly gave an exhibition of horsemanship and when someone put a newspaperman, Powe, whom Belle didn't like on her horse, she raced horse, throwing Powe . . . Belle was not mentioned in the contemporary newspaper accounts of the Fair. It is possible, however, that Belle did play such a role at the Fair two years later.

1885 In May, Belle, while deserting Sam and eloping with John Middleton a horse thief from Paris, Logan County, Arkansas, rode on ahead on a different fork of the road in a wagon with Pearl. Middleton rode alone on horseback. While trying to ford the Poteau River, 25 miles above Fort Smith, he was drowned and four days later his body was found, badly decomposed. The horse wore Belle's cartridge belt and pistol. This later implicated Belle in theft of the horse, which was a horse stolen from one A. G. McCarthy; but Belle pleaded in court that she didn't know this when she bought the horse from Fayette Barnette, a white man (who had a Choctaw woman) for $50 in gold coin, she said. Strange that the prosecutor didn't think to ask her how she ever got $50 in gold coin.

1885 Belle indicted at Fort Smith as one of four implicated in robbery of one Ferrell in May in Cherokee Nation, Indian Territory. Gave bond and got continuance. Indicted also at same time for horse stealing.

1886 Blue Duck, Belle Starr's Cherokee Indian sweetheart, was convicted of murder on January 30th. Sentenced on April 30th to be hanged on July 23rd. Belle employed extra counsel, after the sentence, who succeeded in having the sentence commuted to life imprisonment at Menard, Illinois. Blue Duck was pardoned, through Belle's efforts, after serving only a year.

1886 Belle arraigned at Fort Smith, Arkansas, May 28th on several charges of horse stealing. Gave bail. Returned to Younger's Bend. September 30th acquitted of Ferrell larceny charge. September 30th in Fort Smith gave interview to reporter of Fort Smith *Elevator* saying a New York publisher had offered her a large price for her memoirs but while she had turned the offer down she had manuscript, partly written. Posed for only photo of her known to exist.

1886 Pearl Younger *enceinte* by man whose name was never revealed.

1886 Belle, in October, threatened to kill Larkin Lareaux, Fort Smith newspaper man who secured interview with her printed on September 30.

1886 Felix Griffin and Sam Starr indicted October 16th at Fort Smith on charge of burglarizing the United States Post Office at Eufaula. Belle also arrested in connection with this robbery, accusers alleging she participated, dressed in man's clothing.

1886 Tom Starr convicted at Fort Smith on November 23rd of introducing liquor into Indian Territory and sentenced to one and one-half years in Menard (Ill.) Federal Penitentiary.

1886 The Fort Smith *Elevator* reports that the 1880 census showed that the Cherokee Nation in Indian Territory had a population of 20,036 citizens, plus 2,745 noncitizens living under permits, and 1,921 white intruders.

1886 On Saturday night, a week before Christmas, Belle and Sam stopped for a dance at "Aunt Lucy" Surratt's, near Turk Brothers' store in the Choctaw Nation, I.T. There Sam saw Frank West who had been one who captured Sam and killed Sam's horse a few weeks before, when West, a member of the Cherokee tribal Indian

Chronology and Necrology

Police, and Deputy U. S. Marshal Tyner Hughes were trying to arrest Sam for robbing post office in Blaine, Choctaw Nation. Sam and West blazed away at each other at the same time and both were killed.

1887 Pearl gives birth to illegitimate daughter whom she named Flossie, in April, in Siloam Springs, Arkansas. Fort Smith liveryman married her, according to Harman, just before the child was born. Belle never saw the child—refused to.

1887 On July 6th, U. S. Indian Agent, Robert L. Owen, wrote Belle Starr and caused the letter to be published in the Eufaula *Indian Journal* of July 28th, saying that, in his opinion, the complaint against her for harboring criminals was not established and that the complaint was dismissed. Owen, a part Cherokee, later became noted Senator from Oklahoma, drafted Federal Reserve Act, etc.

1888 Ed Reed, son of Belle Starr, sentenced July 12th to seven years in Federal Penitentiary at Columbus, Ohio, for larceny. Later paroled, after serving short term.

1889 On February 2nd, Jim July (alias Jim Starr), started for Fort Smith to answer an old larceny charge. Belle accompanied him from Younger's Bend to San Bois in the Choctaw Nation, 29 miles southwest of Whitefield. They stopped there for the night and Sunday morning, Belle returned home, Jim going on to Fort Smith.

1889 Belle Starr murdered February 3 between her home on Younger's Bend and the ferry across the Canadian near Briartown. At funeral next day Jim Starr (July) and a deputy U. S. marshal arrested a neighbor, Edgar Watson, for the murder. Watson taken to Fort Smith. Ed Reed, Pearl Younger, Jim Starr and others witnesses; but evidence was contradictory. Defendant's witnesses gave Watson a good character and charges against him were dismissed. Strong suspicion and local belief was that Ed killed his mother. They hated each other, and she was constantly humiliating him.

1889 Bob Younger died in Stillwater, Minn., prison, September 16th of tuberculosis. Was serving life term for being accessory to the murder of Asst. Cashier J. L. Heywood in the robbery of the Northfield, Minn., First National Bank.

1889 Jack Spaniard, one of Belle's numerous lovers, hanged on August 30th at Fort Smith for the murder of William H. Irwin in Indian Territory.

1890 Jim July (alias Jim Starr), Belle's last lover, killed by U. S. Marshal Heck Thomas on January 26th while resisting arrest on robbery charge and for jumping bond. Killed near Ardmore, Okla.

1891 Ed Reed, Belle's son, convicted at Fort Smith of bootlegging in Indian Territory and sentenced to seven years in Columbus, Ohio, Federal Penitentiary. Served few years of sentence and pardoned by President Harrison at the instance of Judge Parker, who had sentenced Reed.

1891 Pearl married Will Harrison (according to Harman) and lived for a time at Tamaha, Choctaw Nation, Indian Territory, but deserted him soon afterwards and entered a bawdy house in Fort Smith as an inmate. After three months she opened a house of her own and at various times moved from one location to another as business improved or declined.

1893 Ed Reed made Deputy Marshal of Judge Parker's Court.

Chronology and Necrology

1895 Ed Reed, on October 24th, shot and killed Dick and Zeke Crittenden, brothers and ex-Deputy U. S. Marshal in Wagoner, Okla., who were drunk and hurrahing the town and had shot a restaurant keeper named Burns. Zeke shot at Ed when he asked Zeke to surrender; Ed shot and killed him; Dick ran up and opened fire on Reed who drove one of Dick's own cartridges from his belt into his side with a pistol shot. Ed exonerated at preliminary hearing.

1896 November. Ed Reed killed while shooting up a saloon in Wagoner, Oklahoma Territory.

1897 Bandit career of Al and Frank Jennings begun on August 18th by a fiasco attempt to hold up a passenger train at Edmond, Okla., ended December 5th when Deputy Sheriff Bud Ledbetter took the whole gang of five single-handed, without firing a shot.

1897 Pearl sold her bawdy house and moved into respectable part of town, taking one of the inmates with her. Later in the year she married again. Her husband died of typhoid on September 13, 1898, according to Harman, leaving Pearl with a baby boy three weeks old.

1902 Jim Younger committed suicide in the Reardon Hotel, St. Paul, Minn.

1916 Cole Younger died at his home at Lee's Summit, Mo., March 21st of heart disease and dyspepsia.

1924 William H. ("Big Bill" or "Uncle Billy") Tilghman shot to death on the evening of November 1, 1924 by a drunken Federal prohibition enforcement officer, Wylie Lynn, in Cromwell, Okla. Big Bill, although seventy years of age, had been brought into the lawless oil boom town by the Citizens Committee of Cromwell as City Marshal to restore order and preserve the peace.

GLOSSARY

GLOSSARY

BALL. Gun-play in which two antagonists or two factions shoot it out in a saloon or in the street. When an old-time Westerner in a narrative says "The ball had commenced," it means that some one had fired the first shot in a fight.

BULLWACKER. Driver of an oxen team.

BUSHWHACKERS. Missouri Confederate guerrillas. Their principal enemies were the Jayhawkers. They preyed upon Union sympathizers. Like the Unionist guerrillas they often burned and plundered indiscriminately.

COWHAND. An earlier and, in the West, still more generally used term than "cowboy."

COWTOWN. A town at or near a railroad to which herds of cattle are driven to be shipped to market. In the wild days before most of the great ranches were divided up and fenced in by homesteaders, a cowtown usually consisted entirely of saloons, gambling joints, bawdy houses, one hotel, a general store and a jail, with courtroom connecting.

DEAL, DEALER. When you encounter the expression "He dealt cards at the Blue Moon," it means that the person was a professional gambler working for the gambling house, his pay being a percentage of the house winnings.

DROP. When a gunman has the "drop" on you, he has his pistol out of the holster and pointing it at you before you have got your revolver out of your holster. It sometimes stopped an argument for one man to get the drop on the other but not always, because the man with the drop sometimes can shoot first, miss and get killed.

FAN. The phrase "fanned the hammer" or "fanning the hammer" means a showy kind of gun play, wherein the gunman has filed off part of the mechanism of a revolver which holds the hammer in place when it is cocked and releases the hammer when the trigger is pulled. By pulling back the hammer with the first joint of the thumb, very rapidly, the effect of firing can be, in the hands of an expert, like that of firing an automatic. Some fancy shooters held the gun in one hand and "fanned" it by rapid movements of the palm of the left hand across the trigger. It's cute to look at in target practice, but, according to the best authorities, it is a quick way to commit suicide in gunplay with a man who is cool and takes deliberate aim.

GUERRILLA. A free-lance soldier not attached to any of the regular forces during the Civil War. The term does not necessarily carry opprobrium, for there were some guerrilla bands on both sides that conducted legitimate warfare despite their status; but the irregular nature of their organization attracted murderers, thieves, plunderers and a bad element generally.

Glossary

HEADRIGHT. Under former laws of Texas, a headright was the inheritable right given to certain immigrating heads of families to grants of free land. The grants carried the condition that the grantee must improve the land and live continuously on it for a period of years.

HOE-MAN. Term of contempt used by cattlemen for farmers. See *nester*.

HURRAH. Verb, meaning to ride through a town yelling and shooting and making people scatter for cover. Favorite sport of Texas cowboys in Kansas cattle towns.

HOMESTEADER. One who accepts a government grant of 160 acres of free public lands on condition that he live on the land and improve it.

JAYHAWKER. Kansas Unionist guerrilla. The jayhawkers preyed upon sympathizers with the Confederacy, particularly Missourians.

LEAN-TO. An addition to a house after it has been built and used, consisting of one room, used as a combined kitchen and dining room, or as a dormitory. The single, slanting roof gave the appearance of the room leaning against the main building.

NECKTIE PARTY. A lynching.

NESTER. Cattlemen's term of contempt for a small farmer who has taken up a government land grant and tried to make a home and a living on it.

PEACE OFFICER. A U. S. marshal or deputy marshal or a sheriff or deputy sheriff, that is, federal or county officers. The term does not include the police, which are local, municipal enforcers of the law. However, the Indian Police of Indian Territory were peace officers because their jurisdiction included a whole Indian nation.

ROAD AGENT. Term used for a stagecoach robber in the days of stagecoaches.

RUSTLER. A cattle thief.

SECTION. A section of land comprises one square mile or 640 acres of land. Allotments of land to Indians were in quarter sections (160 acres), eighths (80 acres) and sixteenths (40 acres).

SCOUT. The phrase "on the scout" means hiding out or on the dodge from officers. Said of a criminal for whom a warrant is out and peace officers or police are looking for him.

TREE. Verb, meaning to intimidate the citizens and officers of a town so badly that the officers fear to make an arrest even for murder. When Texas cowboys had a Kansas cattle town thoroughly frightened or buffaloed, they said they had the town "treed."

WRANGLER. A ranch hand who can handle horses and cattle.

BIBLIOGRAPHICAL REVIEW

BIBLIOGRAPHICAL REVIEW

———•—•———

Advancing the Frontier. By Grant Foreman. University of
Oklahoma Press, Norman, Okla., 1933. Mr. Foreman is
practically alone in the field as historian of the Five Civilized Tribes—the Cherokees, Choctaws, Chickasaws, Seminoles and Creeks; and, so thoroughly has he done his work,
it is not likely that anybody will ever supplant him. As
legal adviser to the Dawes Commission, which was set up
to solve the land disputes among the Indians in Indian
Territory, Mr. Foreman discovered that, aside from the
newspapers published in Cherokee and English, there was
little historical material regarding the Five Civilized
Tribes. He was forced to devote years of study of the reports and letters in the government archives in Washington. *Advancing the Frontier* carries on the history of the
Five Civilized Tribes to the beginning of the Civil War,
from the point where his previous volume, *Indian Removal,* left off. The latter is a history of the Southern Indians prior to the Treaty of New Echota until the last of
them had passed over "The Trail of Tears" in their en-
forced removal—driven out by the whites. *Advancing the
Frontier* filled an important hiatus in American history.
*Adventure on Red River: Report on the Exploration of Red
River by Captain Randolph C. Marcy and G. B. McClellan.*

Belle Starr

By Grant Foreman, Editor. University of Oklahoma Press, Norman, Okla., 1937. Captain Randolph C. Marcy in 1852 was commissioned by the United States Government to explore the country bordering on the headwaters of the Red River from Central Oklahoma to New Mexico, a vast region hitherto uncharted. His and McClellan's reports were published in 1853 by the Government but have long been out of print and scarce. Foreman rescued the book and edited it with abridgments, notes and comments. It is a lively and charming collection of historical, geological and anthropological lore; and the University of Oklahoma Press has illustrated it with valuable old photographs and prints. I found it valuable in my efforts to get a complete picture of the background of this country, which, before any part of it was opened for white settlement, had no laws or government except those of the Indian councils and courts, and hence it was an attractive hiding place for murderers, outlaws, robbers and scapegraces of all kinds.

The Arkansas. By Clyde Brion Davis. Farrar & Rinehart, New York, 1940. One of the uniformly entertaining and informative books in the American River series begun under the editorship of the late Constance Lindsay Skinner and continued, after her death, under the editorship of Stephen Vincent Benét and Carl Carmer. Two pages herein are devoted, uncritically, to legends about the Murrell gang; there is a brief but accurate sketch of Federal Judge Isaac C. Parker and his famous court at Fort Smith; a succinct, accurate and affectionate sketch of the exploits and death of William H. (Big Bill or Uncle Billy) Tilghman, one of the most famous peace officers of Kansas and, later, Oklahoma; and Davis pays his respects to Dodge City, Kansas, and its bad men and peace officers, at no point being sucked in by the silly legends created by ''Ned Bunt-line,'' the anonymous writers of the *National Police Gazette* and the literary fabrications alleged to have been the life stories of various bad men, written by themselves, and sold in paper-back editions at twenty-five cents a copy, which serious but credulous historians have too often accepted as authentic and made use of in their work. This is an excellent, well-documented book.

An Autobiography. By Mark Twain. Harper & Bros., New York, 1924. One of the great books of all times, by the first great writer to use the American idiom for literary purposes instead of a dessicated English idiom, and to use it in masterly fashion. Here we have a great writer and a great man dancing with arms and legs, putting down, without conscious order, anything that comes to his mind, without any of the inhibitions caused by fear of shocking or hurting or offending people, because he was to leave an injunction that the greater part of it was not to be published until long after his death. I restudied it, for this book, because of the picture it gives of the Mississippi valley, and particularly of Missouri, in Mark Twain's boyhood and youth.

An Autobiography of America. By Mark Van Doren, Editor. Albert & Charles Boni, New York, 1929. This is one of the most shamefully neglected books of my time. It is a magnificently selected and edited anthology of excerpts from books, journals, letters and official reports of men who helped to make America, from Captain John Smith to Jack London, and including such things as Benjamin Franklin's autobiographical account of the beginning of his career; a British army officer's depiction of the curious but delightful (though sometimes complicated in outcome) New Eng-

land custom of bundling; the letters in the quarrel between George Washington and Gen. Charles Lee; the whole
story of the astounding naïveté and stupidity Alexander
Hamilton displayed in his illicit love affair with Mrs.
James Reynolds, wife of a blackmailer; an outburst by
the brilliant but crazy John Randolph of Roanoke;
Boone's journal, Davy Crockett's courtship; P. T. Bar-
num's egotism; Josiah Gregg's experience on the Santa Fé
Trail, Buffalo Bill's ghosted account of his exploits; Frederick Law Olmstead's journal of his travels on horseback
through the South in the 1850's (a forgotten classic)—
and delightful bits of a kind usually ignored by anthol-
ogists.

Bella Starr, the Bandit Queen, or the Female Jesse James.
Anonymous. Richard K. Fox, New York, 1889. This rare
item (there is no copy in the Library of Congress, the New
York Public Library, the Morgan Library, the Columbia
University Library or any other public library in New
York) is the basic source of nearly every one of the legends
about Belle Starr—legends which have been repeated by
word of mouth and copied by ''historians'' who had copied
from other ''historians'' who had copied from still other
''historians''—most of them never knowing where the
''data'' originally came from. The existent stuff about
Belle Starr, from Harman's *Hell on the Border* (1898)
to Duncan Aiken's in *Calamity Jane and Other Wildcats*
(1927), E. D. Nix's *Oklahombres* (1929) and the stuff
written by a woman who signs herself ''Flossie'' and alleges she is the granddaughter of Belle Starr (Dallas Sunday *News,* April 30, May 6, 1933), is mostly second-, third-
or fourth-hand rehashing from the fiction written by the
clever but highly imaginative and unscrupulous anony-

mous hacks on the staff of Richard K. Fox's *National Police Gazette*. Fox's rewrite men usually managed to get names and dates and essential facts fairly correct, however much they might embroider on them; but this book has every essential fact wrong, from name and date of birth and family of Belle Starr to the very end of the book. It is patched out with plausible-sounding alleged excerpts from Belle's own journal and letters—every one of which contains slips that, as I have explained elsewhere in this book, show they are pure fabrications. The genesis of every false legend about Belle's career is in this book; and I have read as many as fifty variations of individual episodes, which first appeared here and later appeared elsewhere. Dozens of people, alleging that they knew Belle Starr intimately in their childhood or youth, have written me folklore stuff originating in this book and garbled in the retelling and have solemnly avowed they saw these things with their own eyes—things that never happened except in the mind of some writer who probably had never been west of Hoboken.

Billy Le Roy. Anonymous. Richard K. Fox, New York, 1881. In August, 1881. Jesse James was not to die until April 3 of the following year and Billy the Kid was not to be killed by Sheriff Pat Garrett for two months. The robberies and killings of these notorious bandits had been exploited by the newspapers, by the "boiler-plate" writers for the American News Co. (which supplied stereotype inside pages for country weeklies) and by the *National Police Gazette* to the full extent of their imaginations. The killings of these two men, alone, if the press figures were added up and believed, would number more dead than had fallen at Gettysburg. Fox had rushed into print an "authentic" book of the lives and crimes of Frank and Jesse James while they were still alive, and it had sold like hotcakes; but people were getting fed up on Billy the Kid and Jesse. So it would appear that Fox created a bandit out of his fertile brain and named him Billy Le Roy, set his writers at work chronicling the desperate and daring exploits of this mythical character every week in the *Police Gazette* and had a life story of him prepared to be rushed into print as soon as Fox decided to kill him off in the columns of the *P. G.* This was the book.

Border Captives. By Charles Coke Rister. University of Oklahoma Press, Norman, Okla., 1940. Authentic, thoroughly researched, and interesting account of the warfare waged by the Kiowa, Comanche, Apache, Cheyenne and Arapahoe Indians on the white settlers of the Southwest —raids wherein the Indians not only burned, pillaged and scalped, but dragged off women and children captives, some to be held for ransom, others to be held as wives of the warriors or as slaves of the tribe. Rister is pro-Indian and anti-white, feeling that the Indians got a rotten deal all around from our treaty-breaking government and that they were forced into reprisals by the cruel, wasteful and senseless slaughter of buffalo—the Indians' meat—by the whites, just for the fun of it, or to sell the hides and bones at about a dollar per animal—and by the whites' usurpation of Indian lands. For two strikingly different opinions of Quanah Parker compare Rister's with Dora Neill Raymond's in *Captain Lee Hall of Texas*, listed below. Quanah was the son of Cynthia Ann Parker, who was captured by Comanches in a raid on a white settlement when she was nine; she was brought up as a member of the tribe, almost lost the ability to understand English, married for love within the tribe and bore her husband one girl and two boys, only one of whom, Quanah, survived to manhood. She refused to be ransomed and pined away and died when she was restored to white civilization. Quanah caused Captain Lee Hall a great deal of trouble, so, understandably, Mrs. Raymond, who fell quite in love with the hero of her book, doesn't like Quanah Parker and lets it be known. Quanah, by the way, has two sons living in Cache, Oklahoma (1940); one of them, White Parker, is a Protestant minister.

Calamity Jane and the Lady Wildcats. By Duncan Aikman. Henry Holt and Co., New York, 1927. The chapter about Belle Starr is much better written than most of the rehashings of *National Police Gazette* fakery that pass for historical accounts of Belle Starr's career, and Aikman makes a conscientious attempt to reconstruct the scene and the times; but if he is as uncritical of legends and as careless about easily verifiable facts and names in his story of the doings of Calamity Jane as he is about Belle Starr, the book must be set down as literary folklore, with little relation to fact. Aikman has John Shirley, Belle's father, abandoning his tavern in Carthage, Mo., after the Civil War and going to Texas. Carthage was burned to the ground on September 22, 1863, the tavern meeting no better fate than the courthouse and other buildings. He makes Ed Shirley a captain, which he was not. He writes of Ellis Starr as being the father of Tom, who was the father of Sam who married (under the Cherokee tribal laws) Belle, and of Ellis' having forced the Cherokee Nation to make a separate peace with him. Ellis and Tom Starr were brothers; their father was named James. Aikman's stuff about Belle's telling Deputy Sheriff Nichols

she would kill him if he didn't release Jim Reed and his
suggestion that Belle killed Nichols was invented by the
Police Gazette writers, even if Aikman never heard of
Bella Starr, the Bandit Queen, or the Female Jesse James,
and got his data from books he believed were authentic.
From there on, about 4,500 words, to the end of the chapter on Belle, is *Police Gazette* fiction.

Captain Lee Hall of Texas. By Dora Neill Raymond. University of Oklahoma Press, Norman, Okla., 1940. An elab-
orately documented biography of probably the most dashing, most courageous and most put-upon-by-fate of the
great leaders of the Texas Rangers. Mrs. Raymond falls
very much in love with Hall, but she is an exact and conscientious historian (her *Oliver's Secretary: John Milton
in an Era of Revolt* is flawless, yet quite unorthodox in
treatment) and she has omitted not a single contemporary
news item, government report, letter or document that she
could sift and compare with other data in making this a
monumental addition to American history, and an exciting
book besides. Her account of the Ben Thompson-Joe Foster
feud and duel is the best on record, and, being the most
cautious, is the most credible version. And if you don't
remember where O. Henry got the material for his cowboy
and rough-rider stories, it was on Lee Hall's ranch, to
which Hall invited Sidney Porter to come and stay as long
as he wanted to, without pay, when young Porter was weak
from incipient tuberculosis. There is a grand chapter in
this book on O. Henry and Hall's ranch.

Cherokee Cavaliers. By Edward Everett Dale and Gaston
Lytton. University of Oklahoma Press, Norman, Okla.,
1939. This book is made up of over two hundred letters that
passed between leaders of the Cherokee tribe, which was

Bibliographical Review

split into two factions when a minority group headed by John Ridge, Stand Watie and Elias Boudinot signed the New Echota Treaty in 1835—which provided that the entire tribe should be removed from their homes in Georgia, Alabama and the Carolinas to lands already occupied by the Cherokees West in Indian Territory—and the Ross faction of full-bloods. These letters, edited with explanatory comments, give an intimate picture of the lives, customs, trials and concerns of the Cherokee leaders. Old Tom Starr, after the murder of his father by assassins of the Treaty Party, personally declared a one-man war on the whole faction and started slitting throats until over sixty murders were attributed to him, and the Cherokee Nation signed a special treaty with him giving him amnesty for his past crimes on his agreement to stop killing Cherokees. Old Tom was the father of Sam Starr, who married Belle Starr.

The Chisholm Trail. By Sam P. Ridings. Co-Operative Publishing Company, Guthrie, Okla., 1936. One of the quickest ways of starting a fight down in Oklahoma is casually to inquire what, when and where the Chisholm Trail was, in the presence of two men (friends or strangers to each other) who have definite but differing opinions on the subject. If you have this book along you can umpire the fight and give the decision, or, as would usually be the case, declare, "No decision," for the argufiers, nine times in ten, are both wrong. This book contains a map which shows the exact line through every one-thirty-second of a section of land that the trail followed from Caldwell, Kansas, through Oklahoma to the Red River, the crossing being about five miles due east of Terral. The trail was laid out and surveyed by Robert Bean and Jesse Chisholm in

1832 and it extended 147 miles over rough country, serving to connect the North- and West-Texas cattle ranches with the cattle markets of Kansas, Omaha, St. Louis and Kansas City. Much of the history of the Southwest revolves around this trail. Ridings' book is a plodding but authentic history of the trail and of the ranches and ranchers along it.

The Dalton Brothers. By an Eye Witness. Laird & Lee, Chicago, 1892. Source book for many later accounts, and fairly accurate. Contains reproductions of photographs taken of the dead bandits and of the Condon bank after the Coffeyville Raid, in which the Dalton gang was practically wiped out.

Dodge City, the Cowboy Capital. By Robert M. Wright. No date or place of issue given. On page 309 Wright observes, ''Since beginning this book, I learn that my old friend, William Tilghman, Chief of Police of Oklahoma City, and mentioned several times in previous pages, is a candidate for the marshalship of Oklahoma. The President could not appoint a better man.'' That places the publication date of this book, I think, as or about, 1914; for Tilghman was an unsuccessful candidate for the office of sheriff of Oklahoma County in that year, after serving as chief of police of Oklahoma City; and Tilghman didn't move to Oklahoma City until 1911. But, if I am right in my deduction, this shows how much you have to discount in this marvelous book when Wright deals with facts, especially outside of his own bailiwick; for there were no President-appointed, Federal marshals in Oklahoma after the Territory became a State on November 16, 1907, and, even before then, one didn't announce oneself as a candidate for a Federal marshalship any more than one announced oneself a candidate for the job of Secretary of State. But it is a grand book. Wright was first mayor of Dodge City and lived through all its wild and woolly days; and this, I feel certain, is one of those great rarities—a book by a non-writer that was not written by a "ghost." Wright was a tough, realistic, dry-humored, hard-drinking, saloon and gambling-hall proprietor, cattleman and merchant, who became wealthy and gave Dodge City a park when it got tamed and civilized. His book has the true savor of the frontier days.

Fighting Men of the West. By Dane Coolidge. E. P. Dutton & Co., New York, 19—. Careless and irresponsible.

The Five Civilized Tribes. By Grant Foreman. University of Oklahoma Press, Norman, Okla., 1934. The only thorough history of the Cherokees, Chickasaws, Choctaws, Seminoles and Creeks of the period when these tribes each enjoyed autonomy, and each was a nation within the Nation of the United States in the old Indian Territory, part of what is now the State of Oklahoma. Other histories can only be elaborations from this source material. A monument of scholarship and yet fascinating. Contains much about the Starrs, whose land Belle horned in on by marrying Sam when she was illegally a squatter on Indian land. Old Tom Starr was an assassin, long outlawed by his own tribe, so he was sympathetic to white outlaws "on the scout" and his place on the north bank of the Canadian River on the old Briartown-Eufaula Trail was a hideout for white desperadoes. When Belle settled on his place for keeps, she made it a rendezvous and haven for cattle thieves, highwaymen and murderers. Old Tom was a pretty good cattle thief himself. And he had no known equal in murder. The Starr family of Cherokees was exceedingly numerous, the majority of them then, as now, highly respectable citizens.

Folklore of Romantic Arkansas. By Fred W. Allsopp. 2 vols. Arkansas State Historical Association, Little Rock, Ark., 1931. Folklore, when it is labeled folklore and not set forth as verifiable history, is always interesting and historically, as well as literarily, valuable. This collection is no exception.

The Formation of the State of Oklahoma. By Roy Gittinger. University of Oklahoma Press, Norman, Okla., 1939. A succinct and accurate account of the development of Oklahoma Territory into a state when it was combined with Indian Territory to become Oklahoma.

The Great American Land Bubble. By A. M. Sakolsky. Harper & Brothers, New York and London, 1932. An exhaustive study of the land speculations in America. It is painful for moralists to reflect that much of "civilization's advance" was based upon fraud and that many of the great improvements of the country in the way of railroads and highways were founded in graft. Contractors bribed legislators and judges; hence great public works from which we all benefit. From this book we learn that Thomas Hart, great grandfather of Thomas Hart Benton, the artist, who apparently had been stuck with some fraudulent Spanish land grants, tried his best to get all Spanish land grants, spurious or otherwise, validated. He succeeded in his mission, in part. He got validations for grants more spurious than his own, but his own claims were disallowed.

Gallant Ladies. By Cameron Rogers. Harcourt, Brace & Co., New York, 1928. The chapter on Belle Starr in this book is a cheap and shoddy rewriting of Duncan Aikman's chapter on Belle in *Calamity Jane and the Lady Wildcats,* noted above. Rogers doesn't seem to have bothered to do

Bibliographical Review

any further research than to read Aikman and rewrite Aikman's stuff in *Zippy Stories* style. There are a dozen easily obtainable books from which he could have lifted worse (and different) nonsense. If any of my readers contemplate an article or a book about Belle, *please* leave out that damned "dramatic incident" of Belle's refusing to identify Jim Reed's body to keep the deputy sheriff who shot Jim from getting the reward offered for Jim Reed "dead or alive." It is in every piece about Belle that is more than a thousand words long, from *Hell on the Border* (1898), to the pieces signed "Flossie," who says she is the granddaughter of Belle Starr, and who wrote two articles about Belle in the Dallas *News*, April-May, 1933, largely lifted from *Hell on the Border*. Jim Reed's body was identified by numerous witnesses, including the sheriff of Lamar County, who served with Reed under Quantrill; besides, the deputy sheriff who killed Reed was his cousin. Belle didn't even go to Paris, Texas, for the burial.

Guns of the Frontier. William MacLeod Raine. Houghton, Mifflin Co., Boston, 1940. Mr. Raine, a writer of refreshing and well-constructed Western stories, and once a cowboy himself, here very soberly and conscientiously debunks much of the stuff that has been written about deadshots of the old West. Critically examining the stories that have come down the years, he selects some of the credible ones, strips them of their implausibilities and gives anecdotes about peace officers and bad men, cleaned of most of the sentimental detritus that has accumulated on them. However, Raine himself falls for a number of stories that are obviously fiction. One of them was such a stock-in-trade gag of the yellow journalists to make bandits seem glamorous and noble-hearted that one wonders why Raine, who

Belle Starr

debunks the glamor and noblesse of outlaws, includes it. It is the yarn about Emmett Dalton's receiving his wound in the Coffeyville raid because he rode back into town to pick up his brother Bob. It is pure fiction. It figures in most of the imagined versions of the James-Younger robbery and the Northfield robbery. Cole Younger being the hero in this gallant rescue of his brother Bob. The incident didn't occur there, either. See Robert Huntington's *Robber and Hero* and Robertus Love's *The Rise and Fall of Jesse James,* both reliable. Also, the story Raine repeats about Jesse's suggesting that they kill Bob Younger was the invention of a *National Police Gazette* writer.

A Handbook of Oklahoma Writers. By Mary Hays Marable and Elaine Boylan. University of Oklahoma Press, Norman, Okla., 1939. Biographical accounts of Oklahomans and former residents, together with bibliographies of their writings. Useful and interesting.

Hands Up! By Fred E. Sutton. As written down by A. B. Macdonald. Bobbs-Merrill Co., Indianapolis, 1927. This book is a treasure, a literary curiosity—the most comical lot of brummagem ever put together with scissors and paste, and doubly comical because Sutton has himself figuring personally in nearly every episode, either as an eye-witness or as one who got his information direct from the persons concerned. According to Sutton, he knew them all, from Wild Bill Hickok (his stuff about Wild Bill is taken from an article by Col. George W. Nichols in *Harper's* for February, 1867) to Henry Starr, to whom Sutton claims to have talked just before Starr was killed in 1921! Mr. Sutton was talking and Mr. Macdonald was writing this book in 1927. There are some comical pictures of Mr. Sutton, wearing chaps, cartridge belt with two guns, and holding a Win-

Bibliographical Review

chester, and another of him holding ''Belle Starr's famous Winchester'' (of course, he knew Belle personally!) which show Mr. Sutton to have been about 55 years old when the book was written. According to the correct chronology in *A Handbook of Oklahoma Writers,* Sutton couldn't have been more than three years old when he says he saved the life of Billy the Kid in a Dodge City dance hall! Besides, there is no record of Billy the Kid's ever having been in Kansas except to pass through it when he was a child. The stuff pasted up in this book, often without changing the wording in the slightest, is from *Outlaw Days* (which was cribbed from Newsom's *The Going Out of the Outlaws*), *Hell on the Border, Dodge City, the Cowboy Capital, Harper's Monthly, The Rise and Fall of Jesse James,* and *The Saga of Billy the Kid.* The chapter ''Old Tascosa'' is entirely faked from page 654 *et sequitur* of *Hell on the Border,* spliced in with stuff stolen from *The Saga of Billy the Kid.* Chapter VII is lifted almost without change from Robertus Love's *The Rise and Fall of Jesse James,* except to make it appear that Sutton lived around the corner from ''Mr. Howard'' in St. Joseph, Mo., often met him in the pool hall and that he went in and saw Jesse James' body only a few minutes after Bob Ford had killed Jesse. Sutton quotes as conversation he heard or as words said to him, the stuff he lifts from Love's book. The story of Judge Parker's court is lifted almost without change from *Hell on the Border,* except that the latter half of Prosecutor Clayton's address to the jury in the trial of Cherokee Bill is given as something that Sutton remembered vividly, after thirty-two years, as an example of Judge Parker's hair-raising denunciations in pronouncing sentence.

In the biographical data furnished apparently by members of the family (Mr. Sutton died in Kansas City, Mo., in 1927) for *A Handbook of Oklahoma Writers* (1939) the information is that Mr. Sutton's service as a deputy marshal in Oklahoma was from 1890 to 1893. Cherokee Bill was not sentenced to be hanged until April 13, 1895. Mr. Sutton, again lifting from *Hell on the Border* describes George Maledon, official hangman at Judge Parker's Court, and reports conversations with Maledon at the jail. Maledon gave up the hangman's job in 1894, thirty-two years before this book was written. From page 514 of *Hell on the Border,* Mr. Sutton took a piece of sentimental verse, which Rufus Buck, a rapist hanged on July 11, 1896, had scrawled on the back of a photograph of his mother, and attributes the verse to Cherokee Bill, saying that ''When they cut the body down they found under his blouse a photograph of his mother, lying over his heart, and upon the back he had scrawled a verse of his own composition.'' . . . What is not pure plagiarism in this book is preposterous, and even the plagiarism often further falsifies the record, as above, wherever something is lifted about one episode and attributed to an episode occurring years apart from it. Incredibly enough, other writers have relied upon the Sutton-Macdonald book, notably Nix and Hines in *Oklahombres.* . . .

About the Sutton collection of firearms to which he often refers in this book, let these two quotations suffice:

''When the frontier had tamed and Bat Masterson had joined Alfred Henry Lewis on a newspaper in New York City, I visited him, told him I was making a collection of firearms of historic interest and asked for one of his six-shooters. He gave me one, and pointing to the notches in its gutta-percha stock, said, 'It has twenty-two credits.'

'You killed twenty-two men with this gun, Bat?' I asked. 'And I didn't count greasers and Indians,' was his answer.''—From *Hands Up!*

''Some rapacious collector of souvenirs pestered Bat (Masterson) half to death with demands for a six-gun that Bat had used on the frontier. This collector called on Bat in his New York office and so insistently that Bat decided to give him a gun to get rid of him. Bat did not want to part with the one he had used, so he went to a pawnshop and bought an old Colt's forty-five which he took to his office in anticipation of the collector's return. With the gun lying on his desk, Bat was struck with the idea that while he was providing a souvenir, he might as well give one worth the trouble it had caused, so he took out his penknife and then and there cut twenty-two 'credits' in the pawnshop gun. When the collector called for his souvenir and Bat handed it to him, he managed to gasp a question as to whether Bat had killed twenty-two men with it. 'I didn't tell him yes, and I didn't tell him no,' Bat said, 'and I didn't exactly lie to him. I simply said I hadn't counted either Mexicans or Indians, and he went away tickled to death.' ''—From Wyatt Earp's alleged story of his own life, quoted in Stuart N. Lake's *Wyatt Earp.*

Hell on the Border: He Hanged Eighty-Eight Men. By S. W. Harman. Compiled by C. P. Sterns. Phoenix Publishing Company, Fort Smith, Ark., 1898. This is an important source book and practically every subsequent history of the famous United States criminal court at Fort Smith, Ark., which was presided over by Judge Isaac C. (''Hanging Judge'') Parker, is based upon it. All of the statistical part of the book, the biographical sketches of those connected with the court and the transcriptions from court records, were the work of C. P. Sterns, and are scrupulously accurate. The narratives, written by Harman, a Fort Worth editor, are fairly reliable, except for dates, whenever he writes of something he knows from the court records and the files of the Fort Smith and Van Buren newspapers, but are completely unreliable when he has to depend upon other sources. His account of the career of Belle Starr, for instance, which so many others have used as about their only source material, was taken almost in toto from the anonymous *Bella Starr, the Bandit Queen, or the Female Jesse James* (see above).

History of American Journalism. By Melvin James Lee. Houghton Mifflin Co., Boston, 1917. Inasmuch as contemporary accounts of historical incidents as they were rendered in the daily and weekly press are among the most reliable source material to which historians have access, it is curious how frequently historians neglect these sources. This is a valuable contribution to American history. Its fault is its brevity. Although it is a large-size, 450-page book and its compass is comprehensive, the treatment of each phase of the history of American journalism is necessarily scanty. A five-volume history of American journalism, with pertinent quotations from contemporary newspaper accounts of events of social, political and economic importance and with more examples of nineteenth-century newspaper humor and editorial comment, would fill a great need.

History of the Cherokee Indians. By Emmett Starr. Oklahoma City, 1921. A slipshod work, one of those subscription books in which all those ''eligible'' for a biographical sketch and picture pay for the privilege of being represented in the book and are asked to subscribe also. However, the book has its value to the historian simply because of that fact, because there are interesting biographies of Cherokees of whom we would have no record if they hadn't paid for getting into this book. Also the book contains genealogical rolls that are so absolutely astounding that one wonders how they were obtained, inasmuch as the Cherokees had no written language until about 1830; and in this book, the family trees of some part-breed Cherokees are traced back to John of Gaunt of England.

A History of the United States Since the Civil War. In 5 vols. Ellis Paxson Oberholtzer. The Macmillan Co., New York, 1922. A passionately written and scrupulously documented classic of American history. It has a readability that is rare in books of historical research as thorough and as accurate as this work is.

Indian Justice, A Cherokee Murder Trial as Reported by John Howard Payne. By Grant Foreman, Editor. Oklahoma State Historical Society, Oklahoma City, 1933. Valuable in that it shows how a murder trial was conducted under the Cherokee tribal laws. The dignity with which these trials were conducted and the absence therefrom of the morbid curiosity which makes a sensational modern American murder trial a sort of macabre circus, might be profitably imitated by our bar and bench.

Jasper County, Missouri, in the Civil War. By Ward L. Schrantz. The Carthage Press, Carthage, Mo., 1923. This book contains the official list of slain, the officer rolls of various companies, both Federal and Confederate, descriptions of Carthage before it was burned by guerrillas, and reminiscences of Jasper County survivors of Civil War days. At the time this book was published, there were some who recalled Belle Starr and the Shirley family, but, as might be expected, their memories are faulty after sixty-odd years, especially as to dates.

Jesse James the Great Train Robber. By William Ward. Arthur Westbrook Co., Cleveland. Undated. Ward wrote thirty-five books about the James brothers in this series, each book devoted to a single episode, and all fictitious.

The Life and Practice of the Wild and Modern Indian, including *Going Out of the Outlaws.* By J. A. Newsom. Harlow Publishing Co., Oklahoma City, Okla., 1923. This book contains stuff about Oklahoma peace officers and outlaws which later appeared, often word for word, in *Outlaw Days,* by Zoe A. Tilghman, and still later, with very little change but with some elaboration, in Sutton and Macdonald's *Hands Up!* and still later in Nix and Hines' *Oklahombres.* It would seem probable that Newsom "ghosted" Mrs. Tilghman's book, inasmuch as his book and Mrs. Tilghman's were both published by the Harlow Publishing Company. Or maybe it was the other way around.

The Life of John Wesley Hardin, as Written by Himself. By John Wesley Hardin. From the *Original Manuscript.* Smith & Moore, Sequin, Texas, 1896. This book, on the face of it, is a forgery; for John Wesley Hardin was almost illiterate and a murderous bandit by the time he was sixteen years old; and this book is written with expert literary skill. In fact, the book is so much better written than most of the stories of outlaws and gunmen even in our own day, that it is a shame that the forger's name has not gone down to posterity. This book, curiously enough, is accepted at its face value not only by Thomas Ripley in his book, *They Died with Their Boots On,* who uses it as the basis for a chronicle largely devoted to Hardin, but also by Dora Neill Raymond in *Captain Lee Hall of Texas.* It is quite possible

Bibliographical Review

that the forger talked with Hardin when Hardin was in jail in Austin in 1878, but, if so, it is curious that the manuscript did not see the light until eighteen years afterwards, particularly inasmuch as Hardin was the most vicious murderer Texas ever had, more notorious than Sam Bass; and he was a hired killer on the Taylor side in the famous Sutton-Taylor cattle war—a feud of passionate interest to Texans. This book is highly plausible, and the real author of it was unusually careful in his names and dates. An important thing about the book is the slant it gives on the Texans' side in the hatred and contempt Texas cattlemen had for Kansans.

Marcy and the Gold Seekers; The Journal of Capt. R. B. Marcy, with an Account of the Gold Rush over the Southern Route. By Grant Foreman, Editor. University of Oklahoma Press, Norman, Okla., 1939. Just what the title describes. A fascinating and historically valuable record of an important event.

The Notorious James Brothers, Jesse—Frank. By Edgar James. I. & M. Ottenheimer, Baltimore, 1913. Typical of dozens of blood-and-thunder accounts, mainly fictitious, of the exploits of the James brothers. Illustrated with crude pen-and-ink drawings. Paper-bound, it sold for twenty-five cents a copy.

My Own, My Native Land. By Thyra Samter Winslow. Doubleday, Doran & Co., New York, 1936. These are charming sketches of scenes and characters that Mrs. Winslow remembers from her childhood in Fort Smith, Ark. One of the more piquant pieces concerns the whore house run there by Pearl Starr (or Pearl Younger), Belle Starr's daughter. Of course Mrs. Winslow never saw the inside of this palace of sin, but all the kids of Fort Smith knew all about it from the hushed gossip of adults and respectable women; and, as a girl in pigtails, Mrs. Winslow used to stand across the street and stare at the place and wonder what mysterious doings were going on in there. Mrs. Winslow tells me that as a girl she thought maybe it was a place where evil men paid for the privilege of smoking cigarettes in the presence of women who had lost the last vestige of shame.

Oklahoma. By Victor E. Harlow. Harlow Publishing Company, Oklahoma City, Okla., 1935. Sketchy but reliable history of Oklahoma down to 1933. Includes the Constitution of the State of Oklahoma and other important state papers, verbatim. Mr. Harlow calls attention to the fact that one of the best cowboy, two-gun men who became a peace officer was the late Charlie Colcord, a gentleman who laid aside his guns to help develop Oklahoma City, built one of the city's most famous skyscrapers and died a millionaire.

Oklahombres. By Evett Dumas Nix. As told to Gordan Hines. Eden Publishing House, St. Louis & Chicago, 1929. E. D. Nix of Paducah, Ky., and one of my remote kin, Charley Meacham of Fulton, Ky., made the Run into Guthrie on that noon, April 22, 1889 when the first part of Oklahoma territory was opened to white settlement. Charley moved on to Oklahoma City and Nix opened up a general store in Guthrie. Later he was appointed U. S. Marshal in Oklahoma Territory and the Cherokee Strip, in which office he had the good sense to appoint as his deputies the peace officers who became known as "The Guardsmen," Bill Tilghman, Heck Thomas, Chris Madsen and Bud Ledbetter. Undoubtedly, Nix had a magnificent story to tell, but his collaborator or "ghost," a fantastic genius who writes well, apparently wouldn't let Nix tell it. Hines preferred to lift stuff from other writers and rewrite it in his own engaging style. He even lifted stuff from Fred Sutton, in fact, a great deal, which, if you refer to the bibliographical review of *Hands Up!*, you will see is the reverse of having a regard for truth and accuracy. The book is delightful entertainment, but you must put very little stock in it as history.

Oklahoma Imprints, 1835-1907. By Caroline Thomas Foreman. University of Oklahoma Press, Norman, Okla., 1936. An exhaustive record of the founding, character, date of first issue, ownership, editorship, development or demise of every newspaper and magazine in Oklahoma and Indian Territories from 1835 to Oklahoma's admission into the Union as a state in 1907. Contains many savory examples of the news and comment the various dailies and weeklies published, and hence is in itself a valuable source book. I found former Senator Robert L. Owen's open letter to Belle Starr in this book, written when he was U. S. Indian Agent located at Muskogee in 1887. Also I found such piquant bits about bandits as these items from the Shawnee, Okla., *Quill,* July 25, 1896: "Mrs. Bill Doolin is shipping eggs. It is hoped that none are as bad as the one she called husband." And, "Charlie Colcord has taken Bill Raidler, a member of the Dalton gang, to Columbus, Ohio, where he will do service for the country for twenty years."

Outlaw Days. By Zoe A. (Mrs. Bill) Tilghman. Harlow Publishing Co., Oklahoma City, Okla., 1926. I can't figure out whether J. A. Newsom wrote this book, or whether Mrs. Tilghman wrote Newsom's *The Life and Practice of the Wild and Modern Indian* (q.v.), or whether somebody else wrote both of them, but both are published by the same company and their stuff about peace officers and bandits is almost word for word the same.

The Ozarks: An American Survival of Primitive Society. By Vance Randolph. Vanguard Press, New York, 1931. A delightful account of the customs, speech, superstitions, religious observances, songs, tales, handicraft and way of living of these highly independent mountain people whom Randolph admires and for whom he has a great affection, unmingled with any note of condescension.

Pioneer Life in Southwest Missouri. By Wiley Britton. Kansas City, 1929. A good source book on just what the title says.

Pistols at Ten Paces. By William Oliver Stevens. Houghton Mifflin Co., Boston, 1940. An inquiry into the origin and persistence of a "code of honor," whereby a grown man who got his feelings ruffled, thought he had to challenge the offender to a duel, and the man thus challenged, even if he never had a duelling pistol in his hands in his life, was disgraced if he didn't accept the challenge and shoot it out, with elaborate formalities, even if his antagonist was an expert pistol shot. Contains excellent accounts of the provocation and outcome of some of the more famous duels in America. Even after duelling was outlawed, a curious residuum of the code was adopted by gun-toters in the wild and woolly West. Thus it was murder if a man shot his antagonist or enemy, in a shooting affair, before his opponent had a chance to draw; but it was "self-defense" if a cold-blooded killer challenged an inexperienced man, under no provocation, to shoot it out with him, and then murdered the man as soon as he reached for his gun.

A Political History of the Cherokee Nation. Morris L. Wardell. University of Oklahoma Press, Norman, Okla., 1938.

Bibliographical Review

Just what the title says, and very thorough, accurate and interesting it is.

Pott County and What Has Come of It: A History of Potta-watomie County. By John Fortson. Pottawatomie County Historical Society, Shawnee, Okla., 1936. A journalistic job, paid for by the local Chambers of Commerce, but accurate as to detail, concerning the names and duration in office of the town and county officials, together with brief histories of the founding of the towns in the county and the highlights of their early history, including the famous county-seat war between Tecumseh and Shawnee.

Quantrill and the Border Wars. By William Elsey Connelly. Cedar Rapids, 1910. Most comprehensive and accurate account of the personnel and deeds of this outfit of murderers, plunderers and pyromaniacs, some of whom were honest-enough yokels, duped into the notion that they were serving the cause of the Confederacy; but most of them were only vicious hoodlums, too ornery to enlist as regular soldiers and led by an unscrupulous, cold-blooded thief and killer. Connelly, remembering that many who served under Quantrill were good, if misguided, men who later became pillars of society, evades the moral issue of condemning Quantrill and his gang as perpetrators of unspeakable crimes; but there are those who condone the Federal guerrillas also, and they were murderers and arsonists, too, having no excuse of military orders for their crimes.

Recollections of the Last Ten Years. By Timothy Flint. Boston, 1826. New edition, edited with an Introduction by C. Hartley Grattan. Alfred A. Knopf, Inc., New York, 1932. One of the classics of early American travel in the interior of the mid-American continent. Charming and enlightening.

≈§ 325 ঌ∾

Belle Starr

The Rise and Fall of Jesse James. By Robertus Love. New York, 1926. Blue Ribbon Books, 1939. This is the nearest approach to a sound and accurate history of the life of a bandit that I have ever encountered, with the honorable exception of Wayne Gard's notable work of scholarship, *Sam Bass.* Love, a Missourian, is prejudiced in favor of the James brothers; but his reasons are understandable: he could never forgive the Pinkerton agents for throwing a bomb into the Samuels' home, on the mere suspicion that the James boys were in there, killing Jesse's stepbrother and blowing Jesse's mother's arm off and wrecking the home of Jesse's stepfather, Dr. Samuels—thus making entirely innocent people suffer for the sake of the miserable money award offered for the James boys, dead or alive. But I regret to report that Love fell for the legend that grew up about the James brothers' alleged daring robbery of the entire gate receipts of the Kansas City State Fair on Sept. 27, 1872, in which the James brothers were supposed to have dashed up and seized a *tin box* containing $10,000 (!) in full view of 25,000 spectators, and dashed away. It is a wonder Love didn't stop to figure out how $10,000 in gate receipts, mostly in nickels, dimes, quarters, halves and silver dollars, would weigh. Moreover, according to Love's account, derived from other lurid versions of the episode, ''About 4 P.M., the treasurer of the fair association counted the day's proceeds, locked the cash-box, and handed it to a young man who was instructed to deposit the money in a bank . . . etc.'' What sort of bank would it be that would be open after four P.M.; and what sort of treasurer would entrust $10,000 in cash in a tin box to a messenger boy in a crowd in a rough town, even if the boy could carry it ? The *National Police Gazette's* version is simply that the treasurer reported that he had been held up by the James boys while everybody was watching the race. The *National Police Gazette* implies (and I suspect correctly) that the treasurer was a liar, that he stole the money himself, and that he had an easy alibi because the heads of everybody at the time were full of stuff about the daring hold-ups of the James brothers, and every stick-up, no matter how big or how small, was attributed to them. Yet the preposterous story about a kid's carrying the money away in a tin box and its being seized by Jesse has been accepted without a lifted eyebrow even by writers as cautious as William Mac-Leod Raine. Also, I regret to report that Love gives currency to a fallacy, later lifted from him by dozens of others, including (strangely enough) Walter Noble Burns (see page 60 of *The Saga of Billy the Kid*). The fallacy, as stated by Love, is this: "Your present chronicler has no prejudicial attitude with regard to blue eyes; in fact, he is measurably fond of them. He states a simple fact when he sets down here that virtually all of the noted outlaws he has known in his one experience as a newspaper writer had blue eyes. The eyes of most of them were of a steel-blue tint. Frank James had such eyes; so also has Jim Cummins. The most spectacular bank robber that ever lived (And here's where Love slips up—B.R.), the late Henry Starr of Oklahoma, who does not belong to the present narrative, sighted along the barrels of his six-shooters with eyes serenely blue." In the first place, Henry Starr was a full-blooded Cherokee Indian; his eyes were almost as black as the ace of spades. In the second place, Henry Starr wasn't a spectacular bank robber at all, much less the most spectacular bank robber that ever lived. In the third place, he carried only one gun, never sighted along the barrels of it, shot only one man in his life, and himself was winged and captured after a bank robbery in Stroud, Oklahoma, by a sixteen-year-old country boy named Paul Curry, who, when Starr was making his getaway in full view of an armed crowd that had gathered around the bank, grabbed a citizen's rifle and knocked Starr off his horse with a bullet in his hip.

Robber and Hero; The Story of the Raid on the First National Bank of Northfield, Minnesota, by the James-Younger Band of Robbers, in 1876. By George Huntington, Compiler. The Christian Way Company, Northfield, Minn., 1895. A careful piece of work, being a compilation of the more credible contemporary newspaper accounts of the famous raid, and a systematic discarding of the obviously false versions of alleged ''eye-witnesses.'' Love bases his account of the Northfield robbery and the apprehension of the Youngers on this text.

Roughing It. By Mark Twain. James R. Osgood, Boston, 1872. Surely there is no need to tell what this book is about.

The Saga of Billy the Kid. By Walter Noble Burns. Doubleday, Page & Co., New York, 1926. It is obvious that Burns, after being driven nearly crazy trying to establish more than three or four verifiable facts out of the immense accumulation of folklore and legend about Billy the Kid, finally decided not to make the book a history at all but an anthology of folklore about the Kid. Thus it is a magnificent job. To be sure that people won't mistake it for accurate history, he doesn't cite a single historical source, disdains a bibliography, and makes use of only about three dates in the entire book.

The Sentimental Years. By E. Douglas Branch. D. Appleton-Century Co., New York, 1934. An amusing study, with

Bibliographical Review

illustrations, of the things that occupied the minds of Americans, in their leisure moments, from 1836 to 1860. We learn here what books, pictures, songs, sentiments, household decorations, games and discussions constituted the taste and culture of the genteel class of that period.

Sins of America. By Edward Van Every. Frederick A. Stokes Co., New York, 1931. An admirable selection of pictures from Nat Fleischer's incomparable files of the *National Police Gazette,* together with paraphrased accounts of notable scandals aired by that sprightly, much-read, but ostensibly disapproved-of weekly treasure-trove of the Americana that is sadly missing from the histories of the academic big-wigs.

Southern Plainsmen. By Carl Coke Rister. University of Oklahoma Press, Norman, Okla., 1938. A historical study of the era of great ranches in Texas and Oklahoma, of herds and trails, of cowboys and Indian fighters, of the wars between rival cattlemen and the wars between cattlemen and homesteaders and of the final passing of the open ranges and the doom of the old-time cowboy, many of whom, thrown out of work, became bandits or peace officers or, at different times, first one and then the other.

The Story of a Common Soldier of Army Life in the Civil War. By Leander Stillwell. Franklin Hudson Publishing Co., Erie, Kansas, 1916. A homely but intensely appealing account of just what a mere common soldier in the Union forces experienced during the Civil War. There are no thrills or glamor here; Stillwell had been through three major battles without ever seeing the enemy or firing his gun, and at Shiloh he couldn't see anything except smoke in the direction he was ordered to fire. It is a record of monotony, mud, terrible rations, dysentery, malaria, general misery—all taken stolidly and without complaint. A picture shows that Stillwell was a remarkably handsome youth when he enlisted; and his account shows that he was filled with idealism. He was an Illinois farm lad who disliked Southerners generally, but positively hated Missourians. He was seventy-three years old when he wrote this book; hence it has a rare charm and flavor. He thought most of his Union officers were numbskulls, including the generals.

The Story of Oklahoma City. By Angelo C. Scott. Times-Journal Publishing Co., Oklahoma City, Okla., 1939. Lively and authentic account of the founding of Oklahoma City, a metropolis that sprang up between noon and midnight on April 22, 1889, when the first unassigned Indian lands were opened for white settlement, in what is now Oklahoma. Dr. Scott, dean of Oklahoma historians, was one of the many who made the run that memorable day into Oklahoma City, and took up a township claim. I saw him in 1940 in Oklahoma City. At eighty-two, this wiry, alert and learned little man was still filling lecture engagements, attending all sorts of Chamber of Commerce and Historical Society meetings, carrying on an immense correspondence and, in general, being as spry as a yearling.

Sure Enough, How Come? By F. W. Van Emden. The Naylor Company, San Antonio, Texas, 1933. Verses in the Texas idiom. These colloquial expressions, used just the way all Texans use them, were an immense surprise to many Texans who hadn't realized they talked that way until they read it in a book. Mrs. Van Emden is an expert in phonetics and linguistics. These illustrations of Texan expressions are set in verses that in themselves are either humorous or witty or both.

Bibliographical Review

Target Shooting: The Elusive Ten. By William Reichenbach. Published by the author, Wantagh, L. I., N. Y., 1935. Mr. Reichenbach, an expert shot with a pistol, here provides a simple manual of instruction in how to handle a pistol and how to ring up the highest score in target shooting. He also describes the best makes of revolvers. I would be willing to bet that Mr. Reichenbach, at target shooting, could make monkeys out of all the famous gunmen of the old days, from Billy the Kid on down. There are authentic instances of some of those old-time "deadshots" firing ten bullets at each other, with a space of only twenty yards between them, without either of them hitting the other.

Texas: A Guide to the Lone Star State. American Guide Series, compiled by Workers of the Writers' Program of W.P.A. in the State of Texas. Hastings House, New York, 1940. All of these books that I have examined are excellent as to text, illustrations, format and printing; and this is no exception. Compiled by many hands working on W.P.A., these books are carefully researched, checked and edited. The presentation is clear, succinct and sound.

Texas Cattle Brands. By Gus L. Ford, Editor. Clyde C. Cockrell Co., Dallas, Texas, 1936. A catalogue, illustrated by line drawings, of the various individual branding designs used by Texas cattlemen, together with brief data about each brand and its owner.

They Had Their Hour. By Marquis James. Bobbs-Merrill Co., Indianapolis and New York, 1934. The Pulitzer Prize-winning biographer of Andy Jackson here gives us some sketches that are the by-products of his prodigious research. Chapters on William Kidd, Paul Revere, Major André, Benedict Arnold, William Barret Travis, Sam

Davis, John Wilkes Booth, Dick Yaeger and the Louisiana
Lottery, as well as sidelights on more prominent figures
and events. The chapter on Dick Yaeger, the outlaw, is the
result of a boyhood interest in the local bandit, when Marquis James was a youngster in Enid, Oklahoma. His chapter about Yaeger, James relates, was written in Enid, after
talking to old-timers, and consulting public records and
newspaper clippings. Nevertheless, James is in error on
two minor points: The father of Al, Frank and Ed Jennings, Judge J. D. F. Jennings, was not, as he states, pro-
bate judge of Woodward County at the time Ed Jennings
was killed by Temple Houston; he was county judge of
Pottawatomie County from 1896 to 1900 (and Ed was
killed in 1894, see chapter, ''The Jennings Gang: Comic
Relief,'' in this book). Temple Houston was not the son
of Gen. Sam Houston, but the grandson. Otherwise, this is
entertaining and authentic history.

Tixier's Travels on the Osage Prairies. Edited by John
Francis McDermott. Translated by Albert J. Salvan. University of Oklahoma Press, Norman, Okla., 1940. Apparently inspired by Chateaubriand's *Les Natchez, Atala* and
René, Victor Tixier, a well-to-do young Frenchman sailed
from France in 1839, landed at New Orleans, explored
Louisiana, traveled up the Mississippi, went inland from
St. Louis to the heart of the Osage country, traveled back
to St. Louis, through Southwestern Missouri, meticulously
and charmingly recording all that he observed that impressed him, and returned home. A small edition of his
journal was published at Clermont-Ferrand, France, in
1848, and for a long time it remained one of the rarest
items of Americana. The book was rescued by John Francis
McDermott and translated by Albert J. Salvan, thus offer-

ing the journal for the first time in English. Tixier's son was living when this book appeared.

Tombstone Dick. By Ned Buntline (E. Z. C. Judson). Beadle Library, New York. Merely cited as a typical example of the dime-novel treatment of bandits of the West in the heydey of stagecoach robberies and high-jinks in Abilene. For an amusing account of "Buntline" in Dodge City, see Wright's *Dodge City, the Cowboy Capital.* "Buntline" was a knowing, generous and amusing fellow, thoroughly on to himself and not vain over the kid stuff he wrote that made him so much money.

Triggernometry. By Eugene Cunningham. New York, 1934. You can take it or leave it; but if you take it, take a five-pound bag of salt along with it. Excellent in spots.

When the Daltons Rode. By Emmett Dalton, in collaboration with Jack Jungmeyer. Doubleday, Doran & Co., New York, 1931. A book without any merit whatever, except that arising from the factitious use of Emmett Dalton's name in connection with it—a use that must have been sanctioned by Emmett Dalton. The book is lifted in the main from *The Dalton Brothers,* by "An Eye Witness," a paper-covered two-bit thriller published in 1892 by Laird & Lee, Chicago. The Laird & Lee book is rather better, in that it contains reproductions of some photographs taken of the dead outlaws after the Coffeyville raid, of the bullet-riddled Condon bank, and of John J. Kloehr who killed Bob Dalton, Grat Dalton and Bill Powers. This book repeats the myth that Emmett would have escaped if he hadn't ridden back to try to rescue Bob. It didn't happen. The same yarn was told of Cole and Bob Younger at the Northfield bank robbery. It didn't happen there, either.

Wild Men of the Wild West. By Edwin L. Sabin. New York,

1929. Re-write stuff, and not very particular about the stuff to rewrite.

Wyatt Earp: Frontier Marshal. By Stuart N. Lake. Houghton Mifflin Co., Boston, 1931. I reserve judgment as to whether Lake is telling the truth or not when he says he is quoting verbatim from Wyatt Earp's own manuscript, especially since the bulk of the book is made up of these alleged writings of Earp put within quotation marks. I can distinguish no difference between the personal rhythm and prose style of Earp and Lake. It is certainly a remarkable coincidence if Earp's and Lake's personal rhythm and style were so indistinguishable, especially inasmuch as Earp was a man of action all his life and Lake is a professional writer of long training and considerable skill. But this problem to one side, this is the best-written, most credible and the most thoroughly absorbing of all the existent books about famous peace officers and notorious bandits.

(Since the above was put into type I have heard from Stuart Lake, admitting that my scepticism is justified. Earp, he says, was inarticulate. In speech, he was at best monosyllabic. Lake plied him with questions for months on end and therefore felt journalistically justified in inventing the Earp manuscript.—B. R.)

I am only superficially acquainted with the facts in Wyatt Earp's career as they emerge in other books; but wherever I have been able to check, Lake's book is sound, and Earp's alleged own story, though revealing a very superior man, is related calmly and without braggadocio. The anonymous contributor of the brief piece about Earp in *Arizona*, in the American Guide Series, says that Earp was a killer in league with the lawless element of Tombstone until he was chased out of the city by the decent citizens—which is a quite different view of matters than the one Lake takes; but perhaps the W.P.A. writer chose to rely upon the testimony of the Tombstone *Nugget*, which was inimical to Earp, whereas Lake says he got hold of some of the extremely rare copies of the *Epitaph* which upheld Earp. This book may be faked from beginning to end, but I don't believe it is, and if it is, it is a magnificent job of fakery—a creative work of first-rate ingenuity, in fact. By nearly all accounts, even excluding Lake's, Wyatt Earp was about the brainiest as well as the bravest and most decent of the old-time gun fighters. Earp, alone of the gun fighters of the old West, lived to a ripe old age and died with his boots off in Los Angeles, Calif., on January 23, 1929, at the age of eighty. Perhaps the reason he lived so long was that he never wore guns, even as a peace officer, except when making an arrest.

The Younger Brothers. By Augustus C. Appler. Copyright 1875 by Augustus C. Appler. New edition published by Laird & Lee, Chicago, 1892. Mr. Appler, who was the editor of the Osceola, Missouri, *Democrat* and a friend of the Younger family, wrote this book before the Northfield, Minnesota, bank robbery, in which two members of the gang, Clell Miller and Bill Chadwell were killed, Bob, Cole and Jim Younger were captured, and the James brothers, Frank and Jesse, escaped. Therefore he was writing while the Younger brothers were still active and at large, a fact which causes him to make the prediction: "It has long since been an established fact that the Youngers cannot be taken alive by force, and all hopes of doing so by those who imagine they can capture them, to the mind of every man in the least acquainted with them, is perfectly ridiculous."

Belle Starr

Mr. Appler was in error there; but, allowing for his strong prejudice in favor of the Younger brothers, his book is factually unassailable, as befits the work of a conscientious newsman of the old school. The Younger brothers were accused of many crimes they did not commit, because it was the habit of irresponsible people, including sensational journalists, to attribute every robbery of any kind to the Youngers during the period when they were on the scout. Mr. Appler succeeded in getting a communication from Cole Younger while Cole was still at large. Cole denied participation in many of the robberies of which he was accused and furnished alibis to prove that he was elsewhere when certain robberies took place—alibis which he asked Mr. Appler to check. Mr. Appler secured affidavits from responsible persons establishing the validity of Cole's alibis. These certificates of good character, however, did not prevent Bob Younger from planning the Northfield bank robbery; nor did it prevent Cole and Jim Younger from participating in it. The robbery was a mistake: the Minnesotans didn't take so kindly to the Younger robberies and killings as the Missourians did. The sanest and best account of the Youngers, much used as a source book by writers who did not have Appler's regard for truth and accuracy and who fictionized many of his plain statements of fact.

INDEX

Belle Starr

Index